The ADHD Parenting Handbook

The ADHD
Parenting Handbook

Practical Advice for Parents from Parents

Colleen Alexander-Roberts

Taylor Publishing Company
Dallas, Texas

© by Colleen Alexander-Roberts

Published by Taylor Publishing Company
1550 West Mockingbird Lane
Dallas, Texas 75235

Designed by Hespenheide Design

Note: This book is not intended to serve in the
place of a physician. Always consult your child's
pediatrician before altering childcare practices.

Library of Congress Cataloging-in-Publication Data

Alexander-Roberts, Colleen
    The ADHD parenting handbook: practical advice
for parents from parents / Colleen Alexander-Roberts
        p.   cm.
    Includes index
    ISBN 0-87833-862-4
    1. Attention-deficit hyperactivity disorder—
Popular works.
    2. Child rearing. I. Title
RJ506.H9A58   1994   94-13847
618.92' 8589—dc20   CIP

Printed in the United States of America

10 9 8 7 6 5 4 3 2 1

To my children,
Christopher and Blake,
for all they have taught me
about a world that
I never knew existed.

Contents

Foreword

A proper and effectual remedy
for this wandering of thought,
I would be glad to find.
—John Locke, 1762

Parenting a child is a rewarding job, yet no child is perfect so it is also extremely difficult and challenging work. The challenge is made even greater if a child demonstrates an excessive amount of impulsivity (acting before thinking), hypermotor or hyperverbal activity, poor focused concentration, insatiability (difficulty becoming satisfied), poor internal feedback monitoring of behavior, and/or distractibility. These symptoms have been combined into a complex disorder now known as Attention Deficit Hyperactivity Disorder (ADHD), which seems to be present in an estimated 5 to 10 percent of the general population. The research of Campbell and others have found that characteristics can be identified even before the age of three years; however, some individuals who manifest attention deficits with less hyperactivity and impulsivity, but more focused concentration problems may not be readily identified until later years of elementary school or junior high. The disorder was first described as long ago as 1845 by a German physician, Heinrich Hoffman. The names we have used to associate these symptoms over the years reflect our level of understanding (or lack of) at the particular time (hyperactivity disorder, post-encephalopathic hyperactive disorder, minimal brain dysfunction, etc.)

Although causes may be multifactoral, they are now postulated to arise basically from dysfunctional regulatory mechanisms in the areas in and around the frontal lobes of the brain. In their landmark study published in 1990, Dr. Alan Zametkin and associates documented, in the families they studied with hyperactivity, that: (1) there seems to be a strong inheritance component, and (2) significant biological differences in brain metabolism can persist even into adulthood. Others have documented attention deficits associated with toxic effects on the brain (e.g.: maternal cocaine, tobacco, and alcohol use before birth, or lead exposure, meningitis, or central nervous system irradiation for malignancies after birth).

More and more, we are learning that attention deficits are not entirely emotionally based or due just to conditioned behavioral responses. We also are finding that the disorder is not uniform or one dimensional. For instance, special blood-flow studies in the brain (SPECT scanning) have shown different patterns in those who respond to different classes of medications (such as stimulants versus antidepressants) and brain-mapping studies have documented different patterns for different subtypes of learning disabilities and attention disorders. Although these are still experimental techniques, they document discernable differences between patients that have to be explained. Therefore, it may behoove us to talk more about different attention deficits than about a one dimensional disorder (ADHD).

Children with attention deficits display myriad combinations of symptoms that sometimes vary from day to day. One could say this inconsistency is probably the hallmark of the problem. Therefore, modes of management (medicinal, behavioral management, language therapy, social skills training, etc.) have to be tailored to meet the individual's needs at any point in time. Parents and professionals cannot just apply one technique and expect it to work for all situations. Success of therapy depends a great deal on addressing coexistent factors—intelligence, mood disorders (depression), language-skill deficits, conduct disorders, oppositional temperament, family stresses, etc. These must be identified and addressed to adequately treat the whole patient. Therefore, the parents of children with ADHD may require help from multiple disciplines (pediatrician, educator, psychologist, language pathologist, etc.). The best situation occurs when a multidisciplinary team works with the family and is able to communicate on the same level without encountering problems related to turf issues and biases.

We should point out here that some of the same symptoms we see as contributing to a disorder may later be hailed as strengths (for example, impulsivity may be perceived as decisiveness in adulthood, distractibility may be seen as creativity or open-mindedness, and insatiability as ambition). During the demystification process, I emphasize these points to the parents of my patients. In learning to describe their children's characteristics in positive terms, not only will parents improve their own outlook, but they will affect the outlook of everyone who deals with their child in a positive way (teachers, grandparents, coaches, etc.).

Psychostimulant medications still remain the most effective medical treatment for attention deficits. They seem to work by nonspecifically arousing an apparently "underaroused" central nervous system. When any of us is sleep-deprived, we become fidgety, distractible, easily fatigued, and impulsive. When fully aroused, such symptoms disappear. The same occurs when taking stimulants, such as Ritalin, which seem to improve concentration by arousing the central nervous system and thereby eliminating the need for the body to work to arouse itself (hence, fidgeting or stretching decreases). (This positive effect on concentration has been shown even in "normal" individuals. When given standardized cognitive testing before and after medication, normal individuals scored better on such testing when medicated.) However, as Ms. Alexander-Roberts will point out, stimulant medications only reduce symptoms. They are not a "cure," nor do they have long-lasting effects. They are just management tools that work to help the individual improve his or her ability to stay focused and on task. In addition, chemical actions of the stimulants are not alike. Each stimulant (Ritalin, Dexedrine, or Cylert) works at a different chemical level in the brain, so one may help even though another seems not to, or may create side effects that another doesn't.

Tricyclic antidepressants (Tofranil and Norpramin) have also been shown to be useful, especially with overanxious or moody individuals, either in combination with stimulants or alone, although they have been associated with significant dose-related adverse reactions (cardiac arrhythmias). Combinations of stimulants with other medications have recently been found to improve comorbid (coexisting) conditions such as anxiety, obsessive-compulsive symptoms, overaggression, or tics. Drugs such as Clonidine, Tegretol, Prozac, and Buspar have been shown to be useful adjuncts in special cases and allow for decreased doses of stimulants particularly in adults; however, combinations need to be monitored very closely by experienced physicians. Side effects of medications such as headaches, stomachaches, insomnia, liver toxicity (particularly in the case of Cylert) and appetite loss are often transient, or dose related but need to be monitored. Medication "vacations" can be instituted on a controlled basis after success is achieved, school placement is appropriate, and strategies for self-monitoring (such as the use of the assignment books, long-range planners, etc.) are made habitual.

Medication should never be the only management tool. Some parents and professionals over-rely on the benefits of medication. Medications undoubtedly help with concentration, but don't always improve organization skills or social skills, nor do they elicit compliance. These skills need to be directly taught to the children, which means extra effort on everyone's part—particularly for the parents—but the effort is usually worth it in the long run.

The ADHD Parenting Handbook reads like a compendium of letters from ADHD support groups. Since their formation, national support groups for parents of children with attention deficits, such as Children and Adults with

Attention Deficit Disorders (in 1987) and Attention-Deficit Disorder Association (in 1989), have been tremendous resources parents could turn to for help. Offering much-needed information and strategies, they have also provided political clout to bring about needed changes in educational systems. Through their efforts, laws, such as Section 504 of the Rehabilitation Act of 1973, have been changed to include offering classroom accommodations to students with attention difficulties. Since attention deficits cover a broad spectrum of different combinations of challenges for parents and teachers, these individuals need many different alternatives to choose from.

As a pediatrician during the last eighteen years, I've suggested many behavioral techniques to parents. No one special technique works for all. As I read this book, it was gratifying to hear how parents have taken many of these same techniques, modified them for their own situations, and found them to work. I have personally witnessed the author and her family go through many difficult times while dealing with the problems of ADHD, and am glad to see the struggle has led to such increased awareness.

Ms. Alexander-Roberts's book is truly a labor of love. She has written of the problems with humor and personal understanding as well as with the knowledge of failures and triumphs. She emphasizes the hard work of parenting a child with attention and behavior problems, and addresses the disappointment parents feel when they realize their parenting experience is far from ideal. However, she also offers some very good tried-and-true practical tips (emphasizing problem solving and listening to our children) that will be helpful to anyone regardless of what stage they're at in dealing with any of these problems. This book will encourage other parents to be advocates for their children, preserving their strengths and sustaining their self-esteem. If we parents do not do so, who else will?

Bruce A. Pasch, M.D., F.A.A.P.
Director, Children's Center for Learning and Development

Acknowledgments

I am grateful for the assistance of Bruce A. Pasch, M.D., F.A.A.P., who reviewed and edited the manuscript and offered numerous suggestions and tips. He also shared his expertise, spent countless hours working on the manuscript, and supported this project. Not only has Dr. Pasch been a great pediatrician to my children, but his work with children who have ADHD and their families is to be commended—it is always above and beyond the call of duty. Thanks to Mary D. Squire, Ph.D., for her assistance in reviewing the manuscript, offering suggestions, and sharing the joys and frustrations of parenting children with ADHD.

I want to thank my dear friend, Judith Gilbert, for the numerous pages of tips she provided, for the parts of her family life she shared in this book, and for her encouragement and belief in this project. I am grateful for the insight Janet Robinson, R.N., Ph.D., provided on parenting adolescents with ADHD and for the advice she shared on working with educators. I also wish to thank Kathy Galbreth, who teaches at Maumee Valley Country Day School in Toledo, Ohio, for reviewing parts of the manuscript; Donna Waghorn, information specialist at The National Information Center for Children and Youth with Disabilities, for clarifying Public Law 101-476, the Individuals with Disabilities Education Act (IDEA), and Section 504 of the Rehabilitation Act of 1973; Mary Jane Johnson, founder of Parents of Hyperactive Children and the ADDult Network, for all of her help; Stella Francis, Ph.D., director of The Psychoeducational Development Center in Toledo, Ohio; and Catherine Pidek of Success by Design.

In writing this book, I relied heavily on the experiences of more than 200 parents who offered their insight, suggestions, tips, and words of advice. My thanks to all of these parents who took the time to send their tips. I would especially like to thank all of my friends who have children with ADHD that shared their stories, especially Debra Graf, Gary and Joanie Hoffer, and Dianne Gladieux, and the many members of Adoptive Families of America and CHADD who graciously shared their thoughts and suggestions, frustrations and fears, and joys, so that this book could be written. To Doreen Harris, my close friend and confidant, who has always been there through the years offering comfort when I needed it the most, and for her interest in this book, I am grateful. Thanks also to Mary I. Garcia and Debbie Morgan who have always assisted me cheerfully by making sure my work gets to my editor on time. I'd also like to express my gratitude to a special editor at Taylor Publishing Company, Lorena Jones, who suggested that I write a book on ADHD after working with me on my first book and listening attentively to my many humorous, but frustrating, stories about my children. Thank you, Lorena, for your vote of confidence. You, perhaps, know better than anyone how much this means to me.

I'd like to also thank two very caring school nurses at Maumee Valley Country Day School: Mary Ann Renda and Linda Hottinger, who have provided a tremendous amount of encouragement and support through the years to my son, Christopher, and to me. Both of you have always been there when we needed you. A special thank you to Jan Samples, Christopher's third-grade teacher, for making this year extra special for him. Her willingness to learn more about ADHD is to be commended.

My husband, Clyde, has helped in numerous ways from picking the children up from school, to surprising me with a computer and a "real" desk, to taking the children on mini trips so I could work on weekends. I couldn't have done it without his help. Thanks to my son, Christopher, my impulsive bundle of energy, who has taught me to be more patient, compassionate, and forgiving. Because of Christopher and his brother, Blake, I have learned to be an effective, loving parent—not a perfect parent, which I strived to be for years. My children were the inspiration for this book. Heartfelt thanks go to Heidi Wymer, who is always here when I need her, for her contributions to the book and help with the appendix. I would also like to thank my parents, Joanne and Stan, for the interest they have shown in this book and for their love and support over the years. And to my courageous father who has always been a hero in my eyes, I'd like to say, "I'm so glad you're here. Thanks for all of your help and taking the time to learn as much as you have about ADHD."

Colleen Alexander-Roberts
June 1994

Introduction

Attention Deficit Hyperactivity Disorder (ADHD) is a disorder characterized by age-inappropriate levels of inattention, impulsiveness, and hyperactivity. ADHD currently is a popular diagnosis, constituting the largest single reason children are referred to child mental health clinics. Because of its popularity, it has come to be viewed as the Yuppie diagnosis, and many people are not taking the diagnosis seriously. Consequently, the child with ADHD and his family are often misunderstood by friends, extended family, teachers, scout leaders, and little league coaches. The child becomes labeled as a behavior problem, lazy, irresponsible, and disorganized. Parents are often accused of failing to control and discipline their children. The developmental tasks of childhood and parenting, which are difficult under normal circumstances, are compounded by ADHD and by society's misunderstanding of the disorder. Parents are left with the task of educating those around them, coping with the associated behavior, advocating for their child with ADHD, and protecting themselves and their immediate family from the disapproval of others.

In spite of the view of many, ADHD does exist, as any parent who has a child with the disorder will attest. It has been shown to have a biological cause, or etiology, which appears to be inherited, although other etiologies (such as lead poisoning, perinatal difficulties, and maternal drug use during pregnancy) may account for a percentage of cases of ADHD as well. Estimates of ADHD's prevalence vary from 3 to 5 percent; some sources suggest it may be higher.

ADHD symptoms may be mild, moderate, or severe. Symptoms are considered mild when there are few, if any, in excess of those required for diagnosis and when there is little impairment in school and social functioning. Severe symptoms are present when they markedly exceed the number required for diagnosis and when there is a significant and pervasive impairment in home, school, and social functioning. Symptoms falling between mild and severe are considered moderate.

Each of the three primary symptoms of ADHD—inattention, impulsivity, and hyperactivity—is multidimensional. Thus, problems with attention can manifest themselves in difficulties with alertness, arousal, selectivity, sustained attention, or distractibility. Impulsivity, also referred to as behavioral disinhibition, is manifested in children with ADHD in their inabillity to delay gratification, their failure to consider the negative, even dangerous, consequences of risk-taking behavior, and the carelessness and destructive handling of their own and others' property. Similarly, children with ADHD often experience difficulty waiting for instructions to be completed resulting in careless errors. Hyperactivity may be manifested either through excessive motor movements or verbalization.

Manifestations of ADHD occur in varying degrees in most situations the child participates in, including home, school, and social situations. Nonetheless, ability to focus in highly stimulating or novel situations is not uncommon. Because of the impulsive nature of children with ADHD, aggressive acting out is common. Difficulty with peer relationships also is common. Noncompliance with parental requests and directives is often observed in home situations. Children with ADHD often have low self-esteem, are emotionally labile and prone to temper outbursts, and have low frustration tolerance. Many children with ADHD have academic difficulties or are academic underachievers due to difficulty concentrating and staying on task to complete assignments.

The behavioral characteristics associated with ADHD are often sources of conflict between children with ADHD and their parents and siblings. Researchers have found interactions with and reactions from parents and siblings of children with ADHD to be different than those in normal families in that they are more negative and stressful to all family members. Moreover, there is considerable evidence that parents and siblings of children with ADHD are more likely than those of non-ADHD children to suffer psychological distress and psychiatric disorders.

The effects of ADHD on family members have been demonstrated in a number of research studies. These studies have found that mothers of children with ADHD often report significantly lower levels of parenting self-esteem and higher levels of depression, self-blame, and social isolation than their counterparts who have non-ADHD children. Marital disturbances are more common among families with a child who has ADHD; some studies show separation and divorce rates are three times that of couples without a child with ADHD. Similarly, strained relationships with extended family appear to be more common among families with a child who has ADHD. Consequently, young parents often are deprived of needed emotional support from family and friends, resulting in a sense of social isolation that is detrimental to emotional well-being.

It is no surprise that the entire family system and the way the family functions together can be affected by ADHD. The family systems theory is based on a general systems theory, which maintains that a change in one part of the system results in a change in the entire system. Thus, a family can be thought of as similar to a mobile. When one portion of the mobile moves, all other parts move as well. When a family experiences stress in one subsystem, whether it is the marital, sibling, or individual subsystem, the entire family reacts with attempts to adapt or cope with that stress. Some of these adaptations may be functional; others may be dysfunctional. Healthy families are those that are able to make appropriate or functional adaptations in reaction to stress.

To cope with the behavioral manifestations of ADHD and the accompanying parenting stress, most families with a child who has ADHD make a variety of attempts to adapt or change the way they react to and handle the child. Some of these attempts are functional and successful, and others are not. Oftentimes parents are at a loss for how to successfully adapt or cope with the behavior of their child with ADHD. This difficulty is compounded by the fact that children with ADHD are often impervious to rewards and consequences. Moreover, rapid habituation to reinforcers, a common characteristic of children with ADHD, means that just when you thought you had the key to coping with a behavior, the technique you are using becomes old hat to your child with ADHD and is no longer effective. Consequently, parents must constantly be creative and remain one step ahead of the child to successfully cope with the behavior.

Resources for learning to cope with the behavioral manifestations of ADHD can be hard to come by. Pediatricians are often helpful in prescribing and monitoring medication but may fall short when it comes to additional suggestions for behavioral interventions. Medication, unfortunately, is only one piece of the puzzle required for dealing with ADHD. Psychologists and family therapists who specialize in the treatment of families and children with ADHD may be helpful. However, many are not specifically trained in this area and may even fail to recognize the symptoms of ADHD, particularly when symptoms are mild. Others may confuse severe symptoms with family dysfunction and view the child with ADHD as the family scapegoat, a position he can fall into very easily. Unless one is fortunate enough to be referred to a psychotherapist or pediatrician who specializes in the treatment of ADHD, few resources for coping with ADHD behavior may be available.

Colleen Alexander-Roberts offers parents a rich source of parenting techniques and sound advice on adapting successfully. She addresses a wide variety of problems at all age levels from preschool to adolescence. She has enlisted the help of many parents of children with ADHD and adds her own sensitivity and parenting successes to their advice. As the parent of two children with ADHD, she is uniquely qualified to understand and communicate the pain, frustration, and—yes!—joys of parenting challenging children.

The ADHD Parenting Handbook is solution-focused and offers hope to parents of children with ADHD. Through Ms. Alexander-Roberts's suggestions, parents will discover how to anticipate problem situations, how to become advocates for their children, and how to make appropriate adaptations to cope with ADHD. Parents undoubtedly will find this book an invaluable tool in their quest for a healthy family.

Mary D. Squire, Ph.D.
The Martin & Johnson Group, Inc.

CHAPTER ONE

Getting Started:
What You Need to Know

Approximately 5 million children in the United States have a medical condition called Attention Deficit Hyperactivity Disorder (ADHD). ADHD is a disorder characterized by developmentally inappropriate levels of inattention, impulsivity, distractibility, and/or hyperactivity, and is pervasive in nature. Onset usually begins in late infancy or early childhood, often by the age of three, but many times it is not recognized until the child begins school. Not all children will manifest the same symptoms. Some, not all, children with ADHD will have one or more learning disabilities along with their attention difficulties. Extreme motor activity is seen more often in males than females, which means females may be diagnosed at a later age than boys, or not at all. Many will have social, emotional, or family problems also, often resulting from the numerous stresses the child experiences daily because of ADHD.

Some professionals use the term ADD (Attention Deficit Disorder). In this book, however, the term Attention Deficit Hyperactivity Disorder (ADHD) will be used to refer to this group of children whether or not they display hyperactivity. In the past, this disorder has been referred to as Hyperkinetic Syndrome, Minimal Brain Damage (MBD), or hyperactivity. Because some professionals still refer to Attention Deficit Hyperactivity Disorder using one of the above terms, it is important for you to realize that they are referring to the same disorder.

ADHD is thought to be generated by a biochemical imbalance in the brain that is either inherited or due to head injury or trauma, perinatal insult, or toxic agents. Some adults with ADHD have been shown to have reduced metabolic activity in those areas of the brain that control movement, emotion, and attention. For about 50 to 60 percent of the children, ADHD symptoms will continue into adulthood. Symptoms like hyperactivity may decrease, but the impulsivity and attention problems will persist. Although ADHD is not related to IQ, it impairs a child's ability to learn, behave, and socialize, to some degree, no matter how bright the child is. (Children with ADHD fall into the same IQ ranges as the general population, including giftedness.)

ADHD is a disorder that affects children of all races and ethnic groups. For years, it has been thought that more males have ADHD than females—studies often cited a 6:1 ratio—and that may well be the case. However, at least one nationally recognized expert, Thomas Phelan, Ph.D., believes otherwise. In his book *All About Attention Deficit Disorders* (Glen Ellyn, IL: Child Management, Inc., 1992), Dr. Phelan places the ratio at 1:1, based on his belief that as many females as males have ADHD.

ADHD influences relationships with parents, teachers, relatives, friends, and siblings. Children with ADHD can stretch the frustration levels of all those who come in contact with them. These children's parents often wrestle with feelings of hopelessness, helplessness, despair, and guilt. Healthy siblings are sometimes denied the attention they deserve because their brother's or sister's behavior draws attention away from them. Relatives, friends, and acquaintances often do not understand and are quick to blame the already frustrated parents for the child's actions.

There are approximately 20 million people, including adults, who have ADHD in the United States. Studies indicate that between 5 and 10 percent of school-age children are affected. One study estimates that the incidence of ADHD among children who were adopted may be as high as 25 or even 40 percent.

Diagnosis and Treatment

The evaluation process for making the diagnosis usually includes obtaining a thorough medical and social history through interviews with the parents, the child, and the child's teacher; a complete pediatric medical examination; observation of the child by the evaluator(s); behavioral assessment (questionnaires completed by the parents, teachers, and often the child if over age thirteen), and educational and psychological testing (the latter when academic performance suggests the possibility of a learning or developmental disability). The evaluation should start with a consultation with your child's physician who then sets up a plan for an appropriate assessment. Usually, a team approach is best (for example, working with a physician, educators, and a psychologist).

Rarely is just one professional involved in the management of a child's ADHD. Successful treatment of the child depends on continuous input from parents, teachers, physicians, and other professionals, and may include a relevant educational plan, the use of medication, behavioral management techniques, self-skills training, and counseling and support for the parents and the child.

Medication

Many parents find the thought of medicating their child for attention or hyperactivity problems frightening. "When the pediatrician, pediatric neurologist, and the psychologist all agreed that Andrea should be placed on medication, my first reaction was to fight the decision," explains Chuck, the father of a five-year-old. "I was willing to try almost anything, but medicating my daughter was not something I wanted to do." The pediatrician gave Chuck and his wife, Sharon, information on the most commonly used stimulant medications (Ritalin, Dexedrine, and Cylert) and suggested that Andrea be placed on Ritalin. Ritalin is the first choice of many physicians and is considered safe and effective. The drug has been in use for thirty years, works quickly, and has relatively minor side effects (e.g., decreased appetite and sleep-pattern changes). Chuck and Sharon decided they wanted to learn more about the medication first. After reading some books and discussing the medication with their local pharmacist, Andrea's parents decided to try the Ritalin.

Within a few days they noticed a remarkable improvement in Andrea's behavior. "Suddenly she was like a new child," says Chuck. "Her temper tantrums were shorter and fewer than before the medication. She was following directions for the first time, not arguing with us over every little thing, and able to sit through meals. We were astonished."

Cathy, of Los Gatos, California, had a similar experience. "I tried to hold off using drugs for ADHD," she recalls. "I really thought that if I just had more patience and I accepted my daughter as she was—a bundle of impulsive energy—that everything would be all right. I watched her day after day in preschool (she was four) pushing kids off swings, throwing sand, knocking over children's block structures, spitting water, etc. I would ask her, 'Why do you do those things?' She would reply tearfully, 'I don't know, Mom. I don't want to do it.' I still hadn't figured out that she couldn't help it.

"I realized that a large group setting, with lots of children and choices of activities, and little structure was not the best setting for her," Cathy adds. "I hired a baby-sitter to stay at home with her and there was an immediate change. Even though she was still an impulsive, active, risk-taker, she was not as anxious at home and we could monitor the stimulation.

"When she was about to start kindergarten I was scared to death that she would repeat the behaviors, as it was also a large group setting with lots of choices. It was a week before kindergarten that I told the pediatrician that I wanted to start her on Ritalin. What a miracle! With Ritalin she got the praise and encouragement she needed for a strong self-image, she was able to cultivate friendships and concentrate on lessons. I only had to remind her of her behavior three times a day compared with twenty times a day. However, I also realized that as the responsible adult in her life, it was my obligation to make sure she took her medication."

Stimulant medication is not, however, a miracle drug; medication does not cure ADHD. Instead, it helps control the symptoms of ADHD. An important aspect of using medication, one that parents must remember, is that many of the symptoms are still evident even when a child uses medication. Stimulant medication helps *improve* alertness, concentration and attention span, *reduce* impulsive and disruptive behavior, and *decrease* noncompliant behavior, but the symptoms continue. All children with ADHD benefit from medication, but some children cannot take medication because the side effects outweigh the benefits at the doses needed. And, parents should never rely on medication as the only form of treatment.

As one parent explained it, "Once my son began taking medication, his quality of life improved greatly. Before medication, all he ever heard was, 'No, no, how many times do I have to tell you no? Why can't you ever listen to me? Why can't you learn not to touch things that don't belong to you? Why can't you sit still in school? Why can't you keep your hands to yourself?' Everything we said to him was negative. With medication that changed. Suddenly, we found we were giving him a lot of positive feedback. We could tell he was happier. His schoolwork improved and he actually made some friends. His social skills improved and his self-esteem was higher than before he began the medication. Most important, as a family we were all much happier."

Most parents hesitate when drug intervention is recommended. Fathers are often more reluctant than mothers to use medication, possibly because they may spend less time with their child on a day-to-day basis. By the time parents approach professionals about their child's behavior, mothers are often at the end of their rope and willing to try anything legitimate that sounds promising. Many parents I interviewed, who were initially hesitant to try medication, said their child's physician suggested a trial period. "Our doctor told us to try Ritalin for two weeks," explained Julie from Billings, Montana, "and if we didn't like what we saw, then we could stop the medication. Our daughter responded favorably to the medication and all of our lives are so much better now. I think all parents should at least try the medication for their child's sake." ("However, a successful trial period does not mean that the child has ADHD—'normal' children respond favorably also," cautions Bruce A. Pasch, M.D., F.A.A.P., Director of the Children's Center for Learning and Development.)

Another class of medications used are the tricyclic antidepressants. The most commonly used drugs are Tofranil (imipramine) and Norpramin (desipramine). The antidepressants are generally used when a child does not respond favorably to stimulant medications. Clonodine (catapres), an antihypertensive, and Tegretol (carbamazepine), an anticonvulsant, have been used successfully with some overly aggressive children. For an excellent discussion on the medications used to treat ADHD, you may want to refer to the book

The Misunderstood Child by Larry B. Silver. (See the recommended reading list at the end of this chapter.)

Not all children need to take medication. But for those children who do, not all will benefit from the same medication or the same dosage. All who are involved in the care of the child must carefully monitor the child until the proper dosage is attained and the desired effects achieved. The continual, successful use of medication relies on parents', teachers', and physicians' constant observation of the child because dosages sometimes need to be increased or medications changed as the child grows and develops. Please remember that medication alone is not the only answer for the child with ADHD. When recommended it should be used, but only as a part of a complete treatment program aimed at supporting the child psychologically, medically, and educationally.

Acceptance Is Tough

Whether you gave birth to or adopted your child, learning that something is wrong with him is very traumatic. Most parents, whether biological or adoptive, rarely consider the possibility that the healthy child they brought into their lives may someday be labeled as having special needs. When your healthy child becomes a child with extra needs, you feel a tremendous loss. This is natural. You have lost your dream child. For those who adopted an infant because of infertility, the loss may be even greater because they have already suffered the loss of a child that was dreamed of but could never be.

As with all major losses, grief is an inherent outcome. Grief is a legitimate response to the loss we feel. When our "healthy" child is diagnosed with ADHD, we grieve. We grieve for our child; we grieve for ourselves. We feel anxious, confused, sad, and angry that this has happened to our child and family. But the day does come when we can accept the loss of our dream child and begin to build on the strengths we discover in our family. The most difficult part of grieving is making the transition from the shock of the diagnosis to the acceptance of it.

Most parents of children with ADHD (or any other medical condition) will eventually reach acceptance and learn to cope and live with their child. Some parents, however, will attain acceptance much faster and easier than others. This also is normal because we all react differently to losses.

When both parents finally reach acceptance and gain an understanding of ADHD, they are then ready to begin working for their child. Parents can then seek to learn more about ADHD from books, videos, newsletters, parent support groups, and professionals. (One can only appropriately advocate for his or her child when armed with a true knowledge of the subject.).

You can learn to cope and live with your child. You can make the necessary changes in your life-style to accommodate his special needs. You may still feel angry and bitter at times or become depressed, but overall you will adjust. "ADHD is frustrating and it can drive you crazy at times," acknowledges Mary Squire, Ph.D., the mother of two children with ADHD, "but in the grand scope of things there are disabilities that are much worse." As the years pass, you will find that you are much stronger and more patient and giving than you ever thought possible. However, if you find you are having difficulty with any of these stages, please speak with your physician.

How this Book Will Help You

Even with the help of the many professionals (pediatricians, psychologists, child psychiatrists, social workers, teachers, therapists, etc.) that are involved in the management of children with ADHD, many parents are still unable to find answers to the many questions they have about parenting the child with ADHD. What you are holding in your hands is a compendium of successful tips and suggestions from over two hundred parents of children with ADHD, especially parents who have children that display hyperactivity. This book is for parents whose children have already been diagnosed with ADHD, and that is why you will not find entire chapters devoted to evaluating and diagnosing ADHD. These topics are covered extensively in other excellent books available on ADHD, many of which you will find in the bibliography.

Where to Find More Information on ADHD

The pharmaceutical company that manufactures the stimulant medication Ritalin (CIBA-Geigy), offers a free booklet to parents titled *ADHD: Attention Deficit-Hyperactivity Disorder and Learning Disabilities* by Larry B. Silver, M.D. The booklet can be obtained free of charge from Children and Adults with Attention Deficit Disorders (CHADD), by calling 305-587-3700.

Several national organizations offer information on ADHD for parents. These organizations are listed here. Other organizations serving both parents of ADHD children and parents of children with learning disabilities are listed in the appendix. I encourage you to contact all of these organizations and specifically tell them you are the parent of a child with ADHD. Request general information on ADHD and membership information.

Children and Adults with Attention Deficit Disorder (CHADD)
National Headquarters
499 NW 70th Avenue, Suite 308
Plantation, FL 33322
305-587-3700

This national organization can help you locate a parent support group in your area. Membership includes a newsletter and the quarterly magazine *ATTENTION!* CHADD organizes an annual national conference on ADHD.

Attention Deficit Disorder Association (ADDA)
P.O. Box 972
Mentor, OH 44061
1-800-487-2282
This national organization can also help you locate a parent support group in your area. Membership includes a subscription to the newsletter *Challenge*.

National Information Center for Children
 and Youth with Disabilities (NICHY)
P.O. Box 1492
Washington, DC 20013-1494
1-800-695-0285
703-893-6061 (local)

CHAPTER TWO

The Symptoms That Characterize Your Child

Parents must become familiar with the characteristics of ADHD, specifically the particular symptoms their child exhibits, to help their child along the challenging path that lies ahead.

Although there have been many theories on the causes of ADHD over the years, and controversies over special diets and the use of medication, all professionals do agree on one thing: no two children with this disorder display the same combination of symptoms. One child may display eight or nine symptoms of ADHD, whereas, another may exhibit many more symptoms than those required to diagnose ADHD. Each child with ADHD displays a different pattern—symptoms that may change in different situations or even change from one moment to the next. Some children, for example, may do quite well in school while others may display behavior or learning problems in the classroom. (If you have ever attended a support group meeting for parents of children with ADHD you know exactly what I mean. Every parent present describes a child with a different combination of symptoms.)

As a parent of a child with ADHD, it is your responsibility to identify (usually with the help of other professionals such as teachers, physicians, psychologists, etc.) the symptoms that characterize your child and determine the best way to approach those problems. Only with the knowledge of the problem areas can you help your child effectively; knowing and understanding these characteristics provides a framework for expectations, management, and foresight.

Primary Symptoms of ADHD:
Inattention, Hyperactivity, Impulsivity, Distractibility

Typically, the child who displays hyperactivity (as well as aggressive actions and impulsivity) is the child who experiences behavioral problems at home, in school, or both. Some parents of hyperactive children say, with all serious-ness, that their children never crawled. One mom recalls, "He just stood up and walked one day and by the next was running through the house, going through drawers, and taking apart the stereo system. As a toddler and a preschooler he was like a tornado releasing his fury in his small world. Actually, he's not much better now at age seven, even when medicated. He's learned to control a few symptoms in some circumstances, but we face new challenges at each age."

Children who display the symptom of hyperactivity are often risk takers. Nothing seems to frighten them. No cupboard or bookcase is too high to climb. No situation is too dangerous. You can't tell them that something is hot, for instance, they must experience it for themselves. Even after a serious burn, they'll often return to the burner on the stove because of their impulsivity. They commonly have difficulty controlling their behavior and examining the consequences of that behavior. Therefore, they end up in the emergency room for stitches, burns, or broken bones more frequently than the average child.

The words "no," "stop," and "don't touch," appear to mean nothing to some children with ADHD (due to their poor self-monitoring). Their intense curiosity compels them to explore everything, even though that curiosity (which is a wonderful trait when channeled properly) sometimes invites trou-ble. One father reported telling his son not to touch the computer many times a day. "Everytime I turned around he was playing on the computer opening and closing files, moving from one program to another haphazardly. One day he erased everything. He immediately denied that he was responsi-ble for the lost files." It is common for children with ADHD to not accept responsibility for their own actions.

Children with ADHD are sometimes overbearing with peers. They can't keep their hands to themselves and tend to poke, grab, and touch other chil-dren. This aggressive behavior may result in physical fights on the play-ground with classmates, neighborhood children, and siblings. When asked who caused the fight, the hyperactive child may place the blame squarely on the shoulders of the other person. He seldom sees any relationship between cause and effect, whether he's burnt himself on the stove, erased a computer disk, or caused a fight on the playground.

Some children with ADHD create other problems within the home set-ting. Some have no respect for closed doors and are forever walking in on a parent or sibling who's using the bathroom. Oftentimes this is not done intentionally. The child simply does not stop to think before he pushes open that door, so locking doors is usually a necessity. But don't be surprised if your child knocks on the door repeatedly demanding entrance, especially if he has a low frustration tolerance. (My son once became so frustrated that he couldn't get into the bathroom because I was in the shower, that he took a metal toy and began hitting the wooden door. The damage was so extensive that the door had to be removed, sanded down, and refinished.) Other children will listen in on telephone conversations, ask inappropriate questions at embarrassing times, take items from siblings and forget to return them, and badger you for explanations when you've said no and then won't accept the explanation you've given.

In the classroom, children who have ADHD and hyperactivity may be noisy and disruptive. Or they may make numerous trips to the pencil sharpener or restroom. They may fidget, squirm, tap their feet, swing their legs, or yawn. Thus, hyperactivity can be displayed as just excessive fidgeting. "This is the hyperactivity most underdiagnosed: hyperactivity manifested as activity without purpose," says Bruce A. Pasch, M.D., F.A.A.P., Director of the Children's Center for Learning and Development.

Interestingly, children with hyperactivity react to negative feedback in the opposite way most children do (negative feedback becomes a positive reinforcement). A non-ADHD child may quiver when you raise your voice, or stop the offending behavior immediately at the threat of physical punishment. But threats of physical punishment may mean nothing to the hyperactive child. And, resorting to punishments such as putting soap or hot sauce in a child's mouth *will not* teach compliance. Raise your voice at your hyperactive child, and he may scream back at you. Spank a hyperactive child for misbehavior, and his misbehavior may escalate rapidly, sometimes reaching violent levels. Or he may just turn around and continue the activity you have just forbidden.

Parents and teachers are usually frustrated by an overactive child on a day-to-day basis, but consider how wonderful it is to have an overabundance of energy. Think of what a child could do with all of that energy as he matures if it is channeled properly.

Children with ADHD have difficulties with distractibility. This means that they have difficulty filtering out unimportant stimuli. In the classroom they may hear not only the teacher talking, but also the truck driving by, the child behind them flipping pages in his textbook, and the church bell ringing halfway down the block. They may also notice the flock of birds flying past the window and the squirrel running up the tree. Children with ADHD who are easily distracted have many stimuli competing for their attention. Although hyperactivity is annoying and frustrating, distractibility is a far worse symptom of ADHD. In fact, children who are severely distracted, and do not display hyperactivity, often go undetected for years. Distractible children frequently experience school failures, and may be labeled lazy or space heads. They suffer in silence and are not identified easily because, unlike hyperactive children, their behavior does not disturb others. Children with ADHD may be both hyperactive and distractible, only hyperactive or distractible, or they may not exhibit either of these symptoms.

The child who is easily distracted is usually unable to stay focused on one activity for any length of time, unless it is something he chooses to do. One may observe this in a preschooler or an elementary-age child, for instance, who becomes bored in a room full of toys. A complaint commonly heard by parents is, "I'm bored. There's nothing to do."

Do you find that you have to tell your child two or three times or more to complete a chore? Does he need to have directions repeated several times? Does he start projects but fail to complete them before moving onto another activity? Does he have difficulty keeping track of his possessions? Does he have difficulty paying attention in school? Does he have problems taking messages, keeping the facts in order? Is he frequently late for appointments or never shows up? Does he have difficulty concentrating or paying attention except when he's doing something he particularly enjoys? When you are speaking with him, does he often have a blank look on his face as if he hasn't heard a word you've said? You're witnessing the symptoms of inattention or distractibility or both.

Social Difficulties

Many children with ADHD tend to act younger than their chronological age. They usually are immature and, as a result, tend to play better with younger children often because they cannot successfully do what their peers do. An eight- or nine-year-old child who has ADHD and comorbid (coexisting) fine motor skill challenges may not be able to play certain sports, but can run, jump, and climb (gross motor skills) successfully—typical play activities for younger children. Therefore, the eight-year-old may feel more comfortable with a five- or six-year-old than a child his own age. Sometimes the child with ADHD will even prefer toys made for younger children. Rarely does he understand why he fits in better with younger children, but his perceived immature behavior often separates him from others his own age. As one mother stated, "He's like a square peg trying to fit into a circle [of peers]. He can't fit in no matter how hard he tries." Yet, the immature child often successfully maintains friendships with younger children.

Some children with ADHD are bossy (telling others how to play the game, and insisting it be done their way), pesty, and annoying (teasing and harassing). They may throw temper tantrums when they don't get their way and be prone to fighting, arguing, lying, and cheating. They may attract and make friends, but are usually unable to keep them. Unlike other children in their age group, children with ADHD often have difficulty picking up on social cues, such as facial and verbal expressions or body language. The child is often unaware of the negative messages being sent from peers and seems surprised to learn that others are upset with them. (Children with social skill deficits, without ADHD, may also do these same things.)

A child with ADHD may grab toys away from others, not wait his turn in games, or not follow the rules—all irritating behaviors to playmates. Yet, this same child, may also have wonderful creative-play ideas and find that he has many friends who are willing to tolerate his bossiness because he is able to organize fun activities (the ability to organize and take the lead are valued skills). Another child with ADHD may consistently interrupt conversations (because he's afraid he might forget what he wants to say) or not pay attention to what others are saying. While friends sit around talking and laughing, he may be staring out into space, inattentive to those around him. So while one child with ADHD might attempt to play with other children and fail miserably, another may be totally oblivious to those around him, thus also failing to make and sustain friendships. Still others, because of their gregariousness, may have no social difficulties. In fact, they might be seen as some of the more popular students in school.

Some children with ADHD are great negotiators. If you offer them fifteen extra minutes of play time, they'll negotiate for more. Before you know it, your offer of fifteen minutes has been upped to thirty minutes. Other children with ADHD are also extremely persistent. If they enjoy a particular activity, or want to learn a specific challenging concept, or tackle a difficult game, they'll stick to it until they've conquered it. They don't give up easily. In the same light, if they desire something they are not hesitant to go after it. Many children with ADHD have sharp observation skills and notice things that others frequently fail to notice. This is a wonderful trait, until you witness your child darting across the street to take a closer look at a bird's nest in the peak of a neighbor's roof. Although these are all marvelous attributes for adults, parents often think these characteristics are overbearing when displayed by their children.

Some children with ADHD have little appreciation of how their negative behavior leads to adverse consequences. Most of these children have no idea what they have done wrong or why friends have ostracized them. They do not feel personally attached to an incident or consider themselves responsible for causing the problem, so they blame others for being angry with them and feel that they are being treated unfairly. However, children with attention deficits often are able to feel genuine remorse for their actions in retrospect. (This is a key point because it distinguishes ADHD from conduct disorder.) This creates confusion in the minds of those closest to them. "If he understands now what he did wrong, why didn't he recognize it at the time?" is a question that often stumps parents and teachers. **The answer: although the child now recognizes the consequences of earlier behavior, it does not necessarily mean he can prevent it from happening again in the future.** Remember children with ADHD are frequently impulsive, insatiable, and often lack the ability to control themselves in many situations.

Emotional Difficulties

Attention Deficit Hyperactivity Disorder is a physiological, not a psychological, condition. If emotional difficulties (depression, anger, anxiety) are evident, they are the result of ADHD, or comorbid, not the cause. This is extremely important for parents, teachers, and other caregivers to understand. Children who exhibit signs of emotional difficulties often have low frustration levels, explosive tempers, and difficulty accepting no for an answer. They experience frequent and rapid mood swings, are especially self-centered and have little or no regard for the feelings of others, and sometimes have an I-don't-care attitude.

One mother sums it up quite well: "Whenever my son is punished by losing a privilege or being sent to time-out, he screams out, 'I don't care what I lose. I hate you and I think you are stupid.' Usually he apologizes later, so I know he has given thought to what he said to me. When he loses control like this because he doesn't get his own way, he's very angry and I feel very frightened for him. I wonder if he'll ever be able to control himself. I wonder if he really doesn't care. I wonder if I am the cause of the behavior and if he really hates me." Children with ADHD usually forgive and forget quickly, but they are also moody and unpredictable. Employ a trained professional to help your child with anger control if it becomes a problem.

Children with ADHD are unusually hard to please. For instance, one mother bought her son a Nintendo game that he had been begging for for months and remembers, "He played the game for about twenty-five minutes and then came to me looking for something to do." They can also be extremely negative and oppositional. "My daughter complains about everything. Nothing is ever good enough," says Kelly from Austin, Texas. Children with ADHD also may be reckless, irresponsible, negligent, and argumentative as is evident in the lighthearted approach they take to completing homework, for instance. Point out an error to them and you're apt to hear, "Who cares?" or "My teacher won't care if one problem is wrong."

Clearly, poor self-esteem is a common emotional difficulty many children with ADHD suffer from and one area parents need to help their children with. Poor self-esteem is the result of many things the child experiences, such as frustration with getting school assignments completed and handed in on time, distress in not being able to follow directions, difficulties in organizing themselves, stress from trying to control impulsive behavior, and the constant struggle to stay on task. Often they feel they are being treated unfairly compared with non-ADHD siblings. As a result, their self-esteem plunges even lower. They hear the frustration in their parents' voice. They regard themselves as "bad," or "troublemakers," and often see themselves as stupid and different from other children. (These feelings usually develop about the time they enter elementary school.) Some children are bombarded with "no" and "can't you behave?" from parents and caretakers. As a result of the constant criticism, some children may develop the I-don't-care attitude. Once a child reaches the point of not caring, he has lost a relevant incentive for adhering to society's rules.

Poor self-esteem can exhibit itself in the form of depression, but the depression is secondary to chronic failure. The child may be gloomy, saddened, and detached. He may cry easily or appear angry at himself or the world in general. Some children may act out their depression in destructive ways, such as trying to hurt themselves or someone they love.

The common symptoms of depression are:

- I-don't-care attitude (about things that used to matter)
- Irritability, anxiety
- Loss of interest
- Loss of zest (fatigue and diminished energy for normal activities)
- Diminished appetite or increase in food intake
- Feelings of sadness, hopelessness, and despair
- Preoccupation with death, suicide, or running away
- Disturbed sleep
- Hopelessness and despair
- Inability to concentrate or make decisions

If your child (or you) experiences these symptoms, please seek professional help.

One excellent defense mechanism against depression, and a way to release anger, is exercise. Studies prove the benefits of exercise in both children and adults. Hyperactive children and children with ADHD who do not display hyperactivity, can profit from regularly scheduled exercise programs. Exercise promotes relaxation and helps build stamina and confidence. It is pleasurable, fun, and distracting. It can be a wonderful family activity, or your child can exercise alone with proper guidance. (Specifically, karate has been shown to help improve self-discipline.) If your child has coordination problems, you may want to avoid team sports in which his performance will be judged by his peers.

Physical Difficulties

Children with hyperactivity are in constant motion whether they're bouncing off the walls, talking nonstop, wandering aimlessly, or frequently moving from one activity to another. You may observe them picking their nails, cuticles, noses, or scabs, or pulling on their hair (one boy I know has a bald spot from pulling his hair out one strand at a time), pulling up their socks, or tugging on an earring. Attempts to break the child of such idiosyncrasies are futile, and one peculiar, distressing trait is often replaced by another when it stops.

Sleeping difficulties are apparent in many children with ADHD who are also hyperactive. Many times, they require less sleep than the average child, so don't expect your child to take a nap or fall asleep peacefully at 8:00 P.M.

like your friends' children do. Many children don't fall asleep until 10 or 11:00 P.M. and are awake by 5:00 or 6:00 A.M., but they usually sleep through the night, often quite soundly. Others may fall asleep without much of a problem, but they sleep lightly and often awake during the night. One mom said her child used to fall asleep every night by 9:00 P.M., but would wake around 1:00 A.M. and not fall back to sleep until 4:00 A.M. Because she couldn't trust her child, she would stay awake to make sure he didn't get into trouble. Whether your child goes to bed at 10:00 P.M. and sleeps until 6:00 A.M., or is awake much of the night, sleep deprivation is a common complaint among parents, especially mothers who are usually with their children the majority of the time. Bedwetting also is not unusual for such children.

Children with ADHD may have difficulties with either fine motor skills (small-muscle coordination) or gross motor skills (large-muscle coordination). Children with poor fine motor skills may have problems with writing, drawing, and coloring, for instance. It is not unusual for some fourth graders to be still drawing stick people, much like the ones four-year-olds draw. Their coloring is still uneven and they can rarely stay within the illustration's lines. Their ability to print and write may be limited. They have difficulty forming letters and may actually form letters differently than the way they were taught. They may always have poor penmanship, but their handwriting does improve with age (in many cases) as small muscles develop.

Children who face challenges with comorbid gross motor skills may have difficulty riding a bicycle, running, skipping, and hopping on one foot. They appear clumsy and uncoordinated and often have difficulty with team sports that require an ability to hit or catch a ball. Children who experience difficulty playing certain team sports like football and baseball usually do much better in sports like golf, swimming, bowling, horseback riding, fishing, diving, and karate. ADHD motor difficulties that are not caused by a co-existing condition are due to poor self-monitoring skills and, consequently, improve with medicine. It is important to note, however, that such difficulties can occur without ADHD.

Some children with ADHD have a high tolerance for pain. As previously mentioned, coupled with their impulsive behavior, this means they are more likely to have accidents that require trips to the emergency room. Your responsibility as a parent is to literally keep your child alive. Supervise your child constantly. Some children will climb bookshelves in a matter of seconds if something they want is on the top shelf. If the bookcase is not bolted to the wall the unit will come tumbling down. Their curiosity and determination (another great trait to have when channeled properly) are so intense that if they want to see how power tools work, for example, they'll test them without your help. They can scale a tall tree in seconds, and fall to the ground in even less time. Pain is felt for only a few seconds, so they don't learn from past mistakes. They will climb that bookshelf, test that power tool, and scale that tree again, no matter how serious their injuries were.

Toilet training is often difficult. It is not uncommon for children with ADHD, especially boys, to still be in diapers during the day at age four (sometimes they just don't want to take the time to use the bathroom and interrupt their play). Often boys, and sometimes girls, will still experience occasional nighttime wetting when they reach elementary school age, or still be in diapers every night. Bedtime wetters are often sound sleepers. If their nervous systems are not fully developed, as is often the case, they should not be punished for what they cannot control. Sometimes patience, understanding, and time is all that is needed. If bedwetting is still a problem after age seven, speak with your pediatrician.

Last, children with ADHD appear to have a higher number of physical ailments than other children, such as ear infections; allergies; speech, hearing, and vision problems; stomachaches and headaches. Headaches and stomachaches may be caused by medication or result from anxiety. Your child may develop a stomachache or headache when facing a test or just from the fear of having to confront a new situation.

Academic Difficulties

Without a doubt, most children with ADHD have academic difficulties. Children with hyperactivity may not be able to sit still in school. They may appear restless, fidgeting and squirming in their seats, or they may not be able to stay seated more than a few minutes at a time. They may be disruptive in class or even assume the role of the class clown. (Their ability to pay attention is limited even when medicated.)

Other children, those without hyperactivity, may be compliant. So compliant, in fact, that they never get into trouble for talking or misbehaving in class. They sit still, but are often found staring out the window or into space. As a result of their inability to concentrate and sustain attention, they also experience academic failure. They may be unable to focus and listen to the teacher when directions are given for assignments and may do the assignment inaccurately or not at all. Often, they start an assignment but never complete it. Timed tests are often impossibile for some children because they work much slower than the average child. It takes them longer to get started on a project, to process the information, to organize needed materials, and complete assignments. They need more time simply because they are not able to attend to the task in the same manner as the student who does not have ADHD. Perhaps the most frustrating aspect of inattentiveness is that the student may be able to attend successfully one day, but not the next. A teacher who does not fully understand the inconsistencies of ADHD, may see the student as lazy or unwilling to do the work.

One child told me, "As class began, I would tell myself over and over 'You must pay attention. You must pay attention.' Before I knew it, the class was over and I hadn't heard a word the teacher said." This eighth-grader was not considered a problem in school, but she had the same basic difficulties in school as the hyperactive child. She was easily distracted and had difficulty paying attention. As a result, her schoolwork suffered. Her problem was not hyperactivity (unable to sit still or restlessness) but daydreaming.

Consequently, the child without hyperactivity often slips through the cracks. He is not disruptive in class, or overly active, so his attention problems are not easily identified by her teachers. Usually, by sixth, seventh, or eighth grade (or even later), his problems will catch up with him (or his ADHD problems may never be identified). After years of frustration and disappointments, children without hyperactivity may come to the attention of teachers only because of behavior changes. They may become withdrawn and depressed. The length0 of time before the ADHD is detected may also depend in part on intelligence level. Those children who have high IQs are usually working at grade level or above. Deficits are often masked. Children with average or below-average intelligence are at a greater disadvantage. A percentage of children with ADHD will also have other learning disabilities. The actual percentage varies between 30 and 80 percent, depending on which doctor, psychologist, or psychiatrist you speak with.

Problems may arise with classwork and homework, beginning in lower school and lasting throughout the child's educational career. Children with ADHD may be slow in completing classroom assignments because they sense a need to overmonitor as they go. Or they may do their work so quickly that they make numerous errors because they hurried through it to move onto something more enjoyable. Others may be impulsive and overlook details, such as addition or subtraction signs, or they may fail to stop and read the directions before beginning the assignment. Additional problems children with ADHD may experience in school are: wandering from the classroom, not focusing on a group activity, poor organizational skills, poor short-term memory, talking out of turn, and bothering classmates who are attempting to complete classwork.

Keep in Mind

Attention Deficit Hyperactivity Disorder is difficult to understand, but it is important that parents keep the characteristics of ADHD in mind when dealing with their child. While many—perhaps most—children with ADHD will not exhibit symptoms as severe as some of those outlined here, it is imperative that parents identify those symptoms their child displays. Parents and other caregivers simply cannot compare a child who has ADHD with other children. It is unfair to the child with ADHD. Parents must keep their expectations of themselves and their child realistic. Never forget that ADHD is a developmentally disabling condition, which, in many cases, will last a lifetime.

CHAPTER THREE

Chronological Patterns of ADHD in Children

Whether you suspected your child had ADHD from the time he was born or learned of it later, you now know that your parenting role is different than other parents'. You know, because you are reminded of it every day by your child's actions and behavior from the time he awakes each morning until he retires for the night. Even when you are out alone, the reminders are there. You observe other families in restaurants, in places of worship, at the mall, and you note the differences.

As the popular saying goes, children do not come with instructions. However, each of us enters parenthood with preconceived ideas of how our child will behave, speak, and, to an extent, dress (even when the child is not biologically related to us). But children do come with their own temperament, personality, likes and dislikes, abilities, and challenges. For many families, this is not a problem. However, for families dealing with a child who has special needs, preconceived notions are just that, and it then becomes necessary for them to make adjustments in their lives. We must first look at our child objectively and determine his talents and abilities, his strengths and his weaknesses. To do this effectively, parents must often rely on the expertise of many professionals, such as pediatricians, pediatric neurologists, psychologists, psychiatrists, teachers, social workers, and therapists. They also must open their private lives to relatives and friends because they, too, will be with the child and will provide the parents with assistance and moral support. With help, most parents eventually learn coping skills, find extra patience, new ways to discipline, and different ways to teach their child.

As your child grows and develops, you will find that each age brings different concerns and unique challenges, and what works one year may not be appropriate the next. Naturally, all families must learn to adapt as parents and children grow and change, but a family with a child who has ADHD will experience more confusion and challenges than the average family. You must learn to expect the unexpected.

Grandparents, other relatives, and friends, also have preconceived ideas about your children. They may also experience a mixed bag of emotions when confronted with difficult or unusual behaviors exhibited by your child. Some may be very straightforward with you, telling you clearly what you are doing wrong. Others may offer suggestions using the backdoor approach, "If I were you. . . ." And still others may just shake their heads in disapproval.

However, some relatives and friends will offer you support and help. I encourage you to accept all of the assistance you are offered because there will be many days when you will need a shoulder to lean on for moral support. Families and friends can provide a tremendous amount of support, but only if you share information with them about your child.

This is not meant to imply that all the days ahead will be dismal and bleak; they will not be. You will have some wonderful times with your child. But, children with ADHD can be so unpredictable. One week they are great, the next two weeks they are awful, then suddenly they're great kids again. The highs and lows are tough to handle (most parents feel as if they're riding an emotional roller coaster). A supportive person can help even out feelings of anger, bitterness, shame, pride, joy, and love.

With these feelings in mind, let's take a look at some extra parenting challenges you might experience at different stages of your child's development and how you might begin to cope.

Infants

"My parents kept telling me I must be doing something wrong when Drake cried continuously," says Kathy, a twenty-eight-year-old mother of a difficult baby who rarely slept, and physically resisted affection and cuddling. "She made a point of telling me that I scarcely cried when I was an infant because she met my needs. She also reminded me that all babies love to be held and cuddled, implying that I was doing something wrong."

Kathy's mother did feel her daughter was an inadequate mother. Instead of looking at the baby as a possible source of the problems Kathy was experiencing, she was quick to blame Kathy. She had her own thoughts, which she shared freely, about how babies (Drake in particular) should behave. Clearly, Drake did not fit her expectations.

ADHD Symptoms in Infants

A small percentage of babies display ADHD symptoms. These infants are not easy babies to care for from day one. They often have sleeping and eating problems. They are rarely on a dependable schedule and often wake up during the night every hour or two for as long as two or three years. They often display sharp mood swings and an intense response to stimuli. Babies may spend many of their waking hours crying or fussing, and efforts to calm them are ineffective. Most babies enjoy being held and cuddled, whereas the baby with ADHD frequently resists holding. Parents report that their babies actually turn away from them, pushing and squirming in their effort to break loose. Many resist being held (wiggling and crying frantically) even for routine bottle feeding, preferring instead to take their bottle propped or holding it themselves, while in an infant seat. Once the parent puts the baby down, the crying usually stops immediately. Parents feel rejected and frustrated, and report difficulty bonding with their new son or daughter during the first year or even longer.

These babies are generally very alert, active, curious, and often display remarkable strength by turning over at two or three weeks of age, for instance. Some reach milestones well before other babies. Other children do not reach milestones at the appropriate age and are considered developmentally delayed.

These symptoms do not necessarily mean that a baby has ADHD. But they do identify babies who are at risk, especially when a family member has been diagnosed with ADHD. Some children with ADHD show signs as infants and are identified at an early age (usually by the age of two or three). However, some children who are diagnosed with ADHD at a later age, may not have shown any subtle signs as infants. Some parents remark that their children seemed normal until they began walking. "It was like a dam had broken," said one parent, "and he was the rushing water. Nothing was safe from destruction."

Adoptive parents of difficult babies should be open to the possibility that their baby may have inherited this disorder from his or her birth family. (Adoptive parents should always make an effort to obtain as much background information on their child as possible. They should not be afraid to ask if ADHD or learning disabilities are evident in the medical history of the birth parents and their families.)

Admitting Something Is Not Right

What can you do if you are experiencing parenting difficulties? First, you have to be able to admit that your baby is not like the average baby. Once you can accept that your baby is different, and difficult not because of anything you have done or not done, you should seek the help of a health professional. Usually, this will be your pediatrician. However, if your pediatrician tells you these behaviors are normal, get a second opinion.

Supportive professionals can offer suggestions and techniques to help you manage your baby. Some hospitals have a child-evaluation program for difficult babies and can offer techniques for coping with your baby on a day-to-day basis. Call your local hospitals for information.

Establish Routines

You can take steps immediately to begin modifying some of the difficulties you are experiencing. Start by establishing routines. Give baths at the same time each day (right after breakfast or before bedtime, for example). Feed your baby at approximately the same time each day. If you cannot hold your baby to feed her with a bottle in the normal manner, try laying her on your lap with the heels of your feet resting on a coffee table or footstool. Your knees will then be propped up so she can't roll off your lap. Then hold the bottle but not the baby, or let her hold the bottle. This will (almost) give you the desired closeness with your baby, without causing her to feel restrained.

According to Bruce Pasch, M.D., F.A.A.P., a pediatrician and the Director of the Children's Center for Learning and Development in Toledo, Ohio, difficulties in breast feeding an infant who does not like to be held are rare. Unlike the bottle-fed baby, Dr. Pasch says breast feeding appears to calm the infant when held in the cradle position. If your infant is under six months of age, and you are experiencing difficulties with breast feeding, he recommends talking with your pediatrician, or a breast-feeding consultant or nurse educator at a local hospital. Some mothers may choose to terminate breast feeding. Others may prefer to express the breast by using a pump and then feed the breast milk through a bottle. For infants over the age of six months, Dr. Pasch recommends placing the baby on your lap in an upright position facing you with your hand on his bottom. If this method doesn't work for your baby, your choices are the same as for the infant under six months of age.

Avoid Overstimulation

Try not to overstimulate your baby. Although many babies love to be gently tossed around and many dads, in particular, enjoy doing so, this type of exciting play will only stimulate your baby more. Although using a rocking chair is calming for most babies, my youngest child hated the rocking motion. He cried when I rocked, yet stopped crying when I ceased rocking. He also cried because he didn't like the feeling of being restrained on my lap. As soon as he could sit up on his own, we then sat next to each other, but I usually had to be sure there was at least one inch between us so our bodies didn't actually touch. Often, we could sit like this for five minutes—not much time, but the closeness helped with bonding. Gradually, the sitting-close time did increase, but not by much. Take whatever closeness you can and feel grateful. Continue to look for other activities you can enjoy together that permit some degree of closeness—like bathing your child or brushing his hair—without stifling him.

Keep Things Soft and Quiet

Use soft colors in the nursery rather than bright or primary colors. Keep a night-light on in the room at all times, so you never have to turn a bright light on during the night or in a room that is naturally dark during the day. This way you won't startle your baby by turning on a light.

Use smooth-textured blankets in the crib, one or two soft, cuddly stuffed animals, and only one toy (even one toy may be too much for your baby). Some infants respond to soothing music at bedtime (try a special tape, but realize that some infants will awake when the recorder turns off, in which case you may need to use a radio). My youngest son, who rarely slept as an infant and toddler, would wake at the slightest noise. At nap time, I turned the phones off and used the answering machine. I also used a fan in his room day and night to block out all sounds. Eventually we had to disconnect the doorbell and leave a note on the front door with other instructions for visitors.

Babies Who Don't Sleep at Night

When tending to a baby who frequently awakens during the night, follow the same routine. Do not turn lights on (this won't be necessary if you use a night-light), and do not pick up the baby. Your goal is to check on his safety, settle him down, and leave. Of course if the baby is wet or it's time for a feeding, care for him, but follow the same procedure night after night.

If your baby never sleeps more than an hour or so, ask your pediatrician for a mild sedative. Once the baby can sleep several hours with a sedative, you will be able to stop the medication because the infant usually will have established a routine. (Some doctors recommend using Benadryl, but **always** check with your doctor before administering any over-the-counter medications to learn what dosage would be appropriate for your baby.)

Time Away from Baby

Whenever possible, spend time away from your baby outside your home. These babies can drain you of every ounce of energy you have. If you can afford a baby-sitter for a few hours a day or every other day, then hire someone. One woman hired a baby-sitter for two hours a day; one hour she used for running; the second hour she took an extra long bath and read. This gave her the time she needed to pull herself together. If you can't afford a baby-sitter, find another mother you can trade baby-sitting time with.

Don't forget about your husband. He, too, needs time away from the baby. Make time to go out together. If you can only find a baby-sitter during the day, then meet your husband for lunch.

Difficult Babies May Become Difficult Toddlers

Many babies who are suspected of having ADHD may become even more troublesome as toddlers. These toddlers may exhibit distractibility and/or hyperactivity, get into everything, exhibit a low frustration level, become accident prone, and have unusually long and intense temper tantrums. Some professionals believe that it is possible to identify 60 to 70 percent of all children with ADHD (only if hyperactivity and impulsivity are the main traits) when they are toddlers or preschoolers.

Toddlers and Preschoolers

Daniel was an easy baby. He ate and slept well and was a good baby overall. As an infant, he loved being held and cuddled. At fourteen months, however, Daniel became extremely active. His mother, Janet, described the next two years: "It was as if he became a different child. Suddenly he was climbing on the furniture, climbing up on the kitchen counters to reach into the cabinets, sneaking outside when I was trying to do laundry. Toys no longer interested him. He found electrical appliances to be much more entertaining. We couldn't keep him away from anything electrical including the outlets. Attempts to child-proof the house were in vain. He would literally break off the child-proof locks we had placed on drawers, cabinets, the refrigerator door, and on electrical outlets. He would throw towels in the toilet bowl, flush the toilet, and I would find him in the bathroom laughing with delight as the toilet bowl overflowed. Once, when he was supposed to be napping, I found him trying to climb out of his bedroom window.

"Three times before his second birthday, he received stitches. Once at twelve months he was trying to stand on his head while on a chair and he fell out of the chair and hit his head on the end table. The second time he ran and tried to jump onto a rocking chair. He missed, and hit the arm of the chair. The third time he climbed a bookcase that was not bolted to the wall. The bookcase fell on top of him and he cut open the back of his head. At four years of age, Daniel was diagnosed with ADHD."

Risk Takers
Many toddlers and preschoolers with ADHD are accident prone because they take risks that most children wouldn't. They are often destructive, noncompliant, and are forever getting into things the average child wouldn't even notice or be interested in. They are unable to see a relationship between cause and effect. When Daniel required stitches after falling off the chair, he surprised his parents by immediately returning to the same chair after coming home from the emergency room. Much to his parents' dismay, he was ready to try the same stunt again.

Speak with Your Child's Doctor
Again, there are things you can do to reduce stress during this age period. If your child's behavior is not like other children of the same age (extreme

temper tantrums, noncompliance, low frustration level, abnormally high energy level, etc.), talk with his physician. Obtain a second opinion if necessary. You may want to contact a local mental health center or a university (if it has a mental health center) to have his learning and behavioral problems assessed. Again, you also can contact local hospitals to see if they have child evaluation services. Whatever you do, don't give up. If you suspect your child has ADHD, it is important that you find appropriate services for him as soon as possible.

Transition Times

As with the difficult infant, keep your child on a schedule so he knows what to expect daily. When you must break the routine, tell the child that day what to expect ahead of time. Give him a five- or ten-minute notice before changing clothes, leaving the house, or arriving at your destination. Remind him what you expect his behavior to be like several times during the drive. For example, on the way to Grandma's house you might say: "Nathan, when we arrive at Grandma's, I expect you to get out of the car quietly." Once in Grandma's driveway: "Nathan, I want you to hold my hand (or I will carry you into Grandma's house) but we must do this quietly." Always tell your child what his behavior is to be like once you are inside, for example: "Nathan, give Grandma a hug and say hello. Then sit on the floor and play with your toys." In other words, don't surprise your child with breaks in routines. Always give warnings. And remember, not all children respond to changes in routines and warnings equally. Some children will always react negatively to change, which becomes an extremely difficult and embarrassing problem for parents to handle. For many, these problems do diminish over time or reduce in intensity on their own, and often dissipate completely when the child begins drug therapy.

Ways to Cope

First, understand your child's temperament. Temperament is your child's natural, innate tendency to behave in certain ways. Is he stubborn? Impulsive? Does he throw temper tantrums? Is he shy? Inattentive? Fussy? Defiant? Overactive? Now, when you witness certain frustrating behaviors remember you cannot *change* your child's temperament because it is inborn. You can, however, learn ways to cope with his behavior.

"When I see Michael getting upset about something and know a temper tantrum is just seconds away, I immediately distract him by offering to play a game or read to him," explains Jennifer from Sacramento, California. "Distraction is a management solution to some problems parents face with young children who have ADHD. Bring out a toy your child enjoys. Offer to take a walk outside with him. Suggest a treasure hunt. Sing a song together."

Be consistent in your disciplining techniques; always praise your child's acceptable behavior. In fact, watch for appropriate behaviors and praise as often as possible. Try to praise your child twenty or twenty-five times a day. Set a goal for yourself and keep track of the positive remarks you make to your child until it becomes a habit.

"Too often parents get caught up in seeing only the negative," says Sue from Cincinnati, Ohio. "If you find yourself constantly saying "No," "Don't," "Stop," then you're missing the positive qualities your child displays. Praise your child each time you see her doing something right."

Children in this age group are not receptive to long talks about appropriate behavior. All small children have a short attention span, but young children with ADHD are especially unreceptive. Make explanations simple, and calmly say what you must in as few words as possible.

Child proof your house, including covering electrical outlets. Lock up cleaning products and lock other cabinets necessary to keep your child from getting into things he shouldn't. Even if your child manages to break the child-proof locks, he probably won't break them all in one day. Keep extra locks in the house, including ones for the refrigerator and toilet bowls. For climbers who enjoy getting into kitchen cabinets, reserve one cabinet at floor level just for them. Let them climb in and out of this cabinet, but be sure to keep some interesting items in there for them, whether it's toys they particularly enjoy, pots and pans, or plastic storage containers. Let them know this is their area and that they will not get into trouble when they play in that cabinet.

For a child who strays out of the house, add a lock at the top of the door that he can't reach. While his temper will soar for a few days after installation, he'll learn that he can't go outside unless you let him out. This frustration usually lasts about a week, but you will no longer have to worry about him leaving the house without your consent.

Remove glass items, priceless keepsakes, and plants from your child's reach. These items appeal to all small children, but children with ADHD won't leave them alone until they are broken. Don't bring these items out again until you are sure they'll be safe from your child's hands (usually around age six or seven).

If your child is always getting into one particular type of item, as Daniel did with electrical appliances, find something similar for him to play with. Daniel's parents gave him an old clock, a broken radio, and an old toaster—all minus the electrical cords. (Always be cautious with items that have small parts for children under the age of three.) As Daniel grew older, he became greatly attracted to computers and electronic games and is now extremely proficient in both. In this case, the child's interests were carefully monitored and channeled in a direction that proved productive and acceptable.

When you ask your child a question, allow ample time for the answer. Your child may need extra time to process the information. If your child doesn't comply with the request or answer the question, rephrase it. A child with ADHD may not understand the question or the request you have made.

The best way to handle the hyperactivity level in this group is to supervise your child constantly. Most parents have no choice but to follow their child around, unless they hire a mother's helper. If you are in tune with your child, then you certainly know what turns him on, whether it's electrical appliances, the refrigerator, stereo, toilet bowls, mom's cosmetics, the home computer, or water. To help him with trouble areas, engage your child in other activities he enjoys and keep those little hands busy. But even then, keep your child in sight because you never know how long it will be before he abandons the coloring book or the television show he's watching. **Never** just tell your child to go paint a picture or watch a video. Instead, get the paints and paper out for him and lead him to the table or turn the television on and insert the movie in the VCR. Most children will give almost any activity a try if everything is laid out for them.

If you are going out and need to get ready, put your child in the bathtub while you dress. While fixing dinner, let your child play with water in the sink, play with pots and pans on the floor away from the stove, or work on a special project (gluing pasta on construction paper) within your sight. Always check on children that should be napping. In a matter of minutes they can destroy their rooms or remove screens from bedroom windows if left awake and unattended. Most parents develop a sixth sense with their children, but parents of children with ADHD must develop a seventh or eighth sense.

One mother, realizing that the house was awfully quiet, found her three-year-old backing her car down the driveway. The car stopped when it hit a tree. The child had always shown an interest in cars and, unbeknownst to anyone, knew exactly where mom kept the car keys. The next day, mom and dad bought their child a battery-operated car. Yes, they are expensive, but this child drove that car in the snow, rain, and sunshine for three years and now their youngest child is enjoying it. These parents accepted that their child's impulsiveness would likely lead to another experiment with the family car; they concluded the play car would cost far less than repairing the family automobile.

As you know, children with ADHD can be a handful, but they are also delightful toddlers and preschoolers. They are creative, bright, curious, and have a boundless supply of energy—qualities we admire in adults. As parents, we need to direct these qualities to generate positive experiences for our children.

Elementary School-Age Children

Half of all children with ADHD are diagnosed during the grade school years. Learning disabilities also become more evident at the elementary school level in some children with ADHD. However, not all children with ADHD will have learning disabilities. There are children with ADHD who are gifted. Anthony, who has been on Ritalin since age four because of hyperactivity and impulsivity, began reading at age three. Now eight years old, Anthony is reading at the eighth-grade level and his comprehension is at the ninth-grade level. He began playing around with computers when he was eighteen months old. In third grade now, he excels in computer science. Everything he knows about computers he has learned on his own. He also speaks two languages. Still other children with ADHD have average or slightly above-average IQs and do not have learning disabilities, and other children have one or more comorbid learning disabilities.

Andrea was in third grade when her teacher approached her mother. Andrea was having difficulty paying attention in class, never completed her classwork on time, and seemed unable to follow directions. The teacher also noted that Andrea seemed withdrawn and isolated, and did not have friends to play with at school. Andrea's teacher suggested that she be evaluated for Attention Deficit Disorder. When Andrea was diagnosed with ADHD, her mother blamed herself for not recognizing the symptoms. Andrea's older brother had been diagnosed with ADHD when he was in kindergarten, but his symptoms were more obvious because he displayed more hyperactivity. Andrea was fortunate in that she was identified at age nine. Many girls are not identified until they are older, usually because they do not often display hyperactivity. Instead, they may appear quiet, shy, and withdrawn.

David's grandfather had waited for the day when he could play baseball with his grandson. The problem was that every time he tried to play with David, he was greatly disappointed. "David always seemed excited about playing ball, but he became bored with the game. It was also difficult for him to take turns with the other neighborhood children. He often got confused about the direction in which he was supposed to run," says his grandfather. "One time I kidded David about falling down, and he became extremely angry, verbally lashed out at me, and then lost total control of himself. I was shocked. When I finally summoned the courage to confront my daughter about David's behavior, she admitted that David had always been like that at home, and recently was displaying the same types of behaviors in school."

Eventually David was diagnosed with ADHD. Grandpa was disappointed and saddened to learn about David's disorder. David's parents, also saddened, were relieved to find there was a name for David's problems.

School-age children will continue to display many of the characteristics they exhibited as toddlers and preschoolers. Many children with ADHD are "immature" for their age, often two to three years behind. Children in this age group may also display poor social skills. Tasks performed in school and at home often indicate inconsistent performance.

Establish Rules and Set Up a Reward System

As a parent, you should clearly state the household rules for your child, your expectations, and the repercussions if those rules are broken. If there are two parents in the home, both must be clear about these rules and consequences, so when your child acts inappropriately you both deliver the same results in the same manner. Be sure your child knows and understands the house rules. Discuss them with your child when he is calm and able to sit and listen. Write them down and post them where your child can easily review them.

Before discussing house rules, be sure you have made eye contact with your child. Then begin the discussion. For a child who always puts his feet up on the chair at the table you might say, "John, we need a new rule in our house. The rule is that no one may ever put their feet up on their chair at the table during meals. We hope you will abide by this rule, but if you can't keep your feet off the chair, you will be excused from the table whether your meal is finished or not. This rule has been written down on the blackboard in the kitchen and the bulletin board in your bedroom." Have your child repeat the new rule so you are sure he understands it. Always decide ahead of time which behaviors bother you the most and begin with no more than three inappropriate behaviors to work on at one time. Even three behaviors may be too much for some children. If so, reduce the number to two or even one.

Do not expect the behavior to change overnight; it may take months. Give positive feedback immediately on those days he can keep his feet off the chair. You can acknowledge this accomplishment by a verbal praise, a hug, a kiss, extra television time, or another appropriate activity.

The reward system is another approach that works well. For it to work successfully, however, parents must make a commitment to use it. Here's how this system works: Let's say that each day your child comes home from school and drops his belongings on the floor right at the door. Each day, you become more frustrated as you remind your child to pick up his backpack, hang up his coat, and put his boots in the utility room. In the example above, you would sit down with the child and establish the new rule. Only this time, you and the child will choose the reward he will receive after remembering to put away his things for three days (the time period may be extended to five days or more for older children). For every day he remembers, you give him a small token, a sticker perhaps, that he places on a chart. When he accumulates three stickers, he is then entitled to receive the reward (an hour playing at the park, or a board game with you, for example). The three days do not have to be in succession for the child to receive the reward. (For younger children, even three days may be too long to wait for a reward. If this is the case with your child, you may need to give the reward daily or even in one-half-day increments.)

In our home we use play money. We have a chart with household rules on it. Each rule is worth a specific amount, anywhere from one dollar to twenty. Each time our son follows a rule, he receives the agreed amount. The money he earns is placed in an envelope for one week. During the week he must spend this money. We charge him five dollars an hour to play Nintendo or Sega Genesis, two dollars an hour to ride his bike, ten dollars an hour for playing games on the computer, three dollars to watch a rented video, and two dollars to watch an hour of television. Every Saturday, he turns in what is left of the money he's earned. For every ten dollars in play money he turns in, he receives one dollar in cash. He may spend this money as he wishes or he may save it for something special he wants to buy. In this case, once we give a reward (the play money, for instance) we never take the reward away. Instead, for noncompliance we might use time-out, take away a privilege, or assign an extra household chore. We do not take away what he has already earned.

We have used this play-money system very successfully now for more than six months. The original household rules were replaced by new house rules two months after we initiated this system because we had achieved the desired effect. However, no reward system works forever, so be ready to substitute another system when needed. Always seek professional help if reward systems do not work with your child.

As with infants, toddlers, and preschool children, establish a daily routine. Children do best when they know what to expect—whether it is on a school day or on a weekend, in the morning or at bedtime. Plan a daily routine together, allowing for his input, and put it in writing. For instance, when he gets ready for bed at night he can have a snack, brush his teeth, and use the bathroom before he puts his pajamas on. Whatever the planned routine, he must follow it. On the nights he cooperates, you might allow him fifteen minutes reading time in bed before he turns off his light, for example.

Devise a routine for mornings and provide a token reward (for every three or five stickers he receives a pack of baseball cards, or she receives a new hair ribbon). Follow the same routine as closely as possible for every day of the week including Saturdays and Sundays. The times may vary (for instance, on a weekend he may stay up an hour longer), or he does not have to do homework on Friday and Saturday nights, but the basic routine stays the same. On weekends, he must still get up, brush his teeth, eat breakfast, and then get dressed—the same daily routine.

Although some professionals will tell you to reward only those positive actions that require no verbal warning, parents should assess their individual child. If your child has short-term memory problems or difficulty with concepts of time, a verbal warning may be necessary until a routine is established. With some children, daily reminders are always needed.

Avoid Physical Punishment

Unless your child is an infant, you may have learned already that physical punishment does not work with your child. Many parents today prefer not to use physical punishment, yet most parents of children with ADHD have at least tried it once—often out of frustration and desperation. If you are one of the few parents who have not administered a spanking at least once, here's an example of what may happen. "I struck my six-year-old one time," admits Jessica, "and couldn't believe what happened next. Bobby became more aggressive, verbally abusive, and lost total control of himself. He actually displayed more strongly the very behaviors we were trying to eliminate."

For Bobby and other children with ADHD, physical punishment becomes a positive reinforcement. If a child is seeking attention, your reaction to a particular behavior, whether it is a positive or a negative reaction, will give the child the attention he is seeking. Thus the behavior, whether positive or negative, will increase because it has been rewarded. Physical punishment also teaches aggression, the very behavior that many parents of children with ADHD are trying to eliminate. For instance, spanking a child teaches that it is acceptable to hit others when angry. Remember you are a role model for your child. If you hit, he learns to strike out. If you scream at him in anger, he learns that this is also a satisfactory way of handling feelings of anger. When angry, if you lose control of yourself and throw objects, you can expect your child to react the same way, since many forms of aggression are learned from others.

Besides the fact that physical punishment can cause extreme negative behavior, many children with ADHD are extremely tolerant of pain because of their short attention span. The pain they feel is there one second, gone the next, unlike the average child who may feel that sting for several agonizing minutes. Remember the mom earlier in this chapter whose son, Daniel, received stitches several times before his second birthday? On each occasion, Daniel never cried—not when the accidents happened nor when he received stitches. If an injury that requires stitches doesn't hurt, how can we expect a swift smack to the rear to hurt?

Time-out

Besides using a reward system, what are other ways can we deal with noncompliance? Many professionals suggest using time-out and many parents use this system effectively. However, some experts believe that time-out should be reserved for the more severe noncompliances you experience with your child. (As with all suggestions in this book, always consult with your physician or other professional who helps you with behavioral management techniques before trying something new.)

Time-out is an easy concept to understand, but may be difficult to enforce at times. A child is sent to time-out when he displays inappropriate behavior, such as casually walking by a sibling and striking her. Time-out is always carried out in isolation from other members of the family. This might be in the kitchen, a bathroom, the child's bedroom (if there are no toys in the room), or a guest room. Time-out can be used for children two years and older. The time spent in time-out depends on the child's age. Parents often use one minute for each year of age until the child reaches the age of five. After that, some professionals feel five minutes is sufficient time because by then many children will have forgotten why they were sent to time-out in the first place. However, other experts advise that you use one minute for each year of age regardless—for a ten-year-old, time-out would be ten minutes.

This is how time-out works: Billy walks by his sister and strikes her. You see this behavior and say, "Billy, striking your sister is unacceptable behavior. Go to time-out and get yourself under control." No other comments should be made, including any conversation the child may initiate. Set a timer that the child can hear go off in five minutes, or in five minutes tell your child he may leave time-out.

Issue only one warning. If your child does not comply, then physically carry him to the designated time-out area. If your child does not stay in time-out during those five minutes, restart the time-out. With children who really test limits, you may physically have to place the child in time-out any number of times. One mom says she had to put her four-year-old daughter back into time-out thirty-six times before the child finally realized that mom meant business.

When parents initially learn about using time-out for children with ADHD, their first reaction is usually, "We've tried everything and you're telling us our child will just walk off to time-out just like that?" Well, it may not be just like that, but if you haven't tried it before, you may be surprised. For some children, the first time they receive this command issued by a *calm* parent, they may go immediately to time-out. The difficulty begins later because children with ADHD, and all children in general, *hate* time-out. It means leaving a room where everyone else is, to go to another room isolated from others. No fun!

If your child comes out of time-out and is still not under control, immediately send him back to time-out. Once he comes out and is under control, reissue your request (if he was told to do something and failed to comply, for instance). If he does not comply, then send him back to time-out.

After using time-out effectively for a length of time, don't be surprised when you tell your child to go to time-out and he immediately begins to apologize saying he won't do "it" again and how sorry he is. Accept his apology, but he must still spend his designated minutes in time-out. You might say, "Billy, I accept your apology, but you did not do as I requested. Go to time-out for five minutes." He may once again apologize, giving you no choice but to take him physically to the time-out area. For children who absolutely refuse to stay in time-out, take away all privileges until the child serves his time. This means he loses access to toys, telephone calls, friends who stop over, television, games, outside play, etc., until he complies. Once he serves his time, he immediately regains full privileges.

You are probably thinking, okay, great, but how can we enforce time-out when we are not at home? Believe me, parents have found ways. "I recall one occasion when my seven-year-old was totally impossible in the car. I pulled into the first parking lot I saw, and he found himself outside of the car sitting on the ground for five minutes," says Sheri from Atlanta, Georgia. "That was absolutely the last time he ever tried that stunt."

If you're shopping, try the floor in a corner away from foot traffic. In a mall, use the seating areas provided but not the ones down the main aisle. Older children will usually march to a seat and sit down. Younger children may need to be physically carried to time-out in the mall. Do what you must, but follow through with the time-out. When visiting others, just ask for a place to use for time-out. People will be quite obliging, especially if the child is being disruptive. Time-out can be used anywhere as long as you use your imagination.

Natural Consequences

Natural consequences also work. For instance, it is thirty-five degrees outside and your child refuses to wear a coat even though you have explained how cold it is outside. You could, of course, send him to time-out for noncompliance or you could let him experience the cold himself. Sometimes a natural consequence is a great way to learn. Of course, you should never use natural consequences as an option if it severely jeopardizes your child's health or safety.

Adolescence

Adolescence is a difficult time for most teenagers, but especially for teenagers who have ADHD. If hyperactivity was a problem in the childhood years, parents may notice that it is no longer a problem in adolescence or only a minor one displayed by a sense of restlessness, such leg wiggling, finger tapping, or getting up every ten or fifteen minutes to sharpen a pencil or get a drink. However, other common characteristics—such as impulsiveness, poor judgment skills, learning problems, and troubles with friendships—may be still evident. Later, we'll take a more in-depth look at the adolescent with ADHD.

Parents during These Stages

With a fleeting vision of their dream child in mind, parents are quick to realize that despite all of their repeated attempts at normalcy, their child is unable to meet their expectations. As the child tries to meet these expectations and fails, parents become confused, frustrated, angry, depressed, and often feel a sense of failure and guilt. As relatives and friends observe, they too become frustrated and saddened by what is happening. Many will empathize and offer their support and love. Others may simply withdraw from your life, believing you have done something wrong to create such a difficult child; or they may prefer not to socialize with what they perceive to be a dysfunctional family. Parents will need to make an extra effort to explain to others that their child has a disability and how it affects his behavior, so they will know that he is not just a "bad" child. For some parents this will not present a problem, but for those who are embarrassed that their child has a medical problem or is not a "perfect" child, the process of telling others will be difficult. In the next chapter, we'll take a look at those people who should know about your child's disability and why.

CHAPTER FOUR

So, Your Child Has ADHD

As a parent of a child with ADHD, it is your responsibility to learn as much as possible about this disorder not only for your child's sake, but because you will be explaining ADHD to family, friends, baby-sitters, teachers, and others caring for your child for many years to come. As you look for information and reference materials, don't forget to utilize medical libraries at nearby universities, and textbooks that teach educators about ADHD (See the Appendix for other specific sources.)

Barbara, a thirty-four-year-old mother, was, like many parents, unsure about what and when to tell others. "My husband doesn't want anyone to know," she says. "He doesn't want people to judge Eric, and feels they will if they learn he has ADHD." The chances are good that people are already judging Eric, especially Sue, his baby-sitter, who sits with him two days a week and his preschool teacher who sees him three days a week. Grandma and grandpa are probably wondering also, as are Eric's neighbors. Eric is a hyperactive child who throws extreme temper tantrums whenever Barbara must leave him. Transitions are very difficult for Eric. He is also a child who is constantly on the go and always getting into things he shouldn't. Undoubtedly, the people who are with Eric weekly have already asked themselves, "What's the matter with this child? Can't he ever sit still? Why can't he control himself like most children his age? Why don't his parents do something about his behavior?"

Eric was recently placed on medication with excellent results. But, this means if Barbara doesn't get home in time to give the second dose when a baby-sitter is in the home, or if the preschool teacher is with Eric when the first dose wears off, his baby-sitter and teacher are seeing two different sides of Eric. Now they are asking Barbara questions and she doesn't know how to respond without explaining the actual situation.

Some parents have little trouble telling others about their child, but other parents feel that the fewer people who know about it the better. Ironically, most people who come in contact with your child already know something is not quite right because children with ADHD usually act differently than other children. If you don't tell them about your child, they will speculate.

Remember, ADHD affects every part of your child's life. It affects his behavior and his ability to learn, socialize, and make and keep friends. It affects him at home, in school, at camp, when you are out shopping, on vacation, or visiting friends, family, and neighbors. If people don't understand why he is the way he is, they will most likely judge him and you. Consequently, your child may be labeled as a troublemaker, a spoiled brat, a space-head, weird, or whatever name people may choose to use. If your child hears people using such labels, his self-esteem will plummet. Fortunately, this scenario can usually be avoided if the people who know your child understand ADHD. Instead of ridiculing, most people will offer support to you and your child.

Who to share this information with, when, and how much to share is a relevant concern of most parents. When you elect to speak with others, you must be prepared to explain ADHD in a simple manner. Your main goal is to elicit the support of those who love and care for your child and those who work with you in a professional capacity. Remember, the majority of the population knows nothing about ADHD.

Physicians and Other Professionals

All professionals who work with your child should be told of his ADHD. Even a simple dentist appointment will be easier for your child and the dentist if he or she understands that your child has ADHD and may not, for example, be able to sit still long enough for a routine examination and cleaning. It's helpful to choose a pediatric dentist or a dentist who routinely works with children. Most understand ADHD and can handle your child tactfully without humiliating him.

A speech or occupational therapist, although used to working with children with special needs, must still be told about your child's short attention span or his difficulty following directions. This knowledge gives all professionals, including teachers (see chapter seven for a complete discussion on teachers), the ability to approach your child in an understanding manner and will make the experience less stressful for all involved.

Journals

All parents need to keep accurate medical records on their children, but especially for their children with special challenges. Keep a journal and record unusual behavior. Note the date and child's age at the time the behavior became evident. Be prepared to give detailed reports to your child's doctor and other professionals, addressing the behavior you are concerned about such as extreme motor activity (how he displays the hyperactivity, whether it's a problem at home, in school, or at school and home, the effect it is having on the family, on classmates, etc.).

Write a brief history of your pregnancy, delivery, when your child reached significant milestones, and update it continuously. Every time you visit a new doctor or other professional you will be asked the same questions, again and again.

Adoptive parents may not have information on a pregnancy or delivery, depending on the type of child they adopted (a child born in another country may not arrive with this sort of information), but an American-born infant may have this information in his hospital records. Although adoptive parents can only share what information they have been given, they can keep accurate records from the time the child is placed with them. Many adoptive parents routinely keep accurate records of their child's milestones because they know how important these records will be to their child when he is older since adopted children usually arrive with little social and medical history.

Making Good Health Care Choices

Questions to Ask about Referrals to Specialists
(From "A Parent's Guide: Doctors, Disabilities, and the Family," volume 1, number 2, May 1990, published by the Information Center for Children and Youth with Disabilities)

1. Specifically, why is this referral being made? Is this a second opinion or are we seeing the specialist for a diagnosis?
2. Are there records I should take with me or will they be sent in advance?
3. Is this specialist comfortable with children like mine? Has he or she been fully informed about my child's disability or would it be useful for me to give him or her a call?
4. Who will get the reports of this evaluation? Who will be interpreting them? Who will be discussing these reports with me?
5. What are this specialist's rates? Can arrangements be made to help cover these expenses?

Questions to Ask When Scheduling an Appointment for Your Child

1. I will be needing a longer appointment than most families. Can we schedule a time when we can have a double appointment?
2. My child has difficulty waiting patiently. Is the first appointment of the morning available or one right after the lunch break?
3. If you don't make appointments, what times of day or which days of the week are least busy?

What Should a Family Do Before the First Visit to Another Doctor?

The new doctor will need information about your child and his/her medical history. Before the first appointment, be sure all medical records are either mailed or delivered to the doctor's office. It would be useful for these records to arrive at least a week before your visit so that the doctor has time to look them over.

If your child has already been seen by specialists, have these reports sent to the doctor, too. If your child has educational assessments, send these along as well. The more the doctor knows about your child, the better able he/she is to discuss your concerns.

Requesting that medical records be sent to another doctor is routine. You should not feel uncomfortable requesting your child's records. If your child has already been seeing a doctor, it is always acceptable to request an additional opinion without insulting the first doctor.

You should write to the first doctor's office (most physicians require written permission to send records) and say, "I am interested in discussing my child's situation with another doctor to get additional opinions. Please send a copy of my child's records to Dr. (fill in the name) at (give the mailing address)."

You might also make a list of topics for discussion with the new doctor. Since many children are shy around doctors, especially ones they've never met before, you may need to bring up problems that the doctor cannot readily see. For instance, if you suspect your child may have a language delay, say so. Then the doctor can try to initiate more conversation with your child to better observe your concerns. If you are worried about possible developmental delays, make a list of things your child does or doesn't do to give the doctor concrete examples of behavior he/she may not be able to observe in the office. If you would like a referral for a hearing screening or vision tests, be sure to mention this. Doctors can conduct preliminary visual, hearing, and speech screening in their offices to help to determine if a specialist is needed.

[Never think a doctor is all-knowing. There is no formal board certification for those who specialize in ADHD.]

What Should You Look for When You Get to the Doctor's Office?

Look around. Is this office child proof? Are there toys for your child to play with? Are there many things he/she should not touch, climb, or get into? Can you let your child move around in this room without undue restraint? Are well children separated from children who may have contagious illnesses?

How helpful is the office staff? Do they seem open and friendly, or do you feel out of place here? Are the nurses who weigh the child, conduct eye exams, and perform some of the examination functions comfortable with your child? Are they pleasant to you? Are they supportive of your needs? Does your child seem comfortable, or at least as comfortable as any child feels in a doctor's office? If he/she is frightened, is the staff warm and reassuring?

After the doctor has examined your child, you might ask if the nurse or receptionist could take the child out of the room for a few minutes so you can talk to the doctor alone. Children who are very active can make conversation difficult for both you and the doctor. If this is not possible, ask if the doctor can phone you later in the day to discuss your child and pick a time when you can talk on the phone uninterrupted.

Questions to Ask about Tests

1. What do you expect to learn from these tests? Always ask a physician to explain in layman's terms what a specific test is for and why it is being ordered.
2. Have these tests been given to my child before? Can we coordinate any of the earlier results with these?
3. Does the school or public health clinic also do these tests? Is there any reason not to have them done there to save on expenses?
4. How long will these tests take and what is involved in them?
5. Is there anything I should tell my child about these tests that will help prepare him?
6. Can he eat before coming?
7. Are there any precautions I should take before or after these tests?

Questions to Ask about Medications

[If the physician prescribes medication, be sure you know what it is for; ask for clarification of anything you don't understand and report any reactions to your physician immediately.]

1. When should I give this medication?
2. When the prescription says "three times a day" does that mean every eight hours even during the night, or three times during the daytime while awake?
3. Should the child take this medication before, during, or after meals?
4. Are there any foods that should not be mixed with this medication?
5. How long should he take this?
6. (If your child has other medications he is currently taking) My child is currently taking (name of medication). Can he take this medicine at the same time?
7. Are there any possible side effects or allergic reactions I should be aware of? How will I recognize them? What should I do if I think he or she is having a reaction?

8. Does this medicine need to be stored at a special temperature? That is, will it go bad if the medicine gets too hot or too cold?

Between visits, write down any questions or concerns you have. When you visit the doctor, take your notes along with you. Be sure to take notes during this, and all, doctor appointments. If you need an additional appointment to cover concerns that were not addressed during this session, make the appointment before leaving the doctor's office.

Family Members and Friends

Discuss ADHD with your family and friends. Because many people believe that hyperactivity in children results from poor parenting, it is vital that the child's grandparents, aunts, uncles, cousins, and siblings realize that ADHD is a medical disability. In many ways, ADHD is a "hidden disability," so parents may be reluctant to share something that they feel is not readily apparent to others. Other parents may hide their child's disability because they are disappointed that their child is not perfect, or embarrassed that their child has inherited this disorder.

Adoptive parents are often especially disinclined to share their child's medical information because they want to be seen as perfect parents of perfect children. Unfortunately, this attitude is perpetuated by society's attitude that adopted children are not the same as other children. Prospective adoptive parents often hear such comments as, "Why do you want to adopt? You never know what you'll get." Parents who adopted their child as an infant may fear hearing, "What did you expect? It's not like you gave birth to him." (As if any parent, biological or adoptive, can look at a child and see what the future will hold!) Whether your child is biological or adopted, you must remember that *no* child is perfect. As parents, we must look beyond our personal feelings and do what is best for our child.

You can help your child greatly by giving family members factsheets and books on ADHD to read. While some family members may be willing to take the time to read such materials, not all are. If your family is unwilling to read about the disorder, then share your thoughts and knowledge with them. Eventually, they will learn about it whether they want to or not. In the meantime, do not expect your family to adjust immediately. If you do entertain ambitious expectations, you will be greatly disappointed when a family member reacts negatively to your child or makes an insensitive remark. Remember, most people know little if anything about ADHD and their remarks are often made out of ignorance, not lack of concern. Learning about ADHD is a daily process for you, but you must be patient with others.

"I've told my father at least fifty times to never yell at Brad when he does something wrong, yet occasionally he does," says Brooke, Brad's mother.

"Then my dad becomes livid when Brad reacts violently to the yelling. The angrier my dad becomes the worse Brad behaves." If family members sometimes care for your child, be sure you provide them with positive disciplining techniques to use when your child displays inappropriate behaviors. (If necessary, write them down.) Never concede to pressures from relatives who try to convince you that all your child needs is a good spanking!

Remember close relatives, especially grandparents, are affected by your child's situation. They, too, may feel guilty, especially when they learn that ADHD is inherited in most cases. They may wonder what part they played in their grandchild's disability. They also may experience fear that future grandchildren will inherit ADHD and confusion about the disorder in general. The method you choose for interacting and sharing information with them will affect the way they support you and interact with your child for years to come.

Invite grandparents to attend workshops and conferences on ADHD with you. This is particularly relevant if grandparents are extremely critical of your parenting style, vehemently oppose the use of stimulant medication, or both. They must be educated. One parent combined a conference with a short family vacation and invited her parents along, at her expense. ("It was worth having to eat on a strict budget for several months," says this parent.) Introduce grandparents to your friends who also have children with ADHD. If possible, let them meet other grandparents who have grandchildren with ADHD. This gives them the opportunity to discuss the disorder with their peers.

Provide special opportunities for grandparents to interact with your child so they, too, can learn to know him as a person, not just as a child who has special challenges. Choose activities that will not overly excite or stress your child. Grandparents can take grandchildren to the park, for an ice cream cone, fishing, bowling, out to eat, to a movie (they can always leave if the child can't sit any longer), and to story time at the library. They can read to the child, initiate craft-making sessions, or attend Grandparent's Day at school. Children usually do well when with grandparents because they are the center of attention.

Finally, don't dwell constantly on the problems associated with ADHD. Relatives, grandparents in particular, like to hear positive stories and feedback about their grandchildren. Always share your child's achievements and milestones with them. Be sure they understand that despite the special parenting problems you encounter, your child is still a unique individual with his own set of talents and abilities and is also an important member of your family.

Siblings

A child with ADHD will affect a younger brother or sister, as all older siblings do. Toddlers and preschool-age children often find their older brother or sister funny when the child displays inappropriate behavior. Because many children with ADHD are "immature" for their age, the younger sibling often sees the older child as someone on his own level. Therefore, the younger sib is quick to imitate the child with ADHD, even though mom and dad constantly point out that the behavior is unacceptable. Removing both children from the scene and placing them in time-out (in separate isolated areas) is one recourse for parents.

Younger siblings need to be exposed to other children so they can learn appropriate behaviors. If there are no younger children in your neighborhood or you live in a rural area, your child is especially vulnerable because his older sibling with ADHD may be his only role model. You may want to enroll your child in a day care center or a preschool class either on a part-time or full-time basis, if you can afford the extra expense.

Some therapy programs and school programs have a special group for siblings who have a brother or sister with special needs. Such groups help siblings understand their brother's or sister's disability, and teach the child how to interact with his sibling. Many groups also encourage role playing so the child can learn what it feels like to have a disability such as ADHD. These groups also provide the opportunity for the non-ADHD sibling to be with children who do not have special needs. If you cannot locate such a group, consider starting one with other parents of children with ADHD who have younger siblings. Since siblings are often embarrassed by a sibling with ADHD, it is important that your child realize that he is not the only child with a brother or sister who is "different."

Explain ADHD in terms your other children can understand. The best time to do this is when you are alone with your other children. Young children do not require long explanations so keep it simple and clear. For example, you might say, "It is difficult for your sister to follow directions and pay attention. We all need to help her." Or say, "It is hard for your brother to sit still. We need to help him." Check your local library or bookstore for children's books that address disabilities in siblings.

If a child asks for more information, give age-appropriate facts. Older children will need a more detailed definition for ADHD so they can try to help their siblings. Never explain ADHD when you are frustrated and disappointed with your child, especially if the inappropriate behavior was displayed in front of your other children. You will be apt to explain the disorder in negative terms and make statements you will later regret. Be sure your younger non-ADHD children understand that they cannot "catch" this disorder and that children do not die of ADHD.

Talk about your child with ADHD with your other children. Let them tell you how they feel about him. "After one particularly difficult morning, my four-year-old son and I sat down exasperated after my child with ADHD finally left for school," says Sally from Fairfax, Virginia. "Ben just looked at me and shook his head slowly from side to side." When Sally asked Ben what was the matter, he replied, 'I'll never act like that Mommy when I go to school. He was awful this morning.' Sally admits that sometimes Ben does find the behavior irritating, yet he usually does follow his older brother's example. "That's why we enrolled him in school next fall," adds Sally. "He needs to be around normal behavior as much as possible."

Many siblings harbor jealous feelings because parents tend to give more attention to their child with ADHD. Parents need to make a harmonized effort to spend quality time with their other children. Strive to strike a balance between the children so all energies are not inadvertently directed toward one child. This is often not easy because children with ADHD can deplete your energy levels quickly.

Although it is often easier to ask your non-ADHD children to help with chores, it is not fair to the other children to have responsibilities while the child with ADHD contributes nothing. Always give your child with ADHD a list of chores that are his responsibility and be sure he completes them, even if it means you must supervise. Be sure the chores you designate are ones he is capable of handling so that you can give positive feedback on a job well done.

A younger sibling may taunt and tease an older sibling with ADHD if he surpasses his older sibling in abilities. For example, toileting problems (particularly bedwetting) linger longer in some boys with ADHD. "Our oldest son is seven and still in diapers at night. Our youngest son is four years old and has been out of diapers for over a year now," explains Troy, their father. "Unfortunately our youngest son points this out almost daily to our oldest son. He's still too young to understand the problems his older brother has." Situations such as this one do improve as the younger sibling matures and understands the problems associated with ADHD, but it's a difficult situation for the child with ADHD to be harassed by a younger brother or sister. Assure your child that (1) neither he nor the ADHD is to blame for the bedwetting, (2) he will not wear diapers forever, and (3) his sibling is too young to understand why this is happening.

Neighbors

Before you send your child off to play at neighbors' homes, be sure your neighbors understand that he has ADHD and what this means in relation to your child (is he hyperactive, impulsive, a risk taker, has difficulty following directions or keeping track of time?). They may not want the responsibility of supervising your child, which means you may find the neighborhood children in your yard on most days. The majority of parents feel most comfortable with this situation. They can supervise the children and interfere, if necessary, before their child alienates himself from all of the neighborhood children. Always invite only one friend at a time to your house and limit the time they spend together. Tell your child your expectations ahead of time. For example: "Andy can stay one hour, as long as you and he can play well together. Then it will be time for you to come in and start your homework." Be sure the other child's mother is aware of the restrictions you have placed on play time, and always let the children know at least ten minutes beforehand that play time will be ending soon.

Baby-sitters

A baby-sitter certainly deserves to be told that your child needs constant supervision and the reasons why. If he is impulsive and often gets into dangerous situations while playing outside, or needs to have directions repeated to him frequently, the baby-sitter must know this. She must also understand that the child is not intentionally trying to make her job more difficult.

For your child's safety you must be able to explain ADHD in a straightforward and concise way, without frightening the baby-sitter and while stressing the need for supervision. (Energetic seventeen- and eighteen-year-olds often make great baby-sitters for children with ADHD.) Never just say, "Sam is hyperactive. Do you know what that means?" Most baby-sitters will answer yes, not wanting to embarrass themselves by telling you they don't understand.

When hiring a baby-sitter, be sure she understands that your child has ADHD before she arrives. Teenagers are usually energetic, but an older person may not have the energy or desire to follow your child around from one place to another or one activity to another.

Always assume that the person you are interviewing to care for your child knows nothing about ADHD. Give a potential baby-sitter information on ADHD to read during an interview and explain how it relates to your child. Then discuss ADHD with her.

If you decide to hire her, ask her to arrive early on her first day so she can spend some time with your child before you leave. Before leaving, give her a list of instructions. This list should include your child's trouble areas (he tends to climb the fence and go into the neighbor's yard when not supervised) and emphasize those activities he may or may not engage in (he's not allowed in the garage). As well, include how he is to be disciplined, what types of reactions to expect from him, and how she is to handle various situations that may arise. Personally, I have found that baby-sitters appreciate this openness and guidance. In nine years, our children have had a total of three baby-sitters. Despite the difficulties these sitters have experienced, including having to take children to the emergency room when I couldn't be reached, one baby-sitter stayed for two years, another for three years, and our present sitter has been with us more than four years.

Scout Leaders, Coaches, and Other Activity Leaders

Children with ADHD can benefit from organized group activities. Groups are great for teaching socialization skills and children with ADHD certainly need help in this area. Children should be encouraged to participate in scouting, religious, and sport activities. However, parents must be honest with group leaders about their child, especially if these people must administer medication. Group leaders also should be given guidance on how to discipline your child. If your child plays a sport, be sure the coach knows exactly what your child's abilities are. You don't want your child standing in the outfield extremely bored if he's capable of being the catcher, but that's exactly where he could end up if you don't explain ADHD adequately.

Coaching the team or being the scout leader certainly will allow you to control your child's interactions, but if your schedule does not permit this level of involvement, either mom or dad should be present for games and volunteer to help at meetings and on special activity days. Be aware that many children come home "hyper" after these events. Interacting with a group of children often provides more stimulation than the child can handle, but these activities also help channel excessive energy into a positive experience.

Be honest with these people if your child also has learning disabilities. If a scout troop is putting on a short play, your child may not be able to remember the lines. But, maybe he can hold a prop or play an instrument or participate in some other way without embarrassing himself.

Acquaintances

While I certainly won't advise you tell every person you meet about your child's disorder, I am convinced that it is beneficial in certain situations. For instance, I regularly shop at the same department stores, grocery stores, etc., and the sales clerks and cashiers know me by name. Because I am often with my oldest son, I have found it helpful that these people understand that he does not act up deliberately and that he has a medical problem. Many times, they have kept an eye on my son while I tried something on in a dressing room. I can hear them asking about school or cub scouts or camp. One woman keeps a special treat in a drawer under the cash register. My son is permitted to open the drawer and take a piece of gum or whatever is in there when I'm in the dressing room. Another woman allows him to arrange clothing by sizes, and still another clerk lets him fill out an application for a charge card.

Telling these people has permitted me to get my shopping done without sales clerks glaring at me or reprimanding my son. Because I never want them to think that I am taking advantage of them, I always thank them for their help and often remember them with little tokens of appreciation. As a result, my son and I are always welcome in the stores we shop in and many more people are now aware of Attention Deficit Hyperactivity Disorder. (Before you make plans to explain ADHD to the salespeople you know, plan to heed this advice: never discuss ADHD in a way that is embarrassing for your child.)

Of course the decision to tell or not to tell is ultimately yours. But I encourage you to tell those closest to your child for your sake and your child's. Secrecy only promotes the notion that you are ashamed of your child. As one mother said, "My son is a good-looking boy and I am proud to be his mother. He has a wonderful personality and a beautiful smile. So he has a disability, so what? No one has a perfect child."

Remember your child's ADHD is no one's fault. With proper intervention, support from loving parents and friends, and guidance, your child can grow to be a happy, productive adult.

CHAPTER FIVE

Problems That Drive
You Wild

Many children with ADHD present challenging behaviors at home that can make living with the child an overwhelming, frustrating experience on a day-to-day basis. As a parent of a child with ADHD, you already know that your child is different from other children and that he cannot be parented in the same manner. For instance, discipline techniques used with other children may not work with children who have ADHD. There are, however, different strategies or techniques that parents can exercise to modify some, if not many, of the problematic challenges their child faces (poor impulse control, poor attention, high distractibility, and/or hyperactivity). Using specific techniques can influence the child's behavior so that the quality of homelife improves both for the parent and the child. In this chapter, you will learn the strategies other parents have used to successfully handle these often complex, but common, behavior problems.

Not all of the following strategies will work with every child who has ADHD. This is because children with ADHD are remarkably different in that their symptoms vary: symptoms may be present in differing degrees, some symptoms may not be present at all, or the symptoms may change from one day to the next. Because of this, what works for one child may not necessarily work with another. Some of these techniques may work for your child. Others may work with slight variations.

Handling School Mornings

School mornings with a child who has ADHD are perhaps one of the most frustrating and annoying daily experiences for many parents. Some parents have children with ADHD who can't get out of bed in the morning, and who move at a snail's pace, with no regard for time schedules, once they're up. Other parents have children who wake up too early on their own (between 5

A.M. and 6 A.M.) seven days a week. These children have an overabundance of energy in the morning and little control over their actions. They not only wake up early, but make sure everyone else in the home is awake also. However, like the slow movers, early risers also move leisurely on school mornings because they, too, have difficulty staying on task. Early risers are just as likely to miss the school bus as the slow movers. Some children experience no problems in the morning, although many of their parents admit to using the same exact routine every day.

Craig, a father from Red Wing, Minnesota, says he and his wife use the following approach in the morning, "We wake Jody up at 7:15 A.M. and she has until 7:30 to get dressed, brush her teeth, and make her bed. From 7:30 until 7:45 A.M. she watches television as a reward for getting her first tasks of the day done on time. From 7:45 to 8:00 she eats her breakfast. She then watches television until 8:15 when she leaves for her five-minute walk to school. This schedule is posted in her bedroom, in the bathroom, and in the kitchen. Jody always procrastinated until we put her on a strict schedule, which she follows successfully most days." Craig says they bought a clock for Jody's bedroom *and* use the timer on the stove from 7:30 to 8:15.

If possible, use an alarm clock to wake your child. Some children with ADHD wake up in a cheerful mood, but others wake up ready for a fight—their arms are swinging and legs kicking as verbal insults flow freely. Better that the alarm clock be the recipient of such abuses, than you or your spouse.

"Mornings always seem to be a struggle, especially if there are brothers and sisters," explains Joanie of Sylvania, Ohio. "I found that picking out clothes the night before helps speed things along in the morning. I also used a timer for all functions, such as getting dressed, eating, and brushing teeth. Start the first day, allowing extra time and gradually shorten the time the child has to do each task until you find a comfortable amount of time for everyone. Eventually you may not need the timer."

"My son wakes up to his own voice in the morning," explains Dan from Santa Barbara, California. "We helped him make a tape, which we turn on in the morning then we leave the room. The tape begins, 'Good morning, Jonathan. It is now seven A.M. and it's time to get up.' Then one of his favorite songs plays for about two minutes. After the song, the tape reminds him (in his own voice) that at the tone he is to get up and get dressed now. Two more songs play (which gives him about five or six minutes to get dressed) and he then tells himself to go downstairs to eat breakfast." Dan admits that until he and his wife implemented this approach, mornings were a disheartening experience in their home.

"Surviving early mornings is still a problem for us as David [who is six years old] takes his medications between 7:30 A.M. and 8:00 A.M., and occasionally he awakes as early as 5:30 A.M.," explains his mother, Kate, from Carlinville, Illinois. "Making beds, getting dressed, can last forever with

David bouncing around, getting everyone else off track. David also hates being alone and will purposely wake his brothers."

"Currently David can have two bad mornings a week, the third time is a strike out. David then loses his bedroom, which he shares with his brothers, for two nights. He then must sleep in a sleeping bag in another room. If he's too rowdy getting ready in the morning, then he loses television time which is a big deal for him. Does it work? Not perfectly, but the situation has improved. As he continues to improve, he will gradually be allowed more privileges, like being able to go to the living room to read upon awakening," explains Kate.

"My husband plays a racing game with our son to see who can get dressed first," says Terri from Moravia, New York. "To concentrate on eating breakfast, we play beat the clock," says Beth from Bow, New Hampshire. "We set the timer on the microwave and my son must finish eating before the beep."

"We have school chores," says Ellen from Oconomowoc, Wisconsin. "They consist of getting dressed, shoes and socks on, hair combed, breakfast eaten, and teeth brushed. If our son finishes by the designated time (7:00 A.M. in our house), he gets a prize. I make up squares of cloth and vary the contents (crackers, pennies, stickers, etc.) and put several items in each surprise package. No chores, no prize."

"The biggest challenge we faced in the morning was trying to get our son up and out of bed," admits Janelle from Ohio. "He had his own alarm clock, which he had to get out of bed to turn off, but usually he would just crawl back into bed. On several occasions, he had missed the school bus. I used to drive him to school, but now if he misses the bus due to his procrastination, he has to walk.

"When I decided to try this approach, I told him what would happen if he missed the bus in the morning. He just sort of chuckled. A few days later his chuckles turned to tears as he set out to walk three miles to school. I telephoned the school and left a message for his teacher." Janelle admitted that the thought of sending her fourth-grader out the door on his own was frightening, but says everything had been prearranged. She had friends along the route who called her when her son passed their homes and the school secretary telephoned when Philip finally reached his destination almost two and a half hours later. "That day was also the first and last time Philip ever missed the school bus," Janelle chuckles.

My own son's behavior in the morning before school was awful for four years. It didn't matter what type of mood Christopher woke up in. Halfway through breakfast (he took his Ritalin while eating breakfast so it had no real effect until he was already gone), he would throw his bowl of cereal up in the air, throw food at his brother, hit his brother, argue, and yell at me. After breakfast, he would run through the house screaming and throwing things around. I would follow him around putting him in time-out, trying to get him dressed, keeping him away from his brother who was also trying to get ready for school. It was a nightmare. When it was time to leave for school, he would go out the front door and run around our property refusing to get into the car with his father and brother. When they finally left, I would break down and cry. On several occasions, his dad left without him because our son refused to get into the car. I would call the school and explain that he would be late. I would then drive him to school (because we were seventeen miles away), take him to his classroom and make him explain to his teacher why he was late. But even that didn't work.

One Sunday evening, in desperation, I made up a chart for the week listing all of the tasks Christopher had to do each morning to get ready for school and noted all of the unacceptable behaviors that had to stop. I then sat down and explained the chart to him. Each morning he was to check off his tasks as he completed them. If he did not complete a task by the time he had to leave for school, or if he misbehaved (ran through the house, threw things, or hit his brother, for example), he would be given extra chores to do after school. Together we drew up a list of chores and I had Christopher write each chore down on an index card. We then estimated the time each chore would take (some tasks would take five minutes, others up to thirty minutes). I explained that for each uncompleted task (not brushing teeth, for instance) and for each behavior rule that was broken before school (screaming), he would have to draw a chore card out of the box. Those chores would then have to be completed immediately after school before he could play outside, use his Nintendo, talk with friends on the telephone, or do any fun activity. In other words, he would be grounded until his chores were completed.

I further explained that school mornings were his responsibility. If he chose to be noncompliant, then he also chose to be grounded and do chores after school. He seemed surprised, yet pleased, at the whole routine I outlined for him. I had him sign a form stating that he understood the terms of our agreement.

Chores and their estimated completion times were listed separately on index cards. (Time estimates are given only as a point of reference. Christopher may complete a task in less time or it may take him longer if he chooses to procrastinate. However, when he draws a chore from the stack of index cards, he's taking a chance. He may be lucky and draw a chore that takes only five minutes, but he also could draw a chore or two that take thirty minutes to one hour to complete.)

The first morning he checked off each task as it was completed. Instead of running around upstairs, I heard him telling his father about the new system Mom had started and how he was going to try real hard not to "get into trouble" because he didn't want any additional chores. Just before he left, I put a gold sticker on the word Monday and handed him a quarter as an additional

Christopher's Morning Schedule

	MON.	TUES.	WED.	THURS.	FRI.
Take medicine					
Eat breakfast					
Get dressed					
Brush teeth					
Comb hair					
No running					
No screaming					
No hitting brother					
No arguments					
Get backpack					
Lunch money					

reward. He gave me a kiss and hug and left that morning with a big smile on his face. We used this system for almost two months. Each week during that time, we watched Christopher's behavior gradually improve. When he finally had two consecutive weeks without any misbehavior, I asked him why his behavior had changed so drastically in the morning. He told me he was tired of doing so many chores after school. He also said that he was trying very hard to be good in the morning so we could be a "happy family."

However, while Christopher's behavior improved in the morning, his younger brother's behavior began to deteriorate. Blake, age four, had always been the "good" child. He always ate his breakfast quickly and would immediately get dressed, brush his teeth, and then watch television until it was time to leave for school. However, when Christopher's behavior improved, Blake initiated arguments with Christopher at breakfast, then began arguing with us, claiming he could no longer get himself dressed. Suddenly, Christopher was the one who was ready for school on time, and Blake wasn't. Once again, we were very frustrated.

The situation that developed here is frustrating for well-meaning parents, but it is actually easy to understand. Blake had been seen as the "good" child and Christopher as the "bad" one. Often, without realizing it, parents promote a sense of competition between their children. In this case, we always praised Blake for his cooperation and admonished Christopher for his misbehavior. As Christopher became cooperative, Blake's place as the "good" boy in the family was threatened, forcing him to change his role to reinstate his position in the family.

It is important to remember that this type of situation can easily develop. It is a normal consequence when parents unknowingly promote competitiveness between their children. (Why can't you be good like your sister?) However, it is generally a temporary development that can be extinguished by:

- Encouraging your children's strengths, rather than criticizing their challenges
- Expressing confidence in your children
- Recognizing their daily efforts and the improvements they make
- Showing respect for your children
- Giving each child your undivided attention for fifteen to thirty minutes each day
- Concentrating on their assets and abilities and the contributions they make to the family

In other words, show and tell your children on a frequent basis how important they are to you and how much you love them. Give them your focused time daily, and show appreciation for the contributions they make to the family. Behavior modification plans will fail if children are not shown love and understanding as you strive to help them develop positive self-esteem and self-control. Competitiveness will decrease as your children recognize they have an important place in the family.

Once rules are established, follow through consistently with the consequences. Immediately, administer rewards (positive check marks, sticker, a quarter, etc.) or punishments (unsatisfactory check marks and randomly drawing cards that list after-school chores). Provide the opportunity to receive multiple rewards during the first few weeks (and use a variety of rewards since children with ADHD grow tired of any single reward easily). You might also want to reward three good days out of five with extra television time, a trip to the park or zoo, or doing something special with your child. Or you may want to let your child choose a reward such as a special activity, a play activity, or a creative activity. When the desired behavior reaches a satisfactory level, begin to gradually decrease the number of rewards given. Follow a behavior management plan for at least two weeks before modifying it. It is impossible to change behavior overnight.

If your plan fails to work, examine the reasons for its failure. Ask yourself the following questions:

1. Did my daughter clearly understand what behaviors were not acceptable before the management plan was initiated? (Write the behaviors down and post them where your child can review them daily.)

2. Did she fully understand the consequences of exhibiting the inappropriate behaviors? (Write consequences down and post as a reminder.)

3. Were the consequences (both reward and punishment) important enough for my child?

4. Was I consistent and immediate in delivering rewards and punishments?

5. Did my spouse (or baby-sitter) fail to follow the management plan, or not follow it consistently?

6. Were we trying to modify too many behaviors at the same time? (Children do best when you work on only one or two behaviors at a time.)

Now, alter your plan and start over again. If repeated attempts at modifying your plan result in failure, you should seek professional help.

Despite our attempts to compensate with our younger son, he still continued to act up in the morning so we made a special chart for him. We used pictures because he can't read yet, although we did use one word for each task in the hope that eventually he would be able to identify the word. When he completes his tasks, he earns a sticker; for every three stickers, he receives fifty cents. We did not add unacceptable behaviors to the chart because we wanted to see if the sticker alone would work for him. It has worked successfully.

Blake's Morning Schedule

	MON.	TUES.	WED.	THURS.	FRI.
Get dressed					
Eat breakfast					
Brush teeth					
Comb hair					
Wash hands					
Prepare backpack					

Older children who awaken too early should not be made to feel guilty for doing so (if they were truly tired they would sleep longer). However, they must learn that although they are ready to start the day before anyone else in the family they are expected to be quiet until other family members have awakened.

"Our son has an alarm clock set for 6:30 A.M.," says Ellen from Oconomowoc, Wisconsin. "He can wake up whenever (who can stop that), but cannot come out until the alarm goes off (bathroom breaks are permitted, of course)."

Provide an incentive for your child to play quietly in the morning. Tell your child, "When you are able to wait quietly in your room until it's time for everyone to wake up, you will earn fifteen extra minutes of television time or computer time after school." Or, you may want to write a contract with your child. For example:

"I, Taylor, will not wake anyone up in the morning. I will play quietly in my room. In return, I will receive an extra fifteen minutes of computer time in the evening."

Signed:

Taylor

Your child signs the contract, then it is posted in his room where he can easily see it each morning. For children who need immediate reinforcements, give them a token that they can exchange for some special reward later in the day.

If your child is a preschooler, or an older child who is impulsive and can't be trusted when left alone, a parent will simply have to get up with the child each morning. Neither group of children should be left unattended.

One final tip: whether your child is an early riser or a slow mover, follow the same routine seven days a week. Cathy from Los Gatos, California, uses the following routine with her six-year-old daughter:

1. Cuddle in bed and talk about the day
2. Make school snacks
3. Brush teeth and hair
4. Collect school items
5. Look at the newspaper together
6. Get dressed together
7. Eat breakfast

"Keeping a familiar routine builds a secure framework in which she can live," adds Cathy. (See chapter three for more information on establishing morning routines.)

Bath Time and Bedtime

Evening bath time signals the beginning of the end of the day—something most children want to delay. If bath time is a battle ground in your household, be sure you have established a routine (for instance, baths are taken each evening or every other evening at 7:00 P.M. with no exceptions). Fifteen minutes before bath time, set a timer (the timer becomes the bad guy, not you) and let your child know he has fifteen minutes left to watch television or finish playing. Remember children with ADHD often have great difficulty with transitions, thus the fifteen-minute warning and the use of the timer. As a parent, your goal is to help your child make a smooth transition between ending the day and falling asleep. Therefore, bedtime preparations should begin early enough to allow sufficient time for bathing and tucking in while still getting the child into bed at the appointed bedtime hour.

Make bath time interesting and enjoyable for your child, so it is something he will look forward to. Bubble baths and foam sculpturing soaps make an ordinary bath fun. Keep a bag of bath toys in the bathroom (only to be played with in the bathtub). Sing songs together or read to him. Give a five-minute warning before ending the bath and again use a timer. Offer a snack before bedtime (use that timer) if this is part of the routine, or take the child directly to his room after his bath. Missy from Bow, New Hampshire, adds, "Our son goes to the bathroom, brushes his teeth and drinks any water he needs. Drinking water before he goes to bed put a stop to the 'I'm thirsty' after he's been tucked in for the night." End the day by reading to your child or giving him a back rub. (All children enjoy having mom or dad read to them, even ten-year-olds.)

All children enjoy spending extra time alone with their parents to talk about the day's events, including any stressful situations they may have encountered or difficulties they may be experiencing in school or with their peers. Helping your child find solutions to these problems often increases his ability to fall asleep more easily. Allocating special time for this at bedtime often reduces conflicts between parent and child. When children know they will receive special attention they are less apt to argue in an attempt to gain attention at bedtime.

After tucking in your child, remind him how much you love him before leaving the room. A simple "I love you" is worth a thousand words, especially to a child who experiences difficulties every day. "I love you" tells your child you still value, appreciate, and love him for the person he is despite a demanding day. These three words are important for all children to hear, but especially for those who may feel they are too old for bedtime kisses and hugs.

Whether you say, "I love you," "See you in the morning," or "Goodnight," before leaving your child's bedroom, use the same words each night. This is your final signal to him that the day has ended and that you will not see him again until morning. Be assured that by the time most children reach second or third grade they have adapted well to their bedtime routine and often require little or no assistance settling down for the night. For elementary school-age children who have never had a bedtime routine, establish one immediately if bedtime is a stressful event in your home.

Some younger children have great difficulty falling asleep. Says one mom from Montana, "I found that my son (from ages three to five) fell asleep within minutes if I laid down next to him." It may seem simplistic, but tell your child how to fall asleep. My son would jump out of bed minutes after I had tucked him in, complaining that he couldn't fall asleep. One evening I said to him, "Of course you can't fall asleep Christopher, you aren't even in bed. You must get into bed, hold your puppy dog tightly and close your eyes. Then you will fall asleep." He was asleep within minutes.

You might take another approach, as Marie from Columbus, Ohio, explains. "Let your child know that she must be in bed by a certain time, but don't expect her to fall asleep immediately. Always praise her when she's in bed on time."

Future problems also may be avoided by alternating bedtime duty with your spouse. "Let your spouse put your child to bed every other night, so neither parent becomes the only one who can tuck your child in," advises Jan from Scottsdale, Arizona. "Both parents must follow the same routine though."

Debra from Crownpoint, Indiana, the mother of two children (her oldest child, Denny, has ADHD) who keeps both children on the same schedule, shared her evening schedule, which begins as soon as her children get home from school.

1. Do homework
2. Playtime
3. Dinner
4. Bath time
5. Twenty-minutes reading time with each child (I read with one child while the other is taking a bath)
6. One television show
7. Bedtime

Another mother suggests giving baths immediately after school or before dinner. She found that waiting until bedtime created a tense situation in her household.

Meal Time

Many children with ADHD have great difficulty sitting still long enough to even eat a simple meal. They would rather eat standing up, or with their feet anywhere but on the floor. They prefer to start an argument with a sibling instead of participating in a family conversation. As a parent, you may wonder if your child will ever learn what the purpose of a napkin is or what utensils are for because he always eats with his fingers.

You basically have three or four choices when it comes to mealtimes. First, you can follow the example outlined in chapter three, whereby you dictate table rules. At the first infraction, your child is excused from the table whether his meal is finished or not. A variation of this would be to tell him to leave the table and then permit him to finish eating alone in another room. On days he abides by the rules he is, of course, rewarded for his appropriate behavior. This approach is often used when parents find mealtimes to be extremely upsetting and agree this is a behavior problem that needs to be worked on and corrected.

As with any behavior you find inappropriate, one must decide how relevant it is. Parents who worry about their child's table manners or the clothes he wears, for example, need to evaluate their motives for changing that behavior. If you're worried that he'll be eating with his fingers, with his feet propped up on the table wearing the same clothes every day when he's an adult, you are looking into the future, instead of concentrating on the present. Sometimes it becomes necessary to let go of the future to work on problems that are more relevant in your child's life today.

Your second choice concerning chaos during mealtimes is to adjust to your child. If he can sit quietly to eat part of his meal, then as parents, accept these few minutes together and plan time together later in the evening for conversing. Active toddlers can sit still about ten minutes as long as they are eating, and sometimes much longer if they have something interesting to play with; preschoolers can sit about ten to fifteen minutes; and elementary school-age children can sit about fifteen minutes, depending on how long it takes them to eat.

Terri from Moravia, New York, says that to keep their son Ryan seated at mealtime they "use a timer set for a predetermined time." Once a child is able to sit through meals using a timer set for five minutes, for instance, then gradually increase the time until the child is able to sit through the entire meal. However, be patient; this won't happen in a week.

The third choice is to occasionally feed your children separately so you and your spouse can enjoy a quiet meal together. Rent a special video for the children to watch while you eat or encourage them to watch something special on television. Try to make this time unique for them also.

The fourth choice is to forget about family mealtimes and concentrate on other issues. "At age eight or nine," advises Heather from Raleigh, North Carolina, "loosen the structure of mealtimes and have some peace. Instead of making our child join us for dinner at a certain time, he comes when he is ready, which is usually when he is really hungry. This gives my husband and me five to thirty minutes of adult quiet time and everyone is happy!"

"Most of what I read and had been told was that Ritalin decreases the appetite, so I would let my son's dose run out then serve food," Patrice from Aurora, Illinois, explains. "The problem then was that he couldn't attend at the table. We have found that by medicating him about forty-five minutes before meals he will actually eat better. . . . I'm sure each child is different, but I did learn to at least try different approaches to find one that works best for him. I also found that if he goes to bed about an hour before his last dose runs out, he falls asleep easier."

Don't engage in battles over food with your child. Children who take stimulant medication are usually very hungry in the morning, eat little for lunch (sometimes not much for dinner also if they take medication after school), and are hungry by bedtime. Serve a nutritious breakfast daily and provide a healthy evening snack. For lunch and dinner, serve at least one food your child particularly enjoys (hopefully he'll be tempted to try a few bites), but don't force him to clean his plate and don't forget to praise him for what he does eat. Rest assured that your child will not starve to death. Children do eat when they are hungry!

Chores

Chores are a necessary part of living in a family. Everyone in the family should have assigned daily and weekly chores. I know it's easier to just complete the tasks yourself rather than involve your child, but you'll be doing your child a great disservice if he isn't assigned household chores. Household chores teach responsibility and self-discipline, provide needed skills for independent living, and make the child a contributing member of the family by sharing in the workload. When assigning chores consider the age of the child, his interests, and his ability to perform the chore.

All children learn to do chores in small steps. Parents can help by first assisting the child with the chore (teaching the task). Let's say you want your eldest child to take responsibility for setting the dinner table. (Be sure he's old enough to handle the task and has the needed ability.) Together count out the number of plates needed. Then help him put the plates in the proper locations. (Older children may only need verbal instructions, rather than verbal and visual directions.) Then count out the number of forks, knives, and spoons needed. Put the utensils in their correct places, then the napkins and glassware. Before you know it, your child will have learned the basics of setting a table. However, learning the basics does not mean he is ready or willing to take full responsibility for the job. He will still need reminders and some supervision before he is able to complete the task completely on his own. Be sure to offer encouragement and praise for all attempts (even if it doesn't quite measure up to your expectations).

Establish a time frame (Bill, I want the table set by 5:30). For younger children who can't tell time, set a timer and let them know that when the buzzer goes off it's time for them to help set the table, pick up toys, or feed the dog. Remember to clarify the task to be completed in detail, step by step. A picture reference showing the steps of a task can be posted on his wall and used as a constant reference until the chore becomes routine.

"Chores actually are a great help to David," says Kate, David's mother. "It's a physical way for him to help us. He enjoys helping and even though he complains at times, he does enjoy vacuuming, preparing snacks, and helping sort laundry. Taking the time to teach him the job and monitoring him has now paid off big for us. His vacuuming is passable and his laundry sense is great."

"We try to show Ryan that a family works together," explains his mother, Terri, from New York. "For example, if Ryan does his chores we will have extra time to play or be with him. If not [doesn't cooperate], we will spend that time doing [his] chores."

Another mom says, "In our home, chores are on a 'paid-for' rather than an 'allowance' basis. Each chore is worth so much. Even at an early age, we felt our son must learn that you have to work for what you want."

Above all, remember that the child with ADHD needs to feel he is an important member of your family. Because he may experience more disappointments, failures, and frustrations than the average child, it is imperative that he knows he is needed in his home. Always choose chores for him that you know he can complete successfully. This will help to build self-esteem.

Riding in the Car

I vividly recall picking my first-grade son up from school one day. It was obvious from the look on his face as he approached the car that he was angry. Something told me he was about to have a temper tantrum. Bracing myself for his explosive temper, I flashed a big smile and said, "How are you sweetheart?" As I pulled out into the center lane of a four-lane highway, he began yelling that today was show and tell and I had forgotten to remind him to bring in something blue in color. Calmly, I reminded him that I had told him several times to pick out one of his blue toys and put it in his backpack. "You should have done it for me," he screamed. "I always forget. It's all your fault and I'm really angry at you." With that remark, he unlocked the door, opened the passenger door, and swung his legs around preparing to jump out of the car, which by then was moving at forty-five miles an hour. Fortunately he had his seat belt on, and the automobile next to us did not hit our open car door. Trembling, I managed to convince him to close the door and as soon as I was able, I pulled into a nearby parking lot. (Please remember that most children with ADHD do not have symptoms as severe as this.)

I learned a valuable lesson that day. As a parent of an impulsive and hyperactive child, I learned that I had to be on guard at all times even in our car, a place that I had always regarded as a relatively safe, confined space—a space I felt I had control over. The incident forced my husband and me to establish the following car rules:

1. Seat belts are to be worn at all times for the safety of all family members.
2. The driver decides which windows, if any, are to be open while the car is moving.

3. Doors are to be locked at all times and no one is to open a door while the car is moving.
4. Hands, arms, head, and legs are to be kept in the car.
5. Items are not to be thrown in the car or outside of the car.
6. Passengers have assigned seats and they are expected to remain in those seats (and in a sitting position) at all times.
7. Children who can not sit next to each other without arguing and fighting will be separated in the car (an adult sits between them or one child is moved to the front seat).
8. All children will be rewarded for following car rules.

Discuss the rules with each of your children, and review them frequently as well as the consequences of breaking those rules. Be sure they understand the relationship between their behavior and the consequences (for example, throwing a toy in the car will result in no toys being permitted in the car, or fighting with your sibling will mean you will be moved to the front seat and will no longer be able to play with each other). Write the rules down and give them a copy. Remind your children of the rules every time you get into the car. Remember to always reward appropriate car behavior. As in any other situation, catch them being good and give positive feedback every few minutes.

When Company Comes to Visit

All children get excited when they learn friends or relatives will be stopping by for an informal visit or a family gathering. Excitement mounts as they watch you prepare food and clean the house. They'll ask you a thousand times how long before grandma and grandpa arrive. If parents are especially anxious, children will pick up on those concerns and tensions and, as a result, may misbehave. Children with ADHD, especially those with hyperactivity, often become inordinately excited when visitors are expected. Parents should acknowledge their building excitement: "When I was your age I remember how excited I used to feel waiting for my cousins to arrive, but we all need to remain calm so we get everything done before they arrive."

Provide your child with soothing activities to occupy him while he waits such as putting a puzzle together, listening to music, reading, or playing a board game or cards with a sibling. If your child wants to help with the preparations, supervise him carefully. If you sense that he is starting to lose control, have him engage in another activity (away from other family members) until he regains control of himself. For instance, suggest that he check the bathrooms for clean towels, soap, and toilet paper.

Clearly state the house rules concerning visitors to your home and the behavior you expect from him several times shortly before guests arrive. Be sure he understands the relationship between his actions and the consequences (time-out for inappropriate behavior, for example). Also, verbally rehearse alternative activities he may choose during the day when he gets bored or overexcited. (Make sure he knows his choices before he gets himself into trouble.)

"Whether it's one visitor or ten coming to our home, Jamie gets extremely excited. When company enters the house, he practically bounces off the walls," explains Cindy from Brooklyn, New York. "Last Christmas Eve we put him in time-out several times immediately after our guests arrived. Each time he would rejoin the group, he'd lose control again and be sent back to his room. My sister-in-law followed him upstairs the fourth time he went to time-out. She gave him her undivided attention for ten minutes. When he came back downstairs, he was completely under control. Now when we know company is coming, I always ask someone beforehand to spend a few minutes with Jamie when they first arrive. I then tell Jamie, 'Aunt Sue is looking forward to seeing your rock collection (or whatever) when she arrives.' This never fails to work for us."

Visiting Friends or Relatives

"I talk with my daughter before we visit family and friends and explain the type of behavior I expect," said Cathy from Los Gatos, California. "For example, when we go to her grandparents' house, I remind her that their dog is just a puppy and very excitable and that I know it's very tempting to run around the living room with the dog, but that the ruckus upsets grandma and the puppy. I ask her how I can help her remember not to get wild with the dog. She usually says I can hold her hand.

"When she forgets and starts to get wild, I take her hand immediately and pull her close to me, remind her with a whisper and give her a hug. I catch her right away because if I let it go, even for a minute, she will reach the point where it will be difficult for her to regain control.

"Visiting new friends is always a problem because it's a new situation with different people," adds Annie of Sylvania, Ohio. "If I forget to tell him what type of behavior I expect ahead of time, he'll lose total control when we arrive. If this happens, I put him in isolated time-out until he settles down. If he comes out of time-out and loses control again, we leave and try it again another day."

Playing with Other Children

ADHD affects all aspects of the child's life including his playing with other children. Children who are impulsive in school and in the home may also be reckless and rash on the playground, with neighborhood children, and siblings. They tend to be bossy, unwilling to take turns, and have little regard for the feelings of others.

When it comes to playing with other children, many children with ADHD do not respond to normal social cues (tone of voice, body language, facial expressions) that are clear to their peers which makes it very difficult for them to maintain friendships. "We allow Colin to play with friends only when he is well rested. If he's tired there are usually arguments with the other children and Colin ends up crying and gets very emotional over everything," Missy from Bow, New Hampshire, explains sadly. "Quiet play is usually achieved when we invite only one friend over at a time. Colin usually does better with children who are easy going and not hyperactive. It seems every time he has a friend over, who is also very active, they accelerate each other to higher levels of hyper and it usually ends up with someone getting hurt, something broken, or the house destroyed! We have also found limiting play-time to a few hours rather than a whole afternoon or day helps to keep down trouble too. Colin is now almost eight and in school all day, so he is allowed one friend for one and a half hours once a week after school and one friend for three hours on the weekend. We continue to remind Colin of the rules before any activity and repeat 'think before you do things.' He is also allowed one sport per season."

"I schedule a visit with another child on a day when I have lots of time," explains Mary from Troy, New York. "What seems to work best is scheduled activities with other children. For example, we work on a project together, play a simple game, or go outdoors. I've also found that going to a playground with the other children seems to cause fewer problems (my son can be as active as he wants and he fits right in with the other screaming active children)."

"Limit the number of children at one time," suggests Terri from Moravia, New Yor.. "We also teach Ryan's friends to share their feelings with Ryan [if Ryan dc_s something they dislike]." Just as one should teach their child to express their feelings verbally rather than physically, it is helpful if playmates are taught to share feelings rather than become hostile or aggressive with the child with ADHD.

"Ryan has trouble keeping his hands to himself," continued Terri. "We place a Ø symbol on his hands as a reminder. He likes this." Parents can have rubber stamps like this made, or one of a hand with a line drawn through it, at most print shops and office supply stores.

Peter from Colorado Springs, Colorado, offers: "Our daughter has the most difficulty on the playground at recess. She would complain that she had no friends, that no one ever wanted to play with her. We talked with her teacher who suggested that Stephanie look for another child who was also alone on the playground and ask that child if he or she wanted to play a game. The next day Stephanie's teacher spotted a child standing alone and encouraged Stephanie to approach her. The two children now play together at recess."

My son had this same problem a few years ago, so I encouraged him to find a friend on the playground. The friend he found, on his own, was a boy a year younger. Christopher came home from school and elatedly told me about him. I was thrilled until he added, "He's hyperactive, but his parents won't let him take medicine." My heart sank, but with a smile I said, "I'm glad you made a friend, but when you are with your friend you must remember the school rules and follow them at all times." Three days later, I received a call from the school. Christopher and his new friend had spent the past two recesses in the school office and that particular day his friend had talked him into turning off the electricity to the entire school. His homebase teacher then spent the next two weeks keeping the children apart while I worked to convince Christopher that his friend was not a good choice. Be sure you talk with your child about appropriate playmates and peer pressure.

Julie, from Newark, Ohio, encourages her son "to play with children who are younger than he and who even look up to him. This builds his self-esteem and allows him to practice getting along with other kids without being made fun of by older kids. My husband and I play act behavior that is particularly difficult to modify in our son with ADHD. Usually, this allows him to see what he is doing wrong. Then we play act other ways to handle a situation." Through role playing, a parent can teach a child to make introductions, express feelings rather than act out against playmates, how to share a toy and when, what not to do when a playmate is using a toy they want to play with, and how to take turns.

"I try to make sure that my fifth-grade son fits in with the crowd as much as possible," continues Julie. "He is usually made fun of by other children for his behavior and any other little thing that kids can pick on. So I try to make sure that his clothing or haircut or even his lunch isn't another thing that will cause him taunting by friends or classmates. I don't tell him I am doing this, of course.

"I avoid team sports with my son. Swimming, golf, and karate are sports in which he seems to be able to excel. I find that he is about two years behind the other boys his age when it comes to his ability to play sports. Putting him on a team with his peers just causes trouble.

"When my son is having difficulty with socialization, I arrange social contacts for him without his knowledge. My son gets along better with one playmate and I try to arrange the playtime in our home so that I can supervise and correct a situation if it should get out of hand. I have even used bribery in the form of movies, swimming, or special trips or activities to get a reluctant playmate to come over and play with my son."

"I have found that my daughter does fairly well in group situations," Tracy from Indianapolis, Indiana, comments. "She seems to have a good handle on how to behave with her friends, but I have also noticed that she can not play indefinitely with them. Group situations are very stimulating for her so eventually she becomes bothersome. Currently, she can stay in control for about one hour and fifteen minutes (she used to lose it after fifteen or twenty minutes so she's making progress). I always give her a specific time frame for playing with friends. When time is up, she's to come inside and find something quiet to do, such as reading or watching an educational program on television. I always make a point of telling her how well she played with her friends (sharing, taking turns, etc.)"

Dan from Santa Barbara, California, advises parents to "establish clear rules for social behavior and then to discuss the rules with your child. Role play. Write the rules down and review them with your child before playtime whenever possible." Also when the child is old enough, around the second grade, he suggests that parents begin teaching about personal space, especially when he gets angry. "Tell your child that when he begins to feel angry or is angry that he is always to keep his hands within his own personal space—that he is not to let his hands reach into another space."

"Having a family playtime has taught our son how to play with others," says Robin from Warren, New Jersey. "We've taught him how to take turns, to talk politely, to accept that his turn is over for a few minutes, to wait his turn—but practice and patience is needed if you want to be an effective teacher to your child."

"My son wanted to play a team sport," explains Ann from Boston. "Instead of discouraging him, we told him to decide what sport he truly wanted to play. He chose baseball. We then taught him everything he needed to know about the sport. And we practiced with him every chance we got until he could hit and catch the ball very well. We told him if he really wanted to play then he had to become an expert at the game so the kids wouldn't tease him. Although he made some mistakes last year, he was considered a valuable player and he got the respect he deserved. But it took a lot of practice to get where he is."

Don't forget to teach your child about personal space because they rarely pick this up on their own. I demonstrated personal space to my sons using a Hula Hoop. The other day I heard Christopher say to his brother, "Blake, move out of my personal space please." Blake moved, but not before he grabbed the toy he had his eye on!

For information on teaching social skills, read *If Your Child is Hyperactive, Inattentive, Impulsive, Distractible . . . Helping the ADD (Attention Deficit Disorder)-Hyperactive Child* by Stephen W. Garber, Ph.D., Marianne Daniels Garber, Ph.D. and Robyn Freedman Spizman (Villard, 1990). This book also provides examples on how to help your child learn impulse control, beat distractions, control activity levels and aggression, follow rules, and lengthen attention span. Another book, *Hyperactivity: Why Won't My Child Pay Attention?*, by Dr. Sam Goldstein and Dr. Michael Goldstein (John Wiley and Sons, 1992), identifies the social skills children must develop and explains in detail how parents can teach these skills to their children.

Another very informative and useful book is *Helping the Child Who Doesn't Fit In* by Marshall Duke and Stephen Nowicki Jr. (Atlanta: Peachtree,

1991). In their book, the authors refer to their area of research using the term "dyssemia," which means a difficulty in using and understanding nonverbal signs and signals. Parents will discover many tips and suggestions that can be used to help teach their children how to fit in.

Siblings

In families with one or more children who have ADHD, the scales are tipped often in favor of the child with ADHD, or so it appears to the non-ADHD sibling. Put yourself in the place of your non-ADHD child. What do you see? You probably aren't surprised to see a sibling who receives a great deal of attention for everything he does, whether its appropriate or not—a child who monopolizes mom's and dad's time. You may also see a sibling who never walks by you without slugging you, who interrupts and pesters you constantly, a brother who never knocks before coming into your bedroom, or a sister who "borrows" your belongings and never returns them because she's lost them.

As the non-ADHD sibling, assess how this makes you feel. You no doubt will discover feelings of resentment, anger, and jealousy. After all, the child with ADHD does receive a great deal more involvement, support, and focused time from his parents, even when mom and dad strive to strike a balance between their children. Even when the sibling is mature enough to understand ADHD and the time commitment parents must make to the child with ADHD, feelings of animosity, indignation, and envy can, and often do, exist. Because of this, it's imperative that parents make a special effort from the start to spend more time with their non-ADHD children because they need extra assistance and nurturing also.

Be sure your non-ADHD child is aware that you know that his sibling violates household rules and as a result appears to get away with many things that are off-limits to them. Assure them that their sibling's behavior is often inappropriate but that you are working diligently to help change the troublesome behavior. Children are less apt to harbor hostile feelings if they understand that you are trying to help their sibling maintain control. Empathize with their feelings and concerns; they are legitimate. Enlist their aid. Teach them to recognize appropriate behavior and praise their sibling, or work with them on strategies to remind their sibling in nonhumiliating ways when they are losing control.

Sibling Rivalry

Debra from Crownpoint, Indiana, notes, "At age ten, Denny cannot walk by his sister without tripping her. He constantly walks in on her when she's in the bathroom or her bedroom. He is also always saying or doing things that aggravate her."

Sibling rivalry usually develops when children feel the need to compete for their parent's time and attention. One way to decrease the competition between your children is to spend quality time with each child. You can do this on a daily basis by spending fifteen to thirty minutes or so with each child, playing a game of their choice or reading a story to them. Your child will look forward to this special time. Consider making a weekly date with your child. Once a week, on a certain day, spend a few hours of uninterrupted quality time together, perhaps seeing a movie or going bowling.

"We leave the child with ADHD at home or have him away from the home for a time," explains Ellen from Oconomowoc, Wisconsin. "We then spend that time doing something with our other two children that we couldn't normally do."

Most parents have extremely tight schedules so you may wonder how you can find the time to make a date with your child. Maybe it won't be quite as difficult as you suspect. Take a good look at your week. Is there something you do with your child once a week anyway that could be extended into a date?

For instance, my son goes to counseling every Thursday at 4:00 P.M. After the counseling session I take him out to eat at his favorite restaurant. This restaurant has been around forever and still has the old-fashioned jukeboxes at each booth. We play song after song and eat lots of pizza and genuinely enjoy each other's company. Afterwards, we stop and play a game of miniature golf, visit a video game arcade, or have ice cream. While we are out enjoying ourselves, my husband is eating dinner out with our youngest child. We give up one family meal a week to spend individual time with each of our children.

Unfortunately, competing for parent's time and attention cannot be eliminated entirely, so children must also be taught to get along with each other. Children should be encouraged to play together cooperatively, as a team. You can help your children learn cooperative play by offering rewards or incentives that promote choices. Consider setting up a system whereby each of your children receives a penny or a marble to add to a jar every time they play together without arguing and fighting (stickers and a chart can also be used). After they collect twenty marbles, for example, they earn a meal at their favorite restaurant or they can choose a family outing of their choice. If, however, they choose not to cooperate and an argument or fight erupts, they are both sent to time-out or they lose a penny or two from their jar. The choice is theirs. Before implementing this system, talk with your children about the rules of fair play and how they can earn special privileges for playing together harmoniously.

Take the opportunity to praise your children when they are playing together cooperatively. Positive reinforcement will reduce sibling fights far more quickly than punishing your children will. Encourage your children to come up with their own solutions to problems. ("You both want to play with the same toy at the same time. How can the two of you work this out?")

For children who fight and argue over toys, consider putting the toys in time-out for the rest of the day. Naturally, your children spend the next five minutes in time-out also. For children whose fighting over a television program gets out of hand, simply turn the television off. Then tell them they can turn the television on in thirty minutes, but it will be turned off again if they can't agree on a program without arguing or fighting. This approach encourages children to settle their differences among themselves without involving a parent.

"Encourage your children to express their angry feelings verbally to their siblings rather than striking out at a sibling," offers Suzanne from Houston, Texas. "Even young children can be taught to label feelings if you help them identify how they feel. Attach a name to a feeling such as anger, then the next time a sibling hits them they can say, 'I get so angry when you hit me. Don't hit me again.' Like everything else though, this takes time for parents to teach, but it's worth it in the long run."

Children can be taught to hit a punching bag, a pillow, or to express their anger on paper through drawing or in a diary. It is the parent's responsibility to teach their children to find creative outlets for anger. Hitting, kicking, biting, pulling hair, or calling a sibling names should not be tolerated in the home. Teach your child how to confront a sibling who hits, bites, kicks, destroys a treasured toy, or borrows items without asking first, in a controlled manner. Don't hesitate to give them specific words to use in such situations. For example: "It makes me so angry when you borrow my clothes without asking me. Please don't go into my room again."

Don't be afraid to share stories with your children about the hassles you had with your siblings. Children will be amazed to learn that you and Uncle _____ used to argue over toys or over what television show to watch, especially when they see how well you and Uncle _____ get along now. A good book to review is *Siblings Without Rivalry: How to Help Your Children Live Together So You Can Live Too* by Adele Faber and Elaine Mazlish (Avon, 1987).

When with a Baby-Sitter

Heidi is a twenty-one-year-old college student from Swanton, Ohio. ADHD runs on both sides of her family. Heidi admits that she also has mild ADHD and often uses Ritalin to study. Heidi has had four years experience baby-sitting two children with ADHD (on both a full- and part-time basis). She offers the following advice to baby-sitters:

1. Find things to do with the children. Don't let them go off on their own or they'll find things to do that will be unacceptable.

2. Include them in what you are doing. If you're fixing dinner for them, let them help. That way you can keep an eye on them.

3. Don't spank or yell when they do something wrong. Use time-out and use it consistently, otherwise the children will end up controlling you.

4. Investigate even if the situation looks normal. You may be surprised by what you find.

5. Try to never let them out of your sight. They can get into trouble in a matter of minutes.

6. Always get instructions from the parents as to what the child can or cannot do. If you are unsure if the child is able to do something, tell him no, but let him know that you will ask his parents when they telephone home.

7. Be sure you know when to give medications, and how much. Write everything down. Set a timer if you think you might need a reminder for giving medications. Once you've been around the child enough, a timer may not be necessary. You will be able to tell when medication has worn off.

Remember, it's important that the behavior reward-and-punishment system you establish be used consistently, even when your children are with a baby-sitter. To help the sitter maintain your system, give him or her a written schedule of what to do and when to do it, including exact guidelines for behavior and rewards and punishments.

Running Errands

Many parents of younger children with ADHD would rather not take their children with them to run errands. Some parents handle this by scheduling errands, such as grocery shopping, banking, going to the post office and the cleaners, for the same day each week and hire a baby-sitter to stay with the children. Unfortunately, this is not an option for some parents, either because they can't afford to hire a sitter just for this purpose or they can't find a sitter for just one day a week. If you feel you have no choice but to include your child in errand running, here are some other options to consider:

1. If you work outside the home, run errands on your lunch hour or plan one stop on your way home from work each day. Nancy from Chicago, Illinois, encourages parents to "Follow a routine such as the library on Monday, the drugstore on Tuesday, the cleaners on Wednesday, the grocery store on Thursday, the bank on Friday. Even if you must pick up your child on the way home, he or she can usually handle an excur-

sion of less than fifteen minutes, especially once a routine is established."

2. "Consider one-stop shopping whenever possible," advises Dan from Tampa, Florida. "Always use the drive-in window for banking if the children are with you." Some of this may cost extra pennies, compared with shopping for bargains, but it's worth it for the efficiency.

3. "Negotiate how the errands will be shared with your spouse," says Greg, a father of two hyperactive children, from Grand Rapids, Michigan. "Every Saturday morning I do the grocery shopping for the week. This way my wife never has to take the children to the grocery store. If we run out of something during the week, I stop at the store on my way home from work."

4. Ask a neighbor to watch the children a few hours a week. If you can't afford to pay for the service or the neighbor won't accept payment, offer to care for her children during the week in exchange, or offer to pick up items she needs while you are out.

Shopping with Your Child

Learning to shop is an educational experience and a task that children need to learn to prepare themselves for independent living. On those days when you decide to include your child, consider the following advice:

1. Take your child along when he or she is well rested and in a cooperative mood. Take along nutritional snacks from home, and toys for him to play with when boredom sets in. Remember to keep those hands busy so they are not tempted to reach out inappropriately. Hand-held video games work well for children over the age of five.

2. Use a stroller or a shopping cart for younger children. A stroller will keep your child safe and secure and save you from needlessly chasing after him. Even toddlers who are hyperactive will often stay in a stroller (and preschoolers in a cart) as long as you provide them with something to do (toys or snacks). But don't expect them to remain seated for hours at a time and remember once you let them out for even a few minutes, chances are they won't want to get back in, so plan your time accordingly.

3. Plan short trips, not major marathons.

4. Establish the rules before entering the store. Says Brenda from Little Rock, Arkansas: "Our rules are: (1) you must stay with mom or dad and you are not to be walking alone, (2) you are

not to touch anything without first asking permission to do so, and (3) we only buy items on our list. If a rule is broken, our son is placed in time-out immediately."

5. Once in a store, praise your child's appropriate behavior every minute or two. For example, "You're staying right next to Mom, good for you," or "Thank you for not touching the Halloween display." Make physical contact with your child frequently by touching him on the shoulder, holding his hand, or giving him a hug.

6. "Know in advance what you must buy. Make a list and take it with you," suggests Peter from Colorado Springs, Colorado. "Then involve your child in the actual shopping process as much as possible. Let your child place items in the cart or tell her what items to select from the shelf. Keep her busy and out of trouble."

7. Should your child break a rule, use time-out. (See chapter three for more hints on using time-out effectively.)

8. "After a good shopping experience, I reward my son with an ice cream cone or take him to the park on the way home," explains Annie from Atlanta, Georgia. "I want him to know that I appreciate his cooperation and that he did a good job controlling himself."

9. Terri from Moravia, New York, explains that they go shopping as a family. "That way," she says, "if our son's behavior becomes inappropriate he is taken from the store to the car while the other person completes the shopping."

10. "Have your grocery list written according to where the food is in the store," adds Jody, "then dash through the aisles, and look for the check-out with the shortest line. Use a drive-through to get milk, bread, or other needed items. If possible, send someone else to the store for you."

11. Avoid taking your child to places where he will experience extreme difficulty settling down and displaying appropriate behavior. "If there's a place I know he'll misbehave, I avoid it," admits Diane, "but we need groceries and clothing. At first I let him push the cart. That worked for a while. Then I gave him coupons of items to look for, but he became frustrated because he couldn't find the items. Now he gets to pick out one special food item on each trip to the store. This has been working great in combination with the coupons and pushing the cart."

Taking Your Child to Restaurants

No time to prepare a meal, but recoil at the thought of taking your son or daughter out to a restaurant? While there is no sure way to prevent your child from creating a scene in a restaurant, you can improve the odds by choosing the right restaurant at the right time of the day and following some of the suggestions other parents offered.

"Take your child to a restaurant that is child-friendly," recommends Nancy from Rockville, Maryland. "A child-friendly restaurant dispenses children's menus, placemats for coloring, and provides crayons. They often have a play area with slides and rides. You know when you are in a child-friendly restaurant—there are always lots of highchairs."

Child-friendly restaurants are not always fast food restaurants. They are often casual family restaurants that serve the type of food adults and child alike enjoy. They provide bibs for babies and toddlers as well as coloring placemats and crayons for preschoolers and their prices fit a family budget. Sometimes these establishments also have video arcades for older children.

Other suggestions from parents:

1. "Eat at restaurants that have salad, fruit, and soup bars. Children can begin eating almost immediately. The same holds true for cafeterias. Children can select their own food, which usually means they'll eat what they choose," said David from Snyder, New York.

2. "Don't choose an intimate restaurant for a family meal," offers Sharon from Indianapolis, Indiana. "If your child has a temper tantrum or raises her voice, you can bet that everyone in the restaurant will be looking unhappily your way. Choose a restaurant where the noise level is high because of other families. That way when she acts up, no one will notice or care."

3. "Take something along from home to entertain your child (like a small travel board game) or read a book to him while you are waiting for your food," advises Mary Jo from Livonia, Michigan. "It's hard for all children to sit quietly and wait for something, but doubly hard for hyperactive children. If necessary, one parent can walk the child around the restaurant or take a walk outside for ten or fifteen minutes until the food arrives. When the meal is finished, don't linger drinking two cups of coffee. You're only asking for trouble. Pay your bill and leave."

4. "For special occasions, we always take a favorite baby-sitter along with us," explains Diane from Northport, Alabama. "She helps our son order his food, amuses him until his meal arrives, and entertains him until it's time to leave. He's happy because he's receiving her undivided attention when we, his parents, are otherwise engaged."

5. Advises George from Wheaton, Illinois: "Don't go to a restaurant during peak dining hours. Waiters are very busy and service is often slower. We have found dining out to be easiest on

all of us if we get to a restaurant around five o'clock in the evening. A nearly empty restaurant seems to have a calming effect on our son."

6. "When our first-grader acts up in a restaurant, we remove him from the table and put him in time-out," explains Debra from Boston, Massachusetts. "Depending on the restaurant this might be in the foyer, the restroom, or in the car. We always bring him back to the table after five minutes of time-out as we don't want him to think that if he acts up the whole family leaves the restaurant. Like any other child, he must learn to act appropriately when out in public."

7. "We only go to restaurants when Grandma and Grandpa insist," said Jody. "They stay at the table and place our orders. I take the children and walk, run, and crawl around until the food comes."

Keeping Bedrooms Tidy

"Clean up your room," may mean one thing to you and another to your child. For instance, when I say "Clean up your room" to my nine-year-old son, I mean make the bed, hang up the clean clothes, pick up the toys, put dirty clothes in the laundry room, clean off the top of the desk, and empty the wastepaper basket. However, if I don't clarify this each time my son will focus on one thing only and believe his work is completed once it has been done.

Most children do best with a chart that clearly defines and organizes the tasks. We use one that is displayed in our son's room. I supervise from a distance to help him remain on target. He checks off each task as it is completed. For children who can't read, use pictures from magazines or draw your own.

Decide ahead of time what the consequence will be if your child does not clean his room. Noncompliance may mean having to withdraw a privilege (no playing with the neighborhood children tonight). Be certain your child understands this before you start any charting system.

For young children, provide plastic baskets for toys. Label baskets with pictures. Cars and trucks go in one basket, dolls in another, stuffed animals in an additional one. Place a small laundry basket in the child's room where she can place dirty clothes. Provide a footstool so children can reach hangers in the closet. Use a small floor bookcase for books. For teaching a young child how to make a bed, start the process at the end rather than the beginning. In other words, teach the child first to pull up the bedspread or comforter. When that is mastered, have him pull up the blanket first then the comforter, and so on, until he has mastered making the bed.

Many parents have children who refuse to pick up their toys. Terri, from Moravia, New York, is one such mom. "If toys are not picked up when requested, our son loses the toys for one day." One father says, "We hold everything hostage that we pick up in the bedroom after our daughter has been issued a warning. She then has to earn everything back, including clothes, cassette tapes, magazines, hair ribbons, etc." Another mother uses what she calls the end-of-the-week box. Everything she picks up during the week that the children were supposed to pick up but didn't, goes into the box and stays there until week's end. Occasionally, she admits, she's willing to negotiate for an item's release before the end of the week.

"Keeping bedrooms tidy was and still is a lost cause," acknowledges one mom. "Part of this is being a boy and part of it is ADHD. Once I accepted that, my life and my son's became a lot easier. Once a week he has to clean his room. He receives payment for this chore. Clothes that are not turned right side out go through the laundry inside out and are hung up inside out. At age twelve, getting ready in the morning is his responsibility. It's to his advantage to turn his clothes right side out before throwing them down the chute."

"We limit the amount of toys available to play with at one time," explains Missy from Bow, New Hampshire. "We also store some toys and rotate them with toys with which Colin has become bored. We got rid of the messy toy box and found shelves (closet or wall variety) have worked better. Carefully selected toys are within easy view for selecting and have a specific place on the shelf which helps in picking up. Buckets are great for small toys, cars, and blocks."

Social Gatherings

Your favorite cousin is getting married and your children are invited to the church wedding and the reception, but you don't feel comfortable including Jimmy in the festivities because of his temper tantrums and wild behavior. Although Jimmy takes medication, you're certain that the change in the daily routine, coupled with the excitement of being with so many friends and relatives, will be too much for him to handle. Yet you don't feel right taking one child and not the other. What can you do to include Jimmy in the celebration gaieties, yet keep his behavior in check (at least most of the time)?

First, take an inventory of your child's strengths and challenges. If he usually attends religious services and is able to sit through much or all of them, then he probably can attend the wedding without being disruptive. But, even if your child is used to attending religious services, try to have a backup plan in case he has difficulty sitting through the ceremony. Is there a baby-sitter you can hire to take along with you? Is there someone who wouldn't mind taking him outside for a few moments during the wedding, such as an older brother, sister, cousin, or favorite relative? Whatever route you choose, be sure to discuss your plan ahead of time with your child and whoever will assist if needed.

Consider the reception. How many other children will be attending? Is it being held indoors or outside? If inside, is it a formal reception at a country club or luxury hotel, or at a Knights of Columbus hall? Obviously, the formal reception may be more difficult for your child to handle. Will cocktails and hors d'oeuvres be served first? If only drinks will be available, how long before meal is served? What will your child do during cocktail hour? How long can he wait to eat? Would it be more appropriate to take your child home or to a sitter's house after the wedding? Is it feasible to take a baby-sitter with you to the reception, preferably one who can then drive your child home when he has reached his limit? Does it make sense for you and your spouse to drive separately and then plan for one of you to leave early with your child? Clearly, there are many options for any type of social gathering, so consider your child's temperament and behavior in certain situations and then devise your plan of action. As one mom from Randolph, New Jersey, advises, "Set reasonable expectations."

Preparing Your Child for a Social Occasion

Before the social event (whether it's a family reunion, wedding, birthday party, picnic, or baptism) talk about it with your child ahead of time, but not weeks in advance since this tends to have a snowball effect with some children. The more you talk about it, the more excited they become to the point where they can't sleep for several nights before the event because they are so intoxicated with anticipation. Not only can't they sleep, but their daytime behavior suffers also. So break the news a few days before, or even the day before the actual event.

"Make sure you talk with your child about the event so he knows what type of day it will be and what is expected of him," offers Janet from Seattle, Washington. "Tell him what the rules are for that day. Explain the rules again before you leave the house and again while you are in route. Have him repeat the rules to you so you are sure he understands them fully. Be sure your child gets enough sleep the night before and has been fed before you leave your house. [For small children, take along a snack and a few small toys.] Always remind him of the consequences of unacceptable behavior (he'll be sent to time-out, sent home with a baby-sitter or with Dad, while the rest of the family enjoys themselves). If he's older, you may want to emphasize that he will also lose the privilege of having a friend spend the night or going fishing with Dad the next evening. Emphasize the benefits of acceptable behavior."

Remember to give praise constantly for good behavior either verbally or with a physical gesture, such as patting his shoulder or his hair, touching his shoulder, giving him a hug, or by giving him tokens, such as stickers, play money, or whatever you use in your home for positive reinforcement.

"Express confidence in your child," suggests Barbara from Mississippi, "and let him know that you appreciate his willingness to be cooperative. If he should fail, don't criticize. Instead, tell him you know he will try to do better the next time."

Birthday Parties

"I have never let my son with ADHD have the kind of birthday party where children are invited to our home, simply because I was afraid that no children would come," laments Julie from Newark, Ohio. "Our son, like many children with ADHD, has been a social outcast throughout most of his school career. So I always have an in-school party because the party goers will always show up! I make sure the treat I take in is extra 'cool' so that my son has at least some time when his peers think he is also 'cool.'

"If my son is invited to another child's birthday party, I always ask the parent of the birthday child if she could use a little help and then I stay for the party, too. That way I can keep an eye on my son and intercede if he starts to get out of hand."

Kate from Carlinville, Illinois, commented that her son David always rained on others' birthday parades. "He grabbed things, tried to be the star, blew out candles, and ultimately pouted or threw a temper tantrum. Oddly enough, seeing his ugly behavior on videotape seemed to shock him a bit and his behavior has improved."

When You Are Trying to Talk on the Phone

Establish age-appropriate rules and explain those rules to your child. "I remind Ryan of the phone rules and if he does not comply, he waits in his room until my conversation has ended," said Terri from Moravia, New York. Jackie from Monroe, Michigan, explains: "Tell your child, 'You are not to interrupt me when I am on the telephone. If you need something, please stand next to me quietly until I notice you.' Never make your child wait longer than a minute and always reward him for following the rules."

"Older children can be encouraged to write a note," offers Mary Squire, Ph.D., "if it's something that just can't wait. A parent can then write the answer to the child." (But do not let children use this method as a means to avoid talking with the parent.)

"Teach your child to say 'excuse me' and then to wait for you to acknowledge him," advises Lynn. "Never allow him to say 'excuse me' and begin to talk with you immediately. He must realize that you are having a conversation with someone else and that you must also say 'excuse me' to the person with whom you are speaking before you can speak with him."

"I tell my children that I need to make a phone call and if they have anything important to discuss with me or ask me they should do it now, before I place the telephone call, " shares Joanne from Iowa. "They do know that it is okay to interrupt me if there is an emergency. In an emergency, they are to say, 'Excuse me, this is an emergency.' Be sure you explain to them what you consider an emergency."

"Teach your children by example," offers Ann from Boston. "Never interrupt them when they are talking and tell them you expect the same courtesy from them when you are talking. Be consistent. Never let them interrupt you one time and punish them for interrupting the next time."

"When I talk on the phone we make it into a contest," says Mary from Troy, New York." Every time I got on the phone I would inform him beforehand and then set the timer. Each time he would try to break his record from the previous call (example: one minute of no interrupting the first call; one minute ten seconds the second call). When he broke his record he received a star (on a chart) and then would receive a special treat."

Bad Manners

"Always use good manners in the home," advises Hanna from Richmond, Virginia. "Children with ADHD seem to have a problem learning appropriate manners. I think if you consistently say 'please' and 'thank you' to your child, eventually she'll learn to say 'please' and 'thank you' to you and to others. We also always use formal table manners at home. We've established the rules for good manners that we expect to be followed at all times. We've written them down for our son and daughter and we remind them to use good manners when they are out with us. For instance, 'When I introduce you to a friend of mine, I expect you to say hello with a smile on your face' or 'Always say excuse me when you must step in front of someone.' Always compliment your child when she displays good manners." Etiquette and manners classes are often available in the community. (You might inquire at the local YMCA or YWCA or other community centers.)

You may want to write down the appropriate way to answer the phone on an index card and place the card next to the phone. Remind your child to use the card every time he answers the phone. With practice, he will soon be answering the phone in the proper manner on his own.

Temper Tantrums

Many children experience temper tantrums, but children with ADHD experience tantrums that are often more frequent and intense. Parents report these tantrums to be "severe," "very explosive," "long in length" (sometimes as long as an hour) and "not age-appropriate." As one mom said, "You expect two-year-olds to have temper tantrums, but not seven-, eight-, or ten-year-olds." Some reported their child's tantrums as violent. "My son has had several tantrums that were so severe that he literally tore his room apart in a matter of a few minutes," one mom sadly admitted. "He was totally out of control." One dad reported that it took him an hour to patch up all of the holes in his son's bedroom walls. (Remember some children with ADHD will not experience such extreme temper tantrums.)

Tantrums usually happen because the child has lost his ability to cope—the result is usually an angry or frustrated child. As parents, you can help your child by looking for the cause of the tantrum. What has upset him? Has he been required to sit still too long? Did you fail to give sufficient notice before changing activities? Is he frustrated by a homework assignment? Were your expectations too high? Is he overstimulated by the day's activities? Was he surprised to find visitors in his home when he came home from school? Slow-to-adapt children may have difficulty with changes in routines.

Every time your child experiences a temper tantrum, record the details: time of day, where it happened, and the perceived cause. Eventually a pattern will develop and you will then have something to work with. For instance, my son generally experiences tantrums after school. He either loses it in the car on the way home or as soon as we get home. He rarely has difficulties with his behavior at school and I believe this is because he works very hard to keep himself under control during school hours. Once he feels he is on safe turf, he loses total control because he's been pressured for hours beyond his ability to cope. Once I recognized the pattern, I was able to formulate a plan. He loves classical music; he finds it very soothing and relaxing, so one of his favorite tapes is always playing now when he gets into the car. On warm or hot days, I always have a cold bottle of fruit juice waiting for him. On cold days, I offer him a snack. Because we have a long drive home (30 minutes), I let him set the pace. Some days he wants to talk, but most days he just sits quietly, sipping his drink and listening to the music. Nine out of ten times this approach works very well.

With a little effort on your part, you, too, can often help your child prevent tantrums that occur at specific times or under certain conditions by tuning into your child's temperament, recording your findings, and devising a plan. The important thing to remember is these types of tantrums are not premeditated nor is the child trying to manipulate you. Your child needs you to help him find a way to prevent the tantrum or to help him stop one that has started. The good news is that eventually the temper tantrums decrease in intensity and finally dissipate.

Ways You Can Help

There are ways you can help your child with these types of tantrums. Not all will work with every child, so you may need to try a few before you find one that works.

"We've tried holding our daughter when she has a temper tantrum, but she only pushes us away and seems to get angrier," recalls one mother from Baton Rouge, Louisiana. "Now, we stay in the same room, wait a few minutes, then start talking to her in a calm, firm voice. We'll say something like, 'I know you are disappointed (or angry), but now it is time to stop. You must stop. Now take a deep breath. Now take another deep breath.' This usually works for her."

"When Ryan's tantrum escalates, we usually hold him until he calms down," says Terri, his mother. "When he's really upset, we stay with him and do holding therapy. We use a one-minute cool down time (the child must remain still and breathe deeply) after the tantrum to make sure the tantrum is really over. If Ryan destroys his room in anger, money is taken from his bank to help with the [cost of] repairs or Ryan is expected to [physically] help repair his room. For detailed information on the holding technique, consult the book *Holding Time* by Martha G. Welch, M.D. (Fireside Press, 1989).

"Baths are a great way to calm down a child," said Janie from Scranton, Pennsylvania. "Whenever my daughter lost control when she was younger (under age six), I'd immediately put her in the bathtub. The water always had a calming effect on her within minutes. I must admit though that sometimes getting her into the bathtub was a real hassle."

"Temper tantrums were a big problem for David before Ritalin," remembers Kate. "Nothing worked really well, but things always went poorly if he managed to draw us in emotionally. We found it necessary to remove him physically from the room, put him in his room, shut the door and walk away. (David rarely tore up anything so this worked.) He would scream and scream, but eventually tire out. To avoid going nuts, we would turn up the television and try our best to ignore him. David hated that! No audience, no fun."

Some children can be sent to their rooms, but most children are safer (and feel safer) if you remain nearby. If your child experiences violent temper tantrums, it is imperative that you stay with him. Don't give him the opportunity to destroy his room, or hit you or anyone else. Set household rules for children who react violently and be sure they understand the consequences. In our home our children may not hit, spit, swear, or throw anything. They can, however, beat on a pillow, jump up and down, throw themselves down on the floor or their bed, or ask for someone to hold them. Should one of them break the rule and throw something, I ask if he is choosing to give up a favorite activity that evening. Sometimes that is enough to halt the behavior. If the throwing continues, I then gently stop it by putting my arm across his arms and speaking calmly to him until the tantrum subsides. Once he has calmed down we talk about what happened (we identify the cause of the tantrum) and discuss other ways that he might have dealt with his feelings.

Children who continue to have temper tantrums often do so because, unlike adults, they lack the necessary vocabulary to adequately express the anger or frustration they feel. Talking to your child about his feelings and labeling those feelings is the first step you can take to begin teaching your child to express his feelings in words rather than in actions. So, listen carefully when your child talks about those feelings. The next time you witness the beginning of a tantrum, intervene. Remove him from the activity and then help him label those feelings verbally. If you remain calm, your child will calm down much faster.

"Show your child how you handle frustrations and disappointments," offers Hanna from Richmond, Virginia. "If you burn dinner, point this out to your child. Say something like, 'Look what I did. Well, I'll just have to microwave last night's leftovers for dinner tonight. We'll have meatloaf tomorrow night instead.' This teaches your child other ways to handle frustrations." Parents who encountered mishaps like Hanna's might want to ask their child if they can think of other ways to handle the problem. Let your child help brainstorm solutions to problems with you.

Unfortunately, for some parents it's easy to get caught up in their child's temper tantrum. You may find yourself striking back at your child if he hits or kicks you. If he's screaming, you may find yourself screaming back. Please realize that this is a high-risk situation. It is during times of stress that parents are at risk of physically or verbally abusing their children with ADHD. If you find yourself getting caught up in the moment, take a giant step or two away from your child, take a deep breath and count to ten. If necessary, leave the room and ask someone else to step in.

Nonstop Talking

"My son will ask the same question over and over again. I answer his questions, then ask him to repeat the answer," explains Kristin from Flint, Michigan. "Once I'm assured he has processed the information, I refuse to answer the same question again."

"We understand our daughter's need to talk about her day and we are willing to spend time listening and discussing it with her," acknowledges Jim from Norfolk, Virginia. "But given the opportunity she'd talk nonstop until bedtime. We now give her scheduled time after school (thirty minutes), after dinner (ten minutes) and just before bedtime (fifteen minutes). She may talk about whatever she wants and we listen carefully, but when the timer goes off the conversation must end shortly after (usually one minute). This generally controls the excessive talking."

"We use *1-2-3 Magic*," offers Missy from Bow, New Hampshire. "For example: 'Please be quiet.' Child continues to talk. 'One!' Child continues talking. 'Two!' Child does not stop talking. 'Three! Take five in your room. When the five minutes are up, you can come out if you are quiet.'" For more information on this technique, refer to *1-2-3 Magic: Training Your Preschoolers and Preteens to Do What You Want* by Thomas Phelan, M.D. (Child Management Press, 1985).

Summertime

Some parents look forward to summer because they no longer have to handle phone calls from teachers, school conferences, hassles with homework, lost school books, torn clothes, broken eye glasses and school mornings. Other parents dread the thought of summer because their children behave appropriately at school and have few problems with schoolwork. The major difficulties they experience with their children take place at home, so the end of the school year signals distress for these parents. How will I find someone who understands that Jessica is impulsive and needs constant supervision even when she's on medication? Who can I trust to handle Matthew's behavior problems in an appropriate manner? How will I manage the stress of being with my impulsive, overactive child twenty-four hours a day? How will I keep him occupied and out of mischief long enough to straighten the house in the morning and get my errands done? I can't trust him to play at the neighbor's house or go off bike riding with his friends, yet I don't want to baby-sit all of the neighborhood children every day either. What will I do with her all day every day for the whole summer? These are real concerns for parents of elementary school-age children who can't be trusted because they are impulsive, distractible, and hyperactive.

"Even during the summertime, my son needs to be on medication three times a day," confesses Jennifer from Cleveland, Ohio. "He's that difficult. At nine years of age, I can't trust him to go off on his own. I worry about his safety and I worry because he's always getting into things he shouldn't. The first week after school let out he and his younger brother started a small fire in our shed, spray painted brown spots on our white garage doors, went into the neighbor's pond uninvited and unsupervised, and dumped a bucket of paint on the garage floor. Although my youngest son does not have ADHD, he'll go along with anything my oldest son suggests. After that week, the children were not allowed outside together all summer unless I was with them. So I made a schedule. One child stayed inside for an hour while the other played outside, then they changed places. I did this for the whole summer. It was exhausting, but it kept them out of trouble."

"We put our son in summer day camp. Last summer he went to one camp for six weeks and when that ended I sent him to Boy Scout camp for two weeks," says Linda from Louisiana. "I wish it didn't have to be this way, but at least with camp he stays on a schedule that is not much different than the one we use during the school year. He enjoys camp and it keeps him busy. Be honest though with the camp staff about your child. Make certain they understand your concerns, and know what time to administer medications."

Always remind camp staff that medicine *must* be given when indicated. If they inadvertently give a medication later than scheduled, they must let you know so you don't give the next dosage at the usual time. Be sure they understand the necessity of sharing this with you. My son once received 40 mg of Ritalin in a two-hour period because the staff failed to inform me that the medication they were to give at noon wasn't administered until two o'clock.

Be sure camp staff understands ADHD. If your child is hyperactive and/or impulsive and is a risk taker make sure camp staff knows he must be monitored closely during unstructured activities, such as swimming or horseback riding, for instance. Accidents do happen. (In an endeavor to fit in by showing off, my son once attempted to dive off the high platform at a community pool. Unfortunately, at that time, he did not know how to dive. His "dive" not only knocked the wind out of him, but he hit the water face first resulting in a badly bruised forehead and two black eyes. A former teacher witnessed the entire incident and later said she forgot that he needed to be supervised constantly.)

"Keep your child on a schedule," advises one mom from Kentucky. "When my daughter wakes up, she eats breakfast, gets dressed, makes her bed, and then can play outside until lunch-time. Lunch and dinner are served at the same time every day. Establish a routine for the summertime, just like you do for the school year. On the first day of vacation, post the schedule and go over it with your child."

If you work and wonder what you should do when summer camp ends, consider Debbie's recommendation: "Hire a baby-sitter to come into your home. I found it's easier and less problematic if your child is allowed to stay in her own home."

"When boredom sets in, children misbehave," observes Darlene from Kansas City, Kansas. "The trick is to keep your child busy outdoors with a friend, preferably a friend who does not have ADHD. Structured activities work better than just sending kids outdoors on their own to find something to do. My daughter loves to play dress-up with her friend (a structured activity). I help them create a special area and use a clothesline to hang clothes on. They play for hours. I also keep a list of activities tacked on the bulletin board that she can consult when she gets bored and is looking for something fun to do. Another fun structured activity is painting our deck. I give them each a bucket of water and a paint brush and let them paint away. We visit the park once a day, and the library once a week where she participates in the summer reading program. We have a community neighborhood pool we visit regularly. She plays with the children while I watch from the sidelines and talk with the other mothers. It's a nice break for me.

"We run errands early in the morning because she's usually in a better mood and more cooperative than she is in the afternoon after playing all day. Once the fun starts, she doesn't want to miss anything. But, if something does come up and I have to leave, I always invite a friend of hers to come along. Every evening before bedtime I tell her what tomorrow's day will be like. This seems to help a lot."

"I work in my home so taking care of my son myself every day is not an option," Liz from Minneapolis, Minnesota, explains. "But I do want him in the home, so I hire a baby-sitter four days a week. It works out well for all of us. She entertains my son, but when he needs something only a mom can provide, I'm available. I take more breaks during the summer because I want to be there when he needs me. I plan my summer work schedule months in advance, so the bulk of my work load is completed during the school year.

"Each summer we rent a cottage for two weeks or take the children camping. Before we leave we all get together and make a schedule outlining our day. It's imperative that we maintain a routine so the children, especially our daughter who has ADHD, know what to expect each day and we try to maintain that schedule."

Parents not employed outside the home, who face most summer days alone with their child or children, can make weekly charts that include educational goals for the child to reach as well as time for fun activities and the usual household chores. Set realistic, but challenging goals. Be sure educational goals and household chores are age-appropriate so they give your child a sense of accomplishment.

WEEK ONE	Mon.	Tues.	Wed.	Thurs.	Fri.

- Make bed each morning
- Pick up clothes every day
- Begin a collection of something (colored stones, shells, stamps, baseball cards or postcards)
- Do assigned chores
- Begin to learn to type (15 minutes a day) (computer programs are especially helpful because they give immediate feedback)
- Help parent with one meal daily
- Spend time with family playing board games, etc.
- Put toys away before bed
- Get ready for bed

(Week One's chart can be *slightly* altered for Week Two.)

Use stickers freely for all completed activities as a means of giving immediate positive feedback. Set a weekly goal that your child can work for and collect on the weekend (sleeping outside in a tent, seeing a movie of her choice on Saturday afternoon, going fishing with Grandpa, baking cookies with mom, horseback riding, a day at the beach, bowling, bicycle riding with dad, etc.) after earning a specific number of stickers. Charts can be revised on weekends for the following week and new goals established. If your child is older, be sure to let her choose the weekend activity with your approval.

"I find that if we have someplace to go almost every day, we seem to do better," notes Patrice from Aurora, Illinois. "This past summer I had a notebook of places to go, people to see, and activities to choose from. Having the notebook cut down on [having to make] big decisions out of the blue. I tend to lose my ability to brainstorm and think clearly when my son has especially noisy, active days. Car rides seem to be easier for me than a lot of physical chasing. I do, however, have to separate the kids; one in the front seat and the other in the back seat. I always carry an activity box and snacks."

Other suggestions for summer activities include: beginning a garden, taking swimming or golf lessons, playing miniature golf, horseback riding, taking weekly field trips to such places as a firehouse, a farm, the airport, the train station, a boat marina, historical sites, the zoo, the art museum, a computer store, a video arcade, a bicycle shop, a dairy, the veterinarian's office, or an amusement park. Before weekly field trips, visit the library and choose books on the subject of your upcoming visit.

Jumping on Furniture

Children who are hyperactive need the opportunity to express their energy through acceptable channels. For parents who have problems with jumping on furniture, several parents suggest using a trampoline (the miniexercise trampoline) which costs approximately $30.00. "We encourage our son to use the trampoline several times a day," explains Joanne. "We set the timer for five minutes and let him jump to his heart's content. This has not completely eliminated the problem, but it has helped."

Other parents who have found jumping on furniture to be an ongoing problem suggest making a jumping area in a playroom or in the basement. The jumping area may only be a couple of old mattresses piled on top of each other, but children appear to relish having a special place for such activities.

Transitions

Shifting from one activity to another is often very difficult for the child with ADHD. "Drew usually doesn't have problems with transitions if it's something he wants to do. If it isn't, you'll pay for it," says Debra from Crownpoint, Indiana. "I try to always tell him ahead of time if there's a change in routine. The other day, though, I scheduled a hair appointment for him after school. Of course, I couldn't forewarn him because I made the appointment that morning. He ended up throwing a temper tantrum in the car. I have to admit it really aggravates me sometimes that I have to schedule appointments around his temperament. My advice is to make appointments the day before, then you can warn about changes in routine in advance."

Making transitions from one activity to another or from one place to another may be extremely difficult for certain children with ADHD. All children, not just children with ADHD, accept changes in routine and act more cooperatively when they are forewarned. As parents, attempt to provide your child with a smooth transition whenever possible. With small children, a ten-minute warning may be sufficient. With some children warnings about changes in schedules may need to be given hours before or even days before, so they can process the information and prepare themselves mentally for a doctor's appointment, a shopping venture, or a visit to Grandma's after school. Other children will think about it and work themselves into a tizzy if you tell them too soon. Children with ADHD are not trying to make life difficult for you, they truly have trouble making transitions, so discover what method works best for your child and use it consistently.

Parents should also be aware that major transition times (meals and bedtime) are especially difficult for children with ADHD. Because of this, it's important that parents—not an alternate caregiver—be present during these times.

When giving warnings that changes are about to occur, make eye contact, and speak clearly and positively to your child. For example: "In ten minutes, when the buzzer goes off, it will be time for all of us to leave for church. I know changing activities is difficult for you. That's why I'm giving you a ten-minute warning."

Watching Too Much Television

Like many other children, children with ADHD enjoy watching television. However, some parents report that their children with ADHD (those displaying hyperactivity) did not watch television until the early elementary-school years (possibly because they couldn't sit still until they reached school age or they simply found other activities more interesting).

My son was one of those children who never watched television or videos until he reached second grade. Instead, he was a whirlwind of activity from morning until bedtime. When I heard other parents complain that their children watched too much television, I was envious. I would have given anything just to have him sit down and watch television for one-half hour so I could let my guard down for a few minutes. When he was finally able to sit through a program, I rejoiced. For the first time in seven years I was able to use the television as an electronic baby-sitter and I must admit it felt good.

However, I did find that I had to closely monitor the types of programs he watched.

One day my husband innocently purchased the video *Home Alone*. The three of us sat down that evening to watch the movie together. Within fifteen minutes I knew the movie was a big mistake when my son excitedly exclaimed, "He's hyperactive, just like me." After that movie, jumping on the beds became the sport of the day. A can of hair spray and a lighter made a torch. Broken Christmas tree ornaments were scattered on the garage floor. A goose-down pillow and a fan (taken from the garage without my knowledge) covered his room in feathers and made a mess that I wouldn't wish on my worst enemy. The rule in our house now is that the children are not permitted to watch a movie unless I have previewed it first.

Certain cartoons are prohibited, as are programs that emphasize violence of any kind. (I've received enough karate chops during temper tantrums to last a lifetime.) The problem with certain types of television programs and movies and some children with ADHD is that the children don't know where to draw the line. They can't just watch Superman; they *become* Superman, or Batman, the Karate Kid or, in our case, a very dangerous Kevin McCallister. Television simply cannot be used as a reward for good behavior in our house. My children would rather spend their time engaged in other activities.

But many parents of ADHD children do use television as a reward and they use it quite successfully. If watching television keeps your child quiet and out of trouble long enough to fix dinner or get dressed, use it, but use it cautiously and monitor all programs closely. If your child is addicted to television, or you want to limit the amount of time spent in front of the television, use a television lock (you put the television's plug in a box and lock the box). "We started very early in life limiting television time," says Ellen, from Oconomowoc, Wisconsin. "To break our son away, I often need to start a project that he can help with. He soon forgets the television and seldom asks to go back and watch."

Parents whose children enjoy television should take advantage of it and use it as a reward for appropriate behavior, such as completing chores, finishing homework, or getting ready for school on time. Television time can be used as a reward or sold. You may tell your child, "When you earn ten dollars in play money, you may purchase television time. However, your limit is one hour per day."

Traveling

Traveling with your ADHD child is not as frightening a prospect as you might believe. Actually, it can be handled quite successfully with proper preparation even with the most difficult children. Before we had children, my husband and I traveled frequently. When our first child arrived we never gave much thought to not taking him. We just packed and went. By the time he was a year and a half old, we knew we had a hyperactive child on our hands. Our choices were to decrease the number of trips we took, eliminate them completely, or take our son along. We opted to take our son with us. We were fortunate in that our son always slept whether we were traveling by car or airplane.

When our second child arrived, we faced the same choices. Again, we opted to take the children with us. We took our first trip with both children when the youngest was three months old. We flew from Ohio to California with a baby who cried nonstop from 5:00 A.M. to 4:00 P.M. Our return trip was the same. (So much for babies who are soothed by the sound and movement of an airplane.) Blake didn't sleep one minute either way. Two months later we flew to New Orleans with both children and this time Blake slept about one hour.

Our friends often ask us how we manage to travel with our children. My answer has always been the same: "We think out each trip very carefully." We make our plans and try to stick to as many routines and schedules as we can, just as we do at home. We have now been traveling many years with both of our children and we've all become seasoned travelers. That's not to say that we never have problems. Actually, it's usually the opposite. We have all kinds of problems, but we have found ways to handle them.

We have taken our children on all sorts of trips and we've traveled by airplane, boat (cruise ship), and car. We've found our children prefer flying simply because it's faster. Car trips of more than two hours are just too long for them and they fight constantly (physically and verbally), but some children do better. We all prefer staying in the same hotel for the entire vacation because we have found it easier to stay on a schedule and keep a routine. When we move from one spot to another, the children have difficulty settling down in a new place day after day.

Here are some tips for traveling with difficult children we and other parents have found helpful:

- Share travel plans with your child, along with the each day's schedule on the appropriate day. Keep to routines as much as possible. Meals and bedtime should be at the same time they are at home, if possible (often impossible on days spent reaching a destination).
- "When traveling by air, if you travel on an actual holiday, instead of the day before or after, the plane is less crowded, which is always easier on a family with a child with ADHD," suggests Julie from Newark, Ohio.
- When your child is an infant or toddler and you are traveling by air and departing very early in the morning, put the baby to

bed in a sweatsuit or other wrinkle-free outfit. Wait until the last minute to wake him, change his diaper, and out the door you go. For older children, lay out clothes the night before. Wake them an hour before you leave. Dress and feed them something light, even if they will get breakfast on the plane. They may still be tired, but at least they won't be hungry.

- "My motto is 'Be prepared' when traveling by air," says Julie. "I try to be prepared for anything especially lost luggage. So I pack a special carry-on bag with enough Ritalin to get us through the entire vacation (in case our luggage is really lost). I pack enough clothes for one day for everyone. I figure that most of the things in our suitcases can easily be purchased at our destination, but trying to replace a lost Ritalin prescription (a controlled substance in the U.S. and some countries) is impossible. And I always carry snacks in my purse for easy access during the flight."

- Even if the flight isn't terribly long, it probably will be a much longer day than usual, so time medication dosages carefully.

- Pack another carry-on bag with snacks, small toys and books, bottles, and diapers, baby wipes, a stuffed animal, and a change of clothes. If you're lucky, your little darling will sleep most of the trip. Older children should be encouraged to carry a small bag of items that they have chosen to occupy themselves. Do check the bag to be sure they've put the right types of toys in and make sure it isn't too heavy, or you'll end up carrying it along with your own carryon.

- "Try to book the bulkhead seats because they have the most room and there is no seat in front of those seats for children to kick," advises Julie. "If those seats are taken, with four of us traveling, I reserve the window and aisle seats in two rows. With three seats in coach, the chances are that the middle one will not be booked and you get extra room, which is always a bonus with a child with ADHD." (The disadvantage of bulkhead seats is that carryons with toys and snacks cannot be stored under the seat, which means a parent or flight attendant must get bags out from the overhead storage compartments.)

- Don't board the plane until the final boarding call. The earlier you board, the longer your child has to sit on the plane.

- For children who don't fall asleep, be prepared to keep them entertained. Hand-held electronic games (consider purchasing a new game or cartridge for the trip) will keep most older kids busy for a few hours. Carry back-up games just in case, along with coloring books, travel games, snacks, and gum for children who may experience ear pain from increased cabin pressure. An audiotape player with headphones is useful also.

- Be prepared to make trips to the restroom. Some children with ADHD can't make it the whole trip without getting up and moving around. If there's an empty seat near you, let them move to that seat for a while. Window seats are great because you have better control over your child's movements (I keep my tray down so they can't move past me), but if your child needs to use the restroom it means she has to crawl over two other people unless you are flying in the first-class section. An aisle seat is convenient, but extremely tempting to children who can't sit still. My son once took off running down the aisle bumping into flight attendants as they were attempting to serve beverages, then threw a temper tantrum when I tried to pick him up. What those people had to say about my abilities to parent!

- If you need pillows or blankets, obtain them as soon as you get on the plane, especially if it's a long flight. Also ask for playing cards, children's magazines, and a set of wings once you've settled in. After takeoff, flight attendants are very busy and you may have to wait for these items. Remember difficult and strong-willed children usually can't wait in silence.

- If your child is a fussy eater, call at least twenty-four hours in advance and request a child's plate or a fruit plate. There's no extra charge for this service.

- Have the flight attendant bring your child's meal before yours so you are able to open his napkin and silverware package, butter a dinner roll, and cut up food without worrying about your tray accidentally tipping over. A five-minute delay will also guarantee that your food will be hot when you are ready to eat.

- When you reach your destination by air, try to get off the plane as quickly as possible. If children have been particularly difficult, most people will step aside so you can exit, especially if your child is still screaming.

- "When traveling by car, we find that making frequent stops at rest areas and letting our son with ADHD run around (under close supervision) helps him during the trip," offers Julie. "What worked best for us on our car trips was to keep the length of the driving days short, even if that meant taking an extra day to get where we were going. When we stopped, we tried to make it no later than 4 P.M., and we always stayed at a motel with a swimming pool. We immediately try to get our son in the pool to swim and play off his excess energy before dinner. Dinner then becomes a more pleasant experience."

- When driving, separate children in the backseat with a small suitcase to define boundaries. Define the car rules. Mom or Dad should plan to spend part of the trip in the backseat (one child moves up front with the driver).
- Try to give five-minute warnings before stopping for a stretch break or a meal (admittedly, this is not always feasible).
- If you are driving through several states and taking back roads, take sandwiches along and stop at rest stops or parks for picnics along the way. Carry a thermos of water or juice, cups with lids and lots of straws to prevent spills.
- Consider leaving early in the morning (after 2 or 3 A.M.) so children can sleep part of the way in the car, although some hyperactive children will not go back to sleep once awake. You know your child better than anyone.
- If possible, consider taking a baby-sitter with you. A sitter who cares for your child on a regular basis is an excellent choice. Take her along as a mother's helper rather than as a baby-sitter. (Be sure she understands exactly what her responsibilities will be.) Your major expense will be food and lodging (and the cost of an airline or cruise ticket if either are your mode of transportation). Mother's helpers can assist with unpacking, share a room with one or two of the children, get up with children who wake up early, walk children around while you are waiting for food to arrive, help with daytime excursions or just baby-sit them around the pool or on the beach, and stay with them if you want a night out.

    Divide responsibilities. For instance, if you have two children, you or your spouse takes responsibility for bathing and dressing one child; she takes responsibility for the other. Or take turns watching children who need daytime naps. Be sure your sitter has time for herself each day, plus time for showering and dressing. Don't dump the workload entirely on her shoulders or she'll never want to travel with you again. The trip has to be enjoyable and fun for her also.
- If your budget will not accommodate a full-time helper, make use of sitters who are available through hotels. If you find someone who works in housekeeping that you particularly like, don't be afraid to ask if she is available for baby-sitting in the evening. Many women who work in housekeeping, baby-sit for guests as a way of supplementing their income. (We have found some excellent sitters this way.) Fees are approximately

five dollars an hour (in resort areas) and often you must pay for their transportation to and from the hotel. If you use a new sitter, be sure you explain the rules your child must follow and the penalty for inappropriate behavior. Write down all instructions and always leave a number where you can be reached.

- Be realistic. Your ADHD child will be very excited for the first day or two and will try your patience. Once they become familiar with surroundings and schedules, most will settle down. If you're staying in a hotel or motel with a pool, the possible loss of swimming privileges for an hour, or half a day, usually are the only incentive a child needs to cooperate. In fact if you want a totally relaxing trip, choose a hotel with a pool and/or beach access. The water will entertain and wear out most children day after day.

- If you find a place you all enjoy, consider returning to it again and again. Children settle in easier and much faster when they are vacationing in a spot they have visited before.

- Take night-lights, a first-aid kit, a potty seat for younger children, acetaminophen, a thermometer, syrup of ipecac, medical insurance card, and prescription medication.

- Take a variety of toys (travel-size board games, cassette player, Legos, dolls, small cars and trucks, paint sets, cards, etc.). If you are driving, keep some of the toys in the trunk and rotate them. Bring along story cassette tapes children can listen to as they follow the book (check your library). On longer vacations we've taken a VCR and several movies for rainy days and evenings with a sitter in the room. Don't forget to pack extra batteries. Disposable cameras also are great for small children.

- One mom who has traveled to Disneyworld advises, "not to give up the Ritalin at this overstimulating place. We found that if we could have a day at the park, a day at the beach, a day at the park, etc., we did a little better. We also discovered that our son always has a huge sleep deficit and increasingly higher activity levels as a result. Even the Ritalin helps very minimally at this point. We just put up with the situation. A purse-pak on my waist or a backpack frees my hands for him when we reach this point."

Problems with Inattention

Children and adolescents with ADHD have difficulty concentrating and sustaining attention in different situations. Their ability to concentrate and pay attention is particulary challenged when they are faced with boring, redundant tasks and activities, such as chores. However, when a child with ADHD is occupied with something he chooses to do, like playing Nintendo or watching a movie, he has little or no difficulty sustaining attention. Because of this inconsistency, people often label children and youth with ADHD as lazy, disorganized, flaky, or even stupid, maintaining they could concentrate and pay attention if they really wanted to or if they really tried. Children and teenagers who have trouble focusing and attending consquently have difficulty hanging onto a thought long enough to get a task completed.

The following are some of the symptoms that fall under the heading of inattention and some ways that parents help their children with attention difficulties in the home:

Easily Distracted

"I have found that my daughter gets distracted whenever she has to do something she's not fond of," says Jolene from Chapel Hill, North Carolina. "When it's time to do homework, for instance, I have to take her to her desk and help her get started. If it's a chore, I have to help her begin it. I then reward her for completing the task using a chart system."

"You can't ever tell my son to do something later," explains AnnaMarie from Evanston, Illinois, "or it will never get done. If it's something that has to be done, he's to do it now while it's fresh on his mind, like getting his Boy Scout uniform out for tomorrow or putting clean gym clothes in his backpack. If I say don't forget to do . . . he'll forget."

"We try to provide an atmosphere free of distractions when Brittany is told to do something like homework or a chore," comments Joanne. "No toys, no television, no radio, no friends, no phone calls. This helps keep her on task."

"We list everything that our daughter needs to do on a chart including the time that she must start the task," offers Michelle from Deer Park, New York. "We also use a timer. She has the same chores each day—ones we know she can do successfully. We help her stay on task by reminding her of the time, setting the stove timer, helping her get started and reminding her daily of the rules and her schedule."

Fails to Listen

"Nikki's biggest problem is with listening," acknowledges her mother, Marsha, from Montreal, Quebec. "As a result, she does things but not correctly because she doesn't listen to the directions. She's capable of cooking an easy dinner for the family as long as she has written directions to follow. So I write down each step for her."

"Always give directions to your child [while] making eye contact," suggests Paul from Princeton, Wisconsin. "Keep directions simple—no more than one or two steps. You're asking for trouble if you give a long list of things to be done without writing each task down. Once you give the directions, ask your child to repeat them back to you so you're sure he understands. If the directions are written down, make sure your son or daughter checks off each step as it is completed."

"Don't try to tell your child how to do something with the television on, the baby screaming, and your other child practicing the piano," advises Kelly from Phoenix, Arizona. "Take him to a room where it's quiet so he's not distracted and can concentrate on listening."

Difficulty Following Verbal Directions

"If something is really important and your child must follow the directions carefully then tell him just that," offers Jolene from Chapel Hill, North Carolina. "I say, 'Katie, it's important that you listen carefully. Please take your blouse out of the dryer right now and hang it up so you don't have to iron it later.' We have found this usually works with our daughter. Sometimes she still doesn't follow through, so she's had to iron a blouse or two, which is the consequence of not listening."

"Verbally give directions, but also write them down or have your children write them down," advises Janey from St. Paul, Minnesota.

Other Behavior That May Confuse or Frustrate You

My sons, and some other children with ADHD I know, have experienced other baffling behaviors that appear to be ADHD related. For instance, some children are what I call "hot" children. Even if it's ten degrees outside, they are hot. Not warm, but hot. Their faces get flushed and they sweat profusely, but often the face and head are the only places where perspiration is noticeable.

My son, Christopher, experienced three years as a "hot" child, from ages four to seven. While everyone else was bundled up in warm clothing at home during cold months, Christopher was sockless, wearing shorts and a T-shirt. One winter day I sent him to school with an undershirt and a shirt. He came out of school wearing only his undershirt, much to my embarrassment. His teacher, sensing how I felt, apologized, saying that he was always complaining about how hot he was and today they had told him to take off his shirt. From that day on, I skipped the undershirt and he's never worn one since.

From preschool through first grade, Christopher changed his clothes constantly. From the time he came home from school until bedtime, it was not unusual for him to change his clothes five times or more. At first, I thought it had something to do with the fact that at age four he had finally learned to dress himself without any help; thus he was practicing. But as the months went by, and he was changing clothes on weekends as often as every half hour, I decided this must have something to do with the ADHD. The behavior in itself was not harmful, so we tried not to make a big deal out of it, but as a mother I found it very frustrating. I was constantly picking up piles of discarded clothing. Then one day, much to our amazement, the behavior stopped as quickly as it had started. I have since spoken with several mothers whose children with ADHD also changed clothes frequently at about the same ages.

Some children with ADHD complain about labels in their clothing, or that their clothes are "itchy." (I know several adults with ADD who still cut labels out of their clothing.) It appears that their sense of touch (sensory defensiveness) is so acute, that the slightest raised edge is extremely uncomfortable for them. If your child says he can't wear a garment, don't force the issue. Let him wear clothing that he finds comfortable. In many cases, this means he'll have to go shopping with you so he can choose clothes with fabrics that feel good to him.

Another unusual behavior I've noticed regarding touch, is that some children with ADHD hate to have anyone touch their face or head. I first noticed this when my son was about fifteen months old. Now at age nine, he still pulls away whenever anyone reaches out to touch his face. Getting a haircut is a very trying experience for him, the stylist, and me. I've also noticed that he even hates to touch his own face. When he washes or puts lotion on his face, he does so very reluctantly using only one finger. Other parents have noticed the same type of behavior with their children.

Certain children with ADHD also appear to be sensitive to smells, sounds, and sights. Children will complain about smells or sounds that you cannot smell or hear. We've had to leave all sorts of places because of a smell or sound that my one son found very unpleasant.

While some children became more excited or hyper when they are someplace with an abundance of stimulation, other children will withdraw. The stimulation is just too much for them to handle. One parent recalled the time she threw a birthday party for her daughter at a popular pizza restaurant that has all sorts of video games and play activities for children. "After the children had eaten pizza and cake and played some games, it was time to open the birthday presents," recalls Becky. "I looked around for my daughter and found her sitting in a booth with her grandparents. I said, 'Come on sweetheart, it's time to open your presents.' She shook her head no that she didn't want to open them. So my husband and I opened the presents and thanked all of the children, while my daughter remained sitting quietly. When we got home she went up to her room and listened to music. She finally looked at her presents the next day. I believe all of the stimulation was just too much for her to handle and she knew it. That's why she withdrew from her friends. Our doctor told us that's a great quality for her to have; to be able to withdraw quietly when things get to be too much for her."

When some children with ADHD become ill they may not need their medication for ADHD. My son, who is extremely overactive, does not require medication when he's sick. During these times, he appears to be just an ordinary, normal child. He's affectionate, sweet, even-tempered, and a pleasure to be with. I hate when he's sick, but I have to admit I enjoy seeing this wonderful side of him. He's also never spent a sick day in bed. However, other children seem to need their medication even when they are ill.

As is common with all aspects of ADHD, your child may display some of these unusual behaviors, other unique ones, or none at all.

CHAPTER SIX

Ways to Prevent Misbehavior

We each have our own parenting style (based on the way we were raised), temperament, past experiences, and ability to deal with child-related stress. Research shows that there are basically four types of parents:

1. the dominant parent;
2. the neglectful parent,
3. the lenient parent, and
4. the firm and loving parent.

The type of parent we are influences our child's behavior.

The Dominant Parent

Dominating parents have high expectations and expect rules to be followed with little or no explanation. They usually want complete control over the child. A dominant parent often believes children are to be seen and not heard, and children are not permitted to question the why's of anything. Freedom of expression is not usually permitted. Obedience is often the parent's goal. Dominating parents may not offer enthusiastic, loving support to the child. As a result, dominant parents may have an aggressive, angry child—a child who may be disrespectful, rebellious, and demanding, with little regard for rules and authority.

The Neglectful Parent

Neglectful parents also do not give tender, loving support to the child, nor do they have any control over the child. Neglectful parents get irritated easily and often lash out at the child when pushed to make time for him. They have plenty of time to pursue their own personal interests, but little or no time for their child. Baby-sitters often spend the most time with the child. As a result, the child may be insecure, rebellious, have low self-esteem, and little motivation to excel.

The Lenient Parent

Lenient parents are usually warm and supportive, but they fail to establish rules and consequences. Lenient parents react strongly against authority figures, believing they are too inflexible and uncompromising. When their child misbehaves, they rarely discipline because they don't want to be seen as rigid parents. Lenient parents believe that children, through choice and experience, will learn how to live within society. They encourage individuality. Children of lenient parents are often manipulative, insecure, have low self-esteem, believe they are in control, and have difficulty abiding by group's rules.

The Firm and Loving Parent

Firm and loving parents establish clearly defined rules and consequences, and freely give love, support, and focused time to their child. Children of firm and loving parents typically feel more secure, have higher self-esteem, and know they are loved unconditionally.

Parents should examine their particular parenting style to see what effect it might be having on their children. The style of parenting used can make a situation with a child with ADHD much worse than it needs to be. I encourage you to explore this with a professional, particularly if you suspect that you might be (unintentionally) a contributing factor to aggressive or noncompliant behavior. The way you respond to misbehavior, what you anticipate from your child and whether he is capable of meeting those expectations, your child's temperament, and how he reacts to your parenting style are all factors that should be examined.

Firm and loving parents attain a delicate balance between domineering and permissive parenting to create effective parenting. The following are suggestions for creating an effective parenting style in your home:

1. **Accept the fact that your child has ADHD.** Trying to hide the fact, or refusing to talk about it, only tells your child that you are uncomfortable and embarrassed by him. Never forget that this is a genuine medical problem that just happens to affect such things as your child's attention span, self-control, schoolwork, social relationships, ability to organize, etc. The earlier you accept his disability, the sooner you can effectively advocate in his behalf.

2. **Think ADHD.** Do not expect your child to display normal age-appropriate behavior regularly. Have realistic expectations.
3. **Establish house rules, routines, and schedules.** Be consistent every day whether you feel like it or not. Do not nag, negotiate, or make exceptions to the rules until you are ready to revise the rules or change the routines. Be sure others caring for your child follow your rules, routines, and schedules at all times. Realize that house rules, routines, and schedules will change as your child grows and matures. Include elementary school-age children and teenagers in discussions when establishing house rules.
4. **Be sure your child understands which behaviors are unacceptable and the consequences for inappropriate behavior.** In other words, be specific when talking to your child, maintain eye contact, and have the child repeat what you say concerning rules. Deliver all consequences, both rewards and punishments, immediately and consistently. When you correct or discipline your child, be sure to establish which type of behavior is expected in that particular situation. Write it down if necessary.
5. **Be prepared.** If you know a specific situation will cause problems for your child, either prepare the child ahead of time or avoid the situation, if at all possible.
6. **Make a lifetime commitment to your child.** This is one of the most important steps in effective parenting. Your child must know that no matter what happens, even if you don't approve of his actions, that you will be there with unconditional love. Children of parents who only show love and approval when their child cooperates, is dressed neatly, or gets good grades will never feel unconditional love.
7. **Plan for and schedule time with your child.** One of the most important gifts we can give our children is our focused time—fifteen to thirty minutes each day doing something they want to do. While this is important for all children, those with ADHD especially need this time because it boosts their self-esteem and shows they are loved. In our home we spend one-half hour of quality time with each child every evening. During this focused time, each child can choose an activity of his choice and we spend that half hour doing what he chooses according to his rules. Some evenings we read together, play a couple of games of pool, take a walk, play a board game, hit golf balls, or just talk. It's very important that the child chooses the activity and the parent respects that decision.

8. **Unscheduled time is also important.** How many times can you remember your child asking for time with you and you've told him, "Not now, I'm busy. Maybe later," but later never came? Whether you were truly too busy at that moment, or had just sat down to read the newspaper, what you were doing is irrelevant. What matters is the message you sent your child. In this case, the only thing the child heard was, "She's too busy for *me*. What she's doing is more important than me." Unscheduled time is also beneficial because children with ADHD are constantly told what to do, how to act, etc., by well-meaning others every day. They need the opportunity to feel they are in control at some point. Be prepared for unscheduled time demands—requests come frequently—so you can handle the situation in a loving and supportive way.

9. **When talking with or listening to your child, make frequent eye contact.** (If your child is younger, get down to his level so you can establish eye contact.) Many children with ADHD have trouble maintaining eye contact, so you may have to turn his face toward you or remind him to look at you while you are talking with him. He's less apt to be distracted if you insist on, and maintain, eye contact.

10. **Treat your child with tenderness and respect.** Screaming or yelling, ridiculing, nagging, and sarcasm only tell children that they are of little value to us, which reduces their self-esteem and often causes behavior to deteriorate. Nagging, lecturing, and arguing can lead to various types of problems for all children, but can be particularly destructive for the adolescent with ADHD, so learn to control such responses now while your children are young. If your child insists on arguing with you or won't drop the subject, walk away from him. (Make sure if you walk away that it is not seen as a sign of giving up). Do not argue. Do not acknowledge their statements. This is a no-win situation. I know at times this is extremely difficult. I have found that when I do lose control, a sincere apology followed by a hug works wonders. I see it in my children's eyes and posture. Remember that the apology is for losing control, not for correcting their misbehavior.

11. **Be patient!** Remember your child may have little self-control and is not intentionally trying to displease you. Patience is another wonderful gift you can give your child.

12. **Show love for your child.** A pat on the head or the shoulder, holding the child's hand, or offering a hug or kiss, assures your child that he is loved. Tell your child you love him at least

once a day. A truly wonderful book to read to preschoolers and young school-age children is *Love You Forever* by Robert Munsch (Canada: Firefly, 1986). It's a warm, sensitive story about a caring mother and her child. I highly recommend it to all families, but particularly for families that struggle with a difficult child.

13. **Praise your child whenever you catch him in appropriate behavior.** Praise can be verbal (I'm pleased to see you set the table) or nonverbal (a smile, pat on the head, a wink, etc.).

14. **Identify feelings with your child.** Reminding your child that you too have felt frustration when faced with a challenging homework assignment, that you have trouble paying attention at times, or that you sometimes say things you regret, tells your child that you understand what he is going through because you have experienced the same types of feelings, disappointments, failures, and hurt.

15. **Don't expect perfection from your child or imply that he must be perfect.** Be sure your child understands that everyone makes mistakes, including adults.

16. **Show faith and confidence in your child.** Believe in your child, so he can believe in himself. Acknowledge all improvements.

17. **Concentrate on your child's strengths and abilities.** Acknowledge your child's strengths and assets. Suggest ways he can use his assets to help others or to make a contribution to the family or school.

18. **No negative labels, please.** A child who is constantly told that he is stupid, bad, lazy, dumb, stubborn, or unable to do something, will begin to believe just that. Not only will he believe it, but you'll witness it in his behavior and see it in his eyes. Remember, egos are fragile and often difficult to repair.

19. **Pick your battles carefully.** If you insist on getting your own way all of the time, you are setting yourself up for constant power struggles. Choose your battles carefully.

Smart Discipline Strategies That Work

While there are many different types of discipline strategies presented here, you must remember that not all of the strategies will work with each child. Try different techniques until you find the ones your child responds to successfully. Remember, your objectives are to *increase* the time your child behaves appropriately, *decrease* the unacceptable behavior, and *teach* your child how to control himself.

1. **Time-out**

   Explain time-out to your child before using it and make sure he understands that this is not a punishment but rather an opportunity to get himself under control (some parents, however, use time-out exclusively as a punishment). Time-out can be used when your child is:

   - In the process of, or has broken the rules
   - Acting foolishly or is irritating
   - Screaming or fighting
   - Talking back

   The advantage of using time-out is that it is an immediate, but brief, consequence to an undesired behavior. Time-out is a very kind way of stopping an inappropriate behavior and allowing the child to calm down without feeling embarrassed. Time-out can be used on the spot, no matter where you are. (See chapter three for more information on using this technique.)

2. **Ignore the Behavior**

   This approach is best used when your child is displaying behavior you find minorly upsetting yet tolerable—often it is a behavior that is used to get a parent's attention, such as whining, swearing, or name calling. Let's say you've told your child to go to time-out immediately and on the way he calls you a butt-head or something worse. Ignore it. Consider it nothing but noise. He's trying to irritate you. If you respond, he knows he has gotten your attention, and thus you have rewarded the misbehavior. Usually the name calling, whining, or swearing will escalate (when you ignore it) before it will dissipate, so don't give up. Without an audience, the behavior will eventually stop.

3. **Give a Prearranged Signal**

   If you are leaving for religious services or a movie and know your child often talks out loudly, arrange a special signal between the two of you that will notify him that his behavior is unacceptable in this place (touch his shoulder or make a time-out sign with your hands). Prearranged signals usually do not work if your child is losing control while with a group of friends who are playing a stimulating game or visiting an amusement park, but there is a time and place for this discipline strategy. Prearranged signals often work well in the classroom when the teacher and the child agree on a special signal that notifies the child that he is not paying attention or is disturbing the child seated next to him.

4. **Offer a Choice**

Rather than telling your child what to do, offer a choice: "Would you like to cut the grass or wash the car?" "Would you like to hold my hand in the mall or should we get the stroller out of the trunk?" Give your child the opportunity to make his own decision, but be sure he understands that if he doesn't make a choice you will assign one. Offering minor choices also directs the debate away from the important non-negotiable rule. For example: "Would you like to do your homework in the dining room or your bedroom?"

5. **Use "Grandmother's Rule"**

Grandmother's rule is basically a simple arrangement that says, "When you have done what you are supposed to do, then you may do what you want to do." For example: "When you make your bed, then you may go outside." "When your homework is finished, then you may use the computer." "When you wash the car, then you may drive it." Grandmother's Rule is appropriate for all ages and is extremely easy to use. However, be careful to never substitute the word "if" for "when." To do so will only invite your child to ask, "If I don't do it, what happens?" Grandmother's Rule works because it is always phrased positively. "You may go to the play, when (or after) you do. . . ." You are never saying, "No, you can't."

6. **Use Positive Reinforcements**

Positive reinforcements motivate children to try harder and encourage good behavior. This is an effective way for parents to reward behaviors they want continued. By rewarding good behavior, the child learns to identify the desired behaviors and receives the much-needed attention he desires. Remember, these children see *all* interaction as positive attention, even negative attention.

Verbal praise and tangible rewards (stickers, play money, hair ribbons, baseball cards, etc.) are positive reinforcements that most children enjoy receiving. However, always be sure you focus any form of praise on the behavior and not the child.

Never give rewards or privileges before the desired behavior is achieved. If you pay your child before he starts his chores, there's a good chance that the chores will never get completed. Once he has his reward he has nothing to work for. Again, remember to always use rewards for positive behaviors. Do not use rewards in an attempt to get a child to stop an undesired behavior (don't pay your child to stop hitting his sister).

7. **Make a Promise**

Some children with ADHD respond positively to promises. Promises made by a parent, teacher, or caretaker encourage a child to behave for a defined time period, to do a particular chore, or to resume an existing behavior for a longer length of time.

Promises are like using rewards for appropriate behaviors. However, I have found that if promises are not used too frequently you will usually get superior results. For instance, let's say you just arrived home with your children and there is a message on your answering machine regarding a job you've applied for. You're elated and you want to return the call immediately, but it's imperative that your children, who are fighting with each other at the moment, are quiet during your conversation. What can you do? Promise that in return for their silence for ten minutes you will give them something they want as soon as you get off the telephone. At a time like this, you're more apt to promise them just about anything in return for their cooperation. So what you promise will be more than a sticker on their chart, and if you've used this method before and have always shown that you keep your promises, your children will respond positively to another promise. Because they have learned from past experiences that promises mean something a bit more special, they are more likely to cooperate. To use this strategy effectively, it's important that promises are *always* kept.

8. **Token System**

With the token system, your child receives stickers, check marks, play money, or some other type of token for following the rules or completing tasks outlined on a chart designed by the parent and discussed with the child. The tokens earned can then be used to buy privileges, such as a trip to the park or zoo or having a friend spend the night. Or the tokens may be saved and exchanged for money to buy a desired item. Many families use a chart in the morning listing the tasks that must be completed before the child leaves for school (see the charts in chapter five). When the child successfully completes the tasks, he receives a sticker or other token for a job well done.

9. **Withdraw Privileges**

Removing privileges (activities a child considers enjoyable and would not want to lose) is an effective discipline technique for parents of elementary school-age children and teenagers. This can involve taking away such things as the use of the telephone, car, computer or video games, television, favorite toys, or bicycles. It's important that the withdrawal be directly proportional to the inappropriate behavior (don't remove a meaningful privilege for a minor violation), and be delivered as quickly as possible after the infraction.

10. **Grounding**

A child who breaks a major household rule, such as not calling home when he decides to take off from school to visit a friend or taking the car without permission, needs to learn the consequences of inappropriate behavior. Grounding the child, that is, removing all privileges for a defined time, is one strategy that can have a positive effect on children. Grounding is the equivalent to jail time. (See chapter eight for information on using grounding effectively.)

In the book, *Why Can't Johnny Concentrate*, by Robert A. Moss, M.D. with Helen Huff Dunlap, the authors recommend grounding in conjunction with completing household chores. Depending on the severity of the violation, the child is assigned a certain number of household chores. Until the chores are completed, the child is grounded (all privileges are removed). Other than attending school, working, or eating, the child will be isolated in his bedroom. In this case, the child is the one who actually determines the length of time spent being grounded. If the child can complete the chores satisfactorily in a few hours, then the child is no longer grounded. If, however, it takes the child an unusually long time (days) to complete the chores, the authors suggest that you reassess the arrangement. It just may be that life isn't quite "dull enough" for him yet.

11. **Natural Consequences**

Children can also learn desired behaviors by allowing natural consequences to occur. Let's say you have a rule in your house prohibiting shorts and short-sleeved shirts from being worn to school unless the temperature is expected to exceed seventy-five degrees. One morning your child comes to breakfast dressed in summer clothes but it's not expected to reach sixty degrees that day. As parent you have two choices: you can insist that he change his clothes, or you can mention that he is dressed inappropriately for the weather but allow him to wear the clothes and hope that he feels the discomfort (natural consequence) of choosing the wrong clothing. If you choose the latter, you are permitting him to learn that wearing summer clothing on a chilly day is unwise (some children with ADHD may need to experience this several times before it truly sinks in). Missing the school bus is a consequence of not getting out of bed on time. Having to walk to school is a consequence of missing the school bus. Of course, if the natural consequence poses a risk to the child, a parent must not back down from enforcing the household rule.

12. **More Is Not Always Better**

When I was teaching school years ago, I had a little boy in my class who I'll call Matthew. Matthew was a good-looking and intelligent child, with blond hair and blue eyes. Although he had been diagnosed with ADHD, he was not a "difficult child." He usually sat when required, and basically did well in school. I liked Matthew, but he had an annoying behavior problem that occasionally surfaced and I was determined to put an end to it: Matthew liked to spit.

For the first three months of the school year, I tried everything to stop the behavior. One day when he was in time-out, he turned around and spit at one of the children seated at her desk. And suddenly I knew what I could do to stop that behavior. I called Matthew to my desk and together we drew a picture of a little boy's face. When it was completed, I tacked it on the wall. I then placed Matthew in front of the picture and told him that for the next five minutes he could spit at that little boy's picture as much as he wanted. Well, Matthew got the biggest smile on his face and said, "You mean I can just stand here and spit and no one will get mad at me?" "That's right," I said. "You can spit and spit for a whole five minutes, and no one will get angry with you. In fact, anytime you want to spit just let me know and I'll hang this picture up for you. Is it a deal?" Matthew readily agreed.

Matthew began spitting, but wanted to stop after a short time. I encouraged him to continue and reminded him of our deal. When time was up, I only had to tell Matthew once. What started out to be a whole lot of fun for Matthew soon lost its appeal after several minutes. Matthew never had a problem with spitting after that. More is not always better.

This same technique can be used with four-letter words. If you don't care to listen, send your child to the bathroom and let him use that swear word as many times as he would like. Reassure him that anytime he chooses to swear he can do so in the bathroom for five minutes, but he's not to swear any other time.

13. Write a Note

Notes are a great way to urge a child to do something that he is supposed to do but occasionally forgets, such as putting his bike away, feeding the dog, etc. An example of this sort of note might read:

Dear Jason,

   I had a horrible day today. First, your mother backed out of the garage and almost ran me over. Then some guy came to fix the washer and almost hit me. To top it off, it rained all afternoon and now I'm soaking wet. I'm waiting for you to put me away and dry me off.

Your Bicycle

Notes also work well when you have something important to say to your teenager. Since teens often tune out when parents are trying to tune in, notes can be an effective way to make a point.

14. Write a Behavior Contract

Writing a contract to encourage good behavior or to eliminate annoying behavior is easy and effective. Sit down with your child and define the problem (e.g.: putting bike in the garage). Then decide on a reward (a friend can spend the night when five points are earned) together. Your contract might read:

I, Jason, agree to put my bike away each day.
Every day that I put my bike away without a reminder, I will earn one point.
When I earn five points, my friend Daniel can spend the night.

Signed, *Jason*

Contracts can be used with young children, but they work best with older children and teenagers.

15. Use a Timer

Make a game of eating, getting dressed, picking up toys, and other tasks by setting a timer and playing Beat the Clock with your child. This strategy works best with younger children. Be sure to give abundant praise, and a small token when your child successfully beats the clock. Remember that not all children respond favorably to Beat the Clock. (See chapter seven.)

16. **Be Explicit When Making Requests or Giving Commands**
    Clearly and simply state your request or give your command.
    Telling your child "stop" or "behave" is usually meaningless. Be
    clear: "Shelly, stop running now," or "William, hitting your
    brother is not acceptable. Go to time-out for five minutes."

17. **Use Praise with a Hidden Message.**
    This strategy permits you to compliment desired behavior while
    mentioning unacceptable behavior at the same time: "Thanks
    for putting your clothes in the hamper, instead of throwing
    them on the bedroom floor." Make sure you sound upbeat and
    encouraging, not sarcastic, when using this method.

18. **Think Ahead**
    Many times, parents can prevent certain problems if they plan
    ahead. If you are going out to eat, take toys or books to enter-
    tain your child while you wait for food to arrive—prevent mis-
    behavior by keeping the child occupied. The more proactive
    you can be in problem solving, the less reactive you have to be.
    Reactive disciplining is much more stressful.

19. **Use "I" Statements**
    Use "I" statements whenever the consequence of a behavior
    interferes with your needs: "When you throw your clothes on
    the bedroom floor at bedtime (behavior), I feel frightened (feel-
    ing) because I trip over them during the night when I check on
    you (consequence)." Or, "When you don't come home on time
    or call to say you'll be late (behavior), I feel scared (feeling)
    because I don't know if something bad as happened to you
    (consequence)."

A Plan for Change

Examine your style of parenting and make any necessary changes. While
your parenting style will not cause the primary symptoms of ADHD, you may
find that specific ways of handling your child may actually cause or escalate
the problems you experience in your home. On the other hand, parents who
are firm and loving may actually reduce the number of behavior problems
because their child responds favorably to such child-rearing practices.
Developing effective parenting skills and remaining committed to those skills
is not easy. However, those who practice effective parenting will find that the
rewards for the child and parents over the years are far too numerous to
count.

CHAPTER SEVEN

Working with Your Child's Teacher and School

When it comes to your child's education it would be a great injustice if you did not take the time to meet with your child's teacher. Appropriate interventions are compulsory for children with ADHD to succeed in school. Always remember you are your child's best advocate and that together with his teacher you can make a tremendous difference in your child's education.

Start the School Year Off Right

"I always find out in August who my son's teacher will be. Then I ask the principal to help me arrange a short meeting of introduction to discuss my son's ADHD with the teacher," explains Julie, a former high school teacher, from Newark, Ohio. "Having the principal relay this information to the teacher is important because I have found I get better cooperation from a teacher if she feels the principal is involved. At this meeting I introduce myself, tell the teacher my son has ADHD, and listen carefully to see if she knows anything about this disorder. I give her written information about ADHD and my phone number. I tell her I am available to help her in any way and not to hesitate to call me if there are any problems or questions. I discuss medication with her and tell her how important it is for my son to be able to take his medication quietly on his way to lunch so that the other children will not make fun of him."

I approach a new school year much the same. When school begins, I make an appointment with each of my sons' homebase teachers. Before the meetings, I put together a packet of information on ADHD that I plan to leave behind with the teachers. I come to this meeting well prepared: I know what I want to discuss, what points I need to stress, and what questions I need answers for. The teachers are left with valuable information about my sons' disability and the fact that I am a strong advocate for them.

Fortunately, my sons' school is family oriented so it is easy to meet other parents. About midyear, I start talking with parents whose children are in the grade my sons will be in the following year. I try to determine what they like or dislike about their child's homebase teacher. In particular, I am interested in their teaching style so I can determine which teachers will be best for my children. I also ask my oldest son what teacher he likes best because I think it's imperative that he have a teacher he likes and who likes him. At the last school conference of the year, I ask my sons' homebase teachers which teacher they feel will be best for the next year. Once I've reached a decision, I then speak with the director of the lower school and ask for his or her input.

If recent surveys are accurate, teachers voice a great deal of frustration about the lack of parental assistance. Most teachers are enthused and delighted to have parents work with them in assisting and teaching their child. What most teachers want is a partnership with the parents—an alliance based on openness, trust, and support.

Don't be afraid to speak up at parent-teacher conferences. Ask questions. For example: "How have you handled Andrea's daydreaming. Has it worked?" "Do you recall at the last meeting I suggested that you initiate a system whereby you would put your hand on Jonathan's shoulder when he starts to lose control? Have you tried this approach? Why not?"

To Tell or Not to Tell

Several years ago, when my son was just beginning preschool at age four, I asked his doctor if it was better to tell teachers he had ADHD or to not say anything. The physician answered, "Would you rather the school knew he had ADHD, which would explain any inappropriate behaviors and school difficulties, or would you rather have him known as a troublemaker who has problems in school?" I decided I would rather not have my son labeled as a "troublemaker" or a "school failure" because of his ADHD (some parents disagree with this approach). I concluded it would be better for him to be labeled as a child with ADHD—at least there would be a medical reason for any behavior problems or difficulties in school. This decision was based on the following considerations:

1. A child spends nearly seven hours a day at school; more time than he spends awake at home on weekdays. During school hours, parents rely on teachers to meet their child's needs. To fulfill those needs, the teacher must know the child has ADHD and understand the disorder. For the child to experience success rather than constant failure during those seven hours, the teacher must also know the child's strengths and challenges.

2. Approximately one-third of the children with ADHD take medication. If a child takes medication and must receive an afternoon dose, someone at school must be there to administer it. Schools require a parent's and doctor's signature and the name of the medication before they can give prescription drugs to students. One mother who did not want her daughter labeled admitted that she used to put her seven-year-old's medication in her lunch box, which meant some days her daughter took the medication and other days she did not. "I finally realized I had no choice but to tell her teacher," she said. "Now the school nurse gives her the medication just before lunch. She's doing better in school now that she takes her medication regularly."

3. Because a teacher spends so much time with the child, parents must rely on their observations for feedback on the medication's effects. Is it working effectively in the morning and afternoon? Is the timing right for the afternoon dose? Has he or she noticed any side effects, such as sadness, irritability, or headaches?

4. If support services are needed, parents are most likely to turn to their child's teacher. He or she can enlist the help of other school personnel, such as the school psychologist or a speech therapist. If a support team of professionals is needed to work with the child, the child's teacher will be part of this team.

5. If a child's ADHD was not shared with the teacher, who would be hurt the most?

What is best for your child? If "telling" means swallowing one's pride and admitting that your child is not perfect, then so be it.

Before School Starts

Prepare your child for the beginning of the school year. Some schools hold an open house a day or two before the first day of school. At the open house, children can meet with their teacher, see a list of their classmates, locate their desk and/or locker, walk around their classroom, and visit a short time with other schoolmates. If your child's school does not have an open house, ask if the two of you can visit his classroom before school starts. For first-timers, visit the classroom and tour the inside of the building. Afterwards, take a walk around the outside of the building, visit the playground area, and show your child where the busses will be parked after school. You also might want to visit your local library and pick up some books about the first day of school. This will give your child some idea of what to expect. For younger children returning to the same school, be sure you inform them that some of the children (maybe even some of their friends) from the previous year may have moved and will not be in class this year.

If your child is a slow mover in the morning, initiate practice runs a week or two before school starts so he can begin adjusting. (Some parents of elementary school-age children keep their children on the same morning schedule the entire year.)

Check out extracurricular activities before school begins. Sit down with your child and determine which activities, if any, he might be interested in. If you do this before school starts, you won't have an angry child two months into the school year demanding to know why all of his friends are involved in soccer and he isn't. Check on Girl or Boy Scout activities, which are great for improving socialization skills in children with ADHD. Look for activities that match your child's abilities. Avoid competitive activities before second grade (you may need to avoid competitive activities even longer for some children with ADHD).

Restrict the number of after-school activities. Children with ADHD often burn out quickly. Because of this, they do much better with a balance of structured and unstructured activities. Free time, time for climbing a tree, is important for all children and unstructured activities teach children to play independently. Set ground rules for free time or you may find your child spends this time doing the same thing, like watching television or playing video games. Together, you can make a list of things he can do during unstructured play time, and then rotate the activities. When planning after-school activities, remember that most activities require commitment on your part, even if it's only picking up your child at 5:00 when he normally takes the school bus home.

The First Day of School

Let your child choose the clothes he wants to wear the night before school starts. Many of us grew up when the first day of school signaled the time to wear a brand-new outfit, complete with new school shoes. Times have changed. If an older child insists on wearing something that wouldn't be your choice, remember peer pressure is high in upper elementary and middle schools. Your child's concern is fitting in with the group; he wants to wear what his friends will be wearing. With younger children, who are not yet capable of making decisions concerning appropriate clothing for school and weather conditions, let them choose from two outfits you have laid out.

Set your alarm for an earlier wake-up time. All family members must adjust to the new routine, which probably includes several members of the family using the same bathroom, fixing breakfast, packing lunches, catching the school bus, and leaving for the office at the same time. It may take a week or two to get back into the swing of things, especially for the slow-to-adapt child. If you use a charting system in the morning, be sure it is hanging up with a pencil nearby. Make certain you have stickers available or whatever reward you offer. If your child buys his lunch at school and you often forget to give him lunch money, include this on a chart system. Make it the child's responsibility to ask for lunch money. Even first-graders can be given this responsibility.

If your child will be riding on the school bus, write down the bus number so he knows which bus to look for when school is dismissed. This number can be written on a luggage tag that is attached to his backpack or pinned inside of a jacket, sweater, shirt, or blouse for younger children. If he is younger, try to find another child in his class who rides the same bus and introduce the children to each other. Your child will feel much more secure knowing that a friend is riding the same bus and he's less apt to panic when school dismisses.

The First Few Weeks of School

All children feel more comfortable when they arrive at school on time. If you drive your child to school, leave the house in plenty of time so he gets to school five or ten minutes early. Some teachers use the first few minutes of each morning to tell children the day's agenda. If there will be changes in the routine, teachers will point them out at this time. Because children with ADHD need routines and have difficulty with schedule changes, it's imperative that your child gets to school on time.

Beginning the first day of school, tell your child where she is to put all notices the teacher sends home. Returning responses to the teacher is also a problem for most children with ADHD. Always put responses in the same place each time so a child knows where to find them. One mother reports that her daughter hand delivers notes to her teacher and has been taught to give the note to her teacher as soon as she gets to school. This mom says nine out of ten times the note reaches its destination using this method.

Check with your child's teacher about field trips ahead of time and write them down on your calendar. If you are able and willing to assist a teacher on a field trip, volunteer your services. Your child will enjoy having you along and you will be able to observe his behavior firsthand. The same holds true for volunteering in the classroom whenever possible. "Volunteering in the classroom helps us to see Colin's performance in the classroom setting," says Missy of Bow, New Hampshire, "and if he is falling behind in specific academic or social areas." Volunteering also gives you the opportunity to meet your child's classmates and discover who his friends are. Consider arranging play dates for your child with his friends—one friend at a time as previously discussed.

Attend all parent-teacher conferences. Also try to attend parent association meetings, school concerts, etc. If you are unable to attend some events, be sure to telephone the school and let them know you are aware of the event, but unable to attend (this shows you are interested in school events). Don't feel like you can't attend certain events because you have small children at home and can't find (or pay) a baby-sitter. Most parents take their young children to school activities. After all, schools are designed to accommodate children. Some schools even provide child care while parents attend conferences with teachers.

The Teacher as an Ally

Do you see your child's teacher as an adversary or as an ally? How you view your child's teacher will have a great effect on your relationship with him or her. If you view him or her as an adversary, you are setting yourself up for a frustrating relationship during the school year. But if you see her as an ally—someone with whom you want to form a partnership—the chances are good that you can work together in your child's best interest.

"This year we are blessed with a wonderful teacher," says Diane, whose son has ADHD. "She admits she does not know much about ADHD. I have been supplying her with articles and ideas to help him in school."

Every parent hopes to find a teacher who is sensitive to the issues facing the child with ADHD. When this is not the case, don't lose hope. With some effort on your part, you usually can form a working relationship with your child's teacher. The following strategies will help you earn the teacher's respect and ensure your child's chances of having a successful school year:

- Meet with your child's teacher either before school starts or within the first few weeks. Call and make an appointment, rather than just showing up after school one day. An appointment tells the teacher that you respect his or her schedule and it emphasizes that what you want to discuss is important enough to warrant a prearranged meeting.
- Think of the teacher as an ally, even if you have heard things about him or her you don't particularly like. Be sincere, friendly, and cheerful. The first few minutes of a meeting often set the tone for the entire discussion time.
- Come to the meeting prepared. Know what issues you want to address (e.g.: which seating arrangements have worked best for your child in previous years—what didn't work and why) and write them down. Ask for the teacher's cooperation in meeting your child's needs.

- "Take along a one-page summary of ADHD and how it affects your child," advises Mary Squire, Ph.D.
- Take notes during the meeting and date them.
- It is acceptable to request that specific tests be handled differently for your child if needed. If your child has difficulty with writing, and as a result cannot write fast enough to keep up with the class, then asking that weekly spelling tests be given orally is not unreasonable. Never hesitate to ask a teacher to write down nightly homework assignments for your child, or to at least check to see if your child has written them down accurately. Also ask if he or she is willing to accept your child's call at home if there is confusion regarding an assignment.
- Be empathetic. You *know* how frustrating dealing with your child can be. Now imagine having your child plus twenty-five others to handle. Make a point of letting the teacher know that you appreciate the fact that he or she has many students to work with and that some require extra assistance. You'll be surprised how much compassion you'll receive when you need it the most just because you have shown him or her empathy.
- Accept the fact that your child has limitations and is not perfect. Do not become defensive when talking with the teacher. It will only create a hostile atmosphere.
- Be honest, open, and offer your support. Speak with the teacher about your child's strengths and limitations, disciplinary methods that work, and effective instructional techniques. This is one of the first steps parents need to take to ensure that their child's needs are met academically, emotionally, and socially in the school setting. Talk with him or her about the ways you work with your child at home and the difficulties you have in certain areas. Share what works for you and what works best for your child. Make the teacher your confidant. Then, he or she is more apt to come to you if a problem arrises because you have shown you care about your child's education and he or she knows you can be counted on for assistance in handling the problem.
- If you would like the teacher's feedback on specific behaviors (being disruptive in class, for example) or certain subjects, ask for it. Be sure he or she understands that you will provide support and suggestions (for consideration) on how to deal with challenges your child may present. Let the teacher know that you will monitor schoolwork and homework and will inform him or her of anything at home that may affect your child's schoolwork and behavior. (If grandpa is in the hospital and you

are under a great deal of stress, this may affect your child in school in ways you may not even be aware of.) Above all, encourage the teacher to contact you concerning any problems. A simple statement, like "Please don't ever hesitate to call me. You won't be telling me anything I haven't heard or seen before," assures the teacher that you are a person who is approachable and open to discussion about your child.

- If you want to have regular communication with the teacher, now is the time to arrange for it. Decide if you want to meet with him or her monthly, talk by phone every other week, or send notes through the assignment pad. Be sure to pass along any favorable comments that your child has made about him or her, or school in general, at these times.

- Ask for information about homework assignments (how often, what subjects, how much time your child should spend on homework) and suggestions for helping with homework.

- Volunteer to help in the classroom or with a class project. This is an effective way to observe the teacher's classroom style and your child's response to her style of teaching.

- After the conference, express appreciation for the time he or she gave you. Write a thank you letter. You may want to summarize the main points of the meeting in your thank you letter. Then if there is a discrepancy between what was agreed, the teacher will undoubtedly notify you immediately. (Many teachers will also follow through by sending a letter to you that summarizes the points discussed and his or her plans to help in specific areas.)

- During the school year, clip magazine and newspaper articles on ADHD and send them to your child's teacher. If you discover a great book on ADHD, share it with your child's teacher. Clip a note to an article or a book that says, "Thought you might be interested in this article (or book)." Most teachers will be pleased to receive additional information on ADHD, but especially pleased to know that you have thought of them.

CIBA-Geigy, the manufacturer of Ritalin, offers a free booklet, titled *Attention Deficit-Hyperactivity Disorder and Learning Disabilities: Booklet for the Classroom Teacher*, by Larry B. Silver, M.D., that parents can give to their child's teacher. The booklet can be obtained free of charge from CHADD (Children and Adults with Attention Deficit Disorders) by calling (305) 587-3700. (Note: this booklet is different than the one created specifically for parents; make sure to ask for both.)

Teenagers may feel embarrassed having their parents contact their teacher directly. If this is a problem in your home, you may want to use a letter that he can hand deliver to his teacher. Consider the following letter, which was written by Mary Squire, Ph.D. to her son's teachers:

Dear _____

_____ has Attention Deficit Hyperactivity Disorder (ADHD). ADHD is a physical/neurological disorder characterized by age-inappropriate levels of inattention, hyperactivity, and/or impulsivity. The primary manifestations for _____ are difficulties with attention and concentration, organizational skills, and difficulty staying on task. In a classroom, he may disturb other children at times by talking but is not disruptive. His attention difficulties are most evident in math, due to the degree of concentration required for accurate calculation.

We will be changing _____ medication in early October due to motor tics that result when he takes Ritalin. He will be taking Ritalin until that time, but his current dosage may be a bit low. Therefore, feedback from teachers will be especially important during the first quarter to help us monitor dosage.

Accommodations that improve _____ classroom functioning and academic performance include the following:

_____ should be seated in the front of the classroom surrounded by the attentive students.

_____ will likely require more time on tests and other assignments than the majority of students in the class. He should be encouraged to check his work, especially in math.

If _____ fails to turn in assignments or comes to class without his homework done, it is important to notify me before his grade is adversely affected.

_____ is capable of doing honors-level work. Superior work should be expected of him, and he should not be placed in lower levels simply because of his attention difficulties. He has very high aspirations for himself, and together we can help him achieve them. If _____ quarter grade average falls below a B (or A in science or English), please call me immediately. I can be reached at home at _____ or work at _____.

Thanks very much for your help.

Mary Squire

Mary Squire

You may wish to use a similar letter, however, it must be tailored to meet the needs of your individual child and note the following:

- The current medication being administered
- Specific difficulties your child experiences in the classroom
- Accommodations that will improve academic performance. (The school district can develop a 504 plan—similar to the Individual Educational Plan (IEP)—which incorporates these accommodations and is legally binding. Parents may have to request it. (The 504 plan is discussed later in this chapter.)

"My teenage son has never been able to talk with his teachers, so I draft a letter to each teacher every year, about the third week of school," says Janet Robinson, R.N., Ph.D., who is the mother of an eighteen-year-old. "In the letter I begin by listing his strengths and abilities, then list the specific problems he has (like disorganization). I only make one request, and that is if he misses more than two assignments that I'm notified. Most of the teachers, when you are real concrete, are supportive. I've seen them write in their roll book, 'misses two assignments, call mother.' They don't have to speak with me necessarily. I give them my voice-mail number. Whenever I see my son going into a self-destructive pattern, I send the teachers a note that says I'm concerned about how he's doing. I put in a self-addressed postcard and all they have to do is make a check mark or fill in a blank." Dr. Robinson's postcard is similar to this:

___ He's doing fine
___ No changes
___ Not doing as well
___ Missing _____ assignment(s)

_____
Teacher's Signature

"Anything we can do to make the teacher's life easier is usually very appreciated," explains Dr. Robinson. "Most high school teachers are surprised that parents don't want to be involved in their kid's lives. I think it's essential every parent of an ADHD student gets to every parent-teacher conference. Teachers have to know we are interested. It's easy to assume that because our kids don't hand in assignments that we don't care either. Stay involved with the school, even when there are problems. I know it's hard to go to conferences and have to sit and hear the negatives, but parents must become involved."

Parents should always assess the teacher's knowledge of ADHD before sending a letter. "Some teachers only think of ADHD as a severe behavior disorder," explains Bruce Pasch, M.D. "One high school teacher thought one of our students was mentally ill and advised other students not to associate with him."

Problems with Teachers

Sometimes, despite your best efforts, problems do develop with a teacher. Your child may complain of being treated unfairly, of never having enough time to finish in-class assignments, or losing recess or physical education on a regular basis as a form of punishment. Any complaint your child voices should be investigated thoroughly before you meet with the teacher. First, try to find out exactly what has happened, or is happening, from your child.

My youngest son once told me that he was caught talking during class. When I asked what his teacher said, he answered, "She didn't say anything. She just put tape on my mouth so I couldn't talk again." My first instinct was to immediately telephone the teacher, but I decided to hold off until I learned more. That evening I asked my son to tell his father what had happened in school. My son told the same story. In fact, he relayed the same story after two additional days of questioning. On the third day he said, "Mom, I was only kidding about the tape on my mouth. My teacher really didn't do that. I was playing a joke on you."

Had I reacted hastily, I may have caused a great deal of unnecessary stress for an excellent teacher, so it's wise to find out what you can from your child first. If the problem appears to be legitimate, speak with a parent who volunteers regularly in the classroom. Had my son not revealed the truth, I would have cautiously asked another parent how the teacher handled children who talked during class. Or, I would have dropped by school unannounced and observed the teacher firsthand.

If you discover there is (or appears to be) a problem, request a parent-teacher conference. When you meet with the teacher, express your concern in a relaxed, nonconfrontational manner. Voice your opinion, but do so respectfully. Discuss what your child needs, rather than focusing on what the teacher is doing incorrectly. This is where your knowledge of ADHD can be greatly beneficial.

Ideally, you should present specific concerns: "Evan seems to be having a problem finishing his math tests. I've noticed the last two rows of problems are rarely answered on the timed tests . This is having an effect on the grades he's receiving and I'm very concerned. As you know, Evan has ADHD and we've found that timed tests are difficult for him because he tends to work slower than the average child. It takes him longer get started, to process the information, and write it down. I know the children are expected to complete one hundred addition problems in five minutes before they can move onto subtraction, but this may be impossible for Evan to achieve."

Together work toward finding a solution to the problem, one that is acceptable to both the teacher and you. A parent might say, "It's my hope that together we can help Evan move on to subtraction. He's becoming very discouraged because he is the last child on addition and many of his classmates are already on multiplication and division. We work with Evan nightly and know he can answer these problems. Do you have any suggestions?" Be sure to give the teacher the opportunity to offer his or her suggestions before offering any of your own. In a case like this, suggestions a parent might make include:

- The number of problems could be reduced to fifty, thereby reducing the amount, not the quality of work
- The test could be given untimed (it's his knowledge that is being tested, not his attention span or how fast he can complete the test)
- The test could be given orally
- The grade scale could be altered

If you use a constructive approach, you will find that the teacher will be more receptive to any suggestions you have to offer and less apt to react negatively to you or your child. Remember that many adaptations or interventions can be implemented in the regular classroom to meet the needs of most children with ADHD. Parents who are interested in learning about various interventions and strategies that work with children who have ADHD, should refer to the book, *How to Reach and Teach ADD/ADHD Children* by Sandra F. Rief (West Nyack, New York: The Center for Applied Research in Education, 1993).

If, despite your best efforts, you are unable to reach a satisfactory solution to a problem, then, and only then, should you take your concern to the principal. Approach the school principal using the guidelines presented above.

What should parents do if their child is experiencing academic failure despite interventions in the regular classroom? If you have been working together with the teacher, he or she may suggest that your child be evaluated to determine if he has a learning disability and the nature and extent of the special education and related services that the child needs. If a teacher does not suggest this, you have the right to ask that your child be evaluated. If a teacher does not feel this is necessary, your next step is to request a conference with the principal. If the school refuses to evaluate your child, then ask the principal for the name of the special education contact person for your area, or the name of the director of special education, and request a conference.

"If you suspect that your child's teacher is not capable of handling a child with ADHD [after parent-teacher conferences have failed to produce results], then talk with the principal and see if there is a more suitable teacher for your child in the school," says Joanie from Sylvania, Ohio.

"With on-going problems, I find that daily communication with the teacher helps," says Julie from Newark, Ohio. "You can do this two ways. Either briefly ask the teacher how things went each day when you pick your child up, or use a message envelope for a daily report. Teachers who will not take the time to write a daily note, will answer you if you appear in person." If a teacher is not willing to write a daily note, she may provide this information if you give him or her a supply of daily checklist forms (noting your child's specific problem areas) that can be filled out within a few minutes and sent home with your child.

Unfortunately, not all teachers are willing to accommodate a child who presents challenges. "My son was switched from a public school to a private school after one quarter in first grade. The problem was both his ADD and his teacher's response to it," explains one mother. "Rather than accept a different child in her class, she made him feel as though he was an outcast and, thus, he became one. Phone calls came at least three times a week. She offered no solutions, nor, in my opinion, did she even try to understand . . . she just complained. Conferences with the principal were to no avail. Eventually, we all benefited . . . she got her wish and ultimately, we got ours (which was a better education for our son). We transferred him to a private school. At the private school, difficulties were discussed with individual teachers and allowances were made for motor skill problems and speech difficulties. He was required to do at least half of the work (half full rather than half empty principle) that the other children were expected to do. With time, these allowances were decreased and now, in seventh grade, he is operating fully with his class. Were changes dramatic when he transferred schools that first year? No. But it was certainly a [positive] start. He was treated as an individual and not as a clone."

"In our experience we have found that young teachers are usually wonderful with children with ADHD," says Dewey from Santa Fe, New Mexico. "Because they are younger, they are energetic, have more patience, are willing to spend extra time reaching the child with ADHD, and are eager to learn more about this disorder. In our opinion they are more open to suggestions from the parents." (Remember, many older teachers are also young at heart and enjoy working with children who have challenges.)

What Type of School Is Best for the Child with ADHD?

Most experts agree that children with ADHD do better in a more structured setting (where prescribed work patterns are the norm) rather than in a school that promotes open-ended choices, yet, some parents I interviewed felt differently. Their children attend schools that are less structured (open-classroom concept) and are doing considerably well.

When my husband and I decided to send our oldest child to the school he now attends (an independent, open-concept school), we did not know that the professionals recommend that children with ADHD be schooled in a structured setting. We looked at the schools in our area and decided this particular school would be best for a child with ADHD because it was the least restrictive. Our son would not be required to sit at a desk all day, nor would he have the same teacher all day long. After we enrolled him that summer, we mentioned this to his psychologist, who was disheartened to learn of our choice. He told us this school would not work for our son, but time has proved otherwise. Parents who have their children in small private and independent schools say that many of these schools offer:

- Small classes—children receive more focused time from teachers, teachers are able to immediately respond to appropriate and inappropriate behavior because of the smaller student-teacher ratio.
- Many one-on-one learning experiences—wonderful for children who have ADHD and experience difficulty staying on task in group situations.
- Hands-on approach to learning—children learn through touch along with sight and sound.
- The use of computers—instant feedback and reinforcement.
- The choice, even in primary grades, to type classroom and homework assignments, which is often much easier for children with fine motor skill difficulties.
- A variety of teachers throughout the day, which lessens the chance of one teacher being drained by the challenges of the child with ADHD—also, children learn how to change classes at an early age rather than having to learn this skill and adapt at the junior high or high school level.
- Morning meetings where students find out what they will be studying that particular day, and are told of schedule changes ahead of time—great for the slow-to-adapt child.
- A weekly check of schoolwork, which requires a parent's signature—an automatic home-school feedback system.
- An organized notebook approach, which often includes color-coded folders for homework and various subjects, a folder for notices sent home, a pencil holder and, most important, an assignment pad folder—this approach helps children improve their organizational skills.
- The choice of learning activities when free time is available during the school day—children are taught to make choices, learn to entertain themselves while developing some skills independently (interests and talents often become evident with this type of learning approach).
- Freedom to get up and move around quietly (within limits)—children are recognized as individuals with varying needs (not

as "problem children") and are not punished if they can't sit still for long periods of time.

- The last hour of the school day is reserved for classes that require less concentration (music, art, physical education, for instance)—excellent for children whose afternoon dose of medication may be wearing off or has worn off.

Says Heather, a former teacher who lives in Raleigh, North Carolina: "Traditional structured classrooms are not required for all kids with ADHD. I taught in an open classroom and the students went off Ritalin in my class because of the flexibility. There were fewer conflicts yet there was structure: (i.e., reading first, then math, then playtime, etc.) Each child had an individualized assignment, but some talking and moving around was allowed." Structure is always needed but it must allow for flexibility.

For information on how to evaluate curriculum and staff, and public and private schools, you may want to take a look at the book, *Your Child's First School: A Handbook for Parents*, by Diana Townsend-Butterworth (New York: Walker, 1992).

Home Schooling

"If school has become a horrid experience and your child's self-esteem is slipping away, consider home schooling," suggests Kate from Carlinville, Illinois. "We home school all of our children. Since David is ADHD/gifted, it affords him the opportunity to study his current interests in-depth. He doesn't compete with thirty others for attention. A four-to-one ratio in a class is great . . . He doesn't have a bad 'rep' at this school. And he can't con this teacher. And no one loves or understands him like I do, so I get the best results. He gets plenty of socialization through neighborhood friends, church, and sports. For David, school socialization would take over academics to negative extremes in both areas."

There is a growing number of parents who teach their children at home. Many school districts permit this and some districts even cooperate with parents by permitting them to use school resources. Home schooling involves a significant commitment, but parents who make that commitment can effectively teach their children at home. For more information on home schooling consult *The Home School Manual, 5th Edition*, by Theodore E. Wade, Jr. and Others (Auburn, California: Gazelle Publications, 1993). Curriculum guides are available through your school system, a local library, or may be ordered through bookstores.

Gifted Children with ADHD

More than three million children in the United States have an IQ of 125 or higher. But having a high IQ is not the only criterion involved in evaluating a gifted child. Often, a child is regarded as gifted when he shows exceptional abilities in one or more areas, including mathematics, music, leadership, language, computer science, creative thinking, or special talent in the performing or visual arts.

In her book, *The Gifted and Talented*, Gilda Berger describes gifted children as those who do things earlier, faster, better, and a little different than other children. But what about gifted children with ADHD? What difficulties will they experience in school and what is their prognosis for the future? Unfortunately, there is little information available on this particular group of children, but it is known that when gifted learning-disabled children receive appropriate intervention they can have a successful, rewarding future.

Appropriate intervention includes many strategies because multiple areas of the child's life are affected. First, psychological counseling may be essential for the child and family. Educational therapy is imperative. Second, intellectual deficits must be identified (the deficits are often masked by the giftedness) and adjustments made that will enable the child to take control and learn to adapt to his unique situation. Third, the child must be taught to deal with anger and stress (often caused by frustration) using distinct behavioral techniques. Finally, the child's teachers and school administrators must be involved in all aspects of the child's educational program.

The following are some hints for parents with gifted children who have ADHD:

- Most gifted children show an early interest in books. Read to your child and discuss the stories with him. Talk about the characters, ideas, actions, and meanings. Have age-appropriate interesting books in your home for young children who are reading on their own.
- Provide access to a computer. Using a computer is good exercise for children with ADHD who may need to stimulate small hand muscles. It's challenging for even the brightest child, and it provides immediate feedback. Nintendo also is great for the same reasons.
- Help your child develop interests and hobbies. Provide space, time, materials, and encouragement for activities he enjoys.
- Buy toys that help to develop mental and physical abilities. Toys that involve problem-solving or decision-making skills are best.
- Provide reference books (encyclopedias, dictionaries, etc.) for young children. Some gifted youngsters intuitively know how to use reference manuals.
- These children are smart; so, say what you mean and mean what you say. They'll catch you every time.

For more information on gifted children contact: The Association for the Gifted, Council for Gifted Children, 1920 Association Drive, Reston, VA 22902, or the National Association for Gifted Children, 1155 15th Street, NW, Suite 1002, Washington, DC 20005. You may also be interested in the book *The Survival Guide for Parents of Gifted Kids: How to Understand, Live with, and Stick Up for Your Gifted Child* by Sally Yahnke Walker (Minneapolis: Free Spirit, 1991).

Homework without Hassles

No matter what type of school your child attends, one thing is certain: your child will have homework. If you are fortunate, your child's teacher will check his assignment pad every day to make certain your child knows what his homework is. Because some teachers are unwilling to do this, believing that the child needs to learn responsibility for taking accurate notes on his own, you may find that your child is not sure what his homework is. Some children take notes, but then can't read their writing or they don't have the appropriate books with them to complete the assignments. Without a doubt, homework can be a very frustrating experience both for the child and for the parents.

Homework Patterns

Homework for younger school-age children may follow a pattern or schedule. For instance, every Monday they have a spelling test and on Tuesday evenings they are expected to write ten sentences, using as many of their spelling words as possible. Ask your child's teacher whether he or she follows such a schedule. If you know what to expect from week to week it will help you and your child tremendously and prevent many nightly battles.

Daily Assignment Pads

Whether or not a homework pattern exists, the daily assignment pad is still the most beneficial tool available. Your child records his assignments during the day and then his teacher checks the assignment pad and signs it before he leaves for home. You, in turn, sign the sheet after the homework is completed and it is taken back to school the next morning. For assignment pads to work parents, teachers, and students must work together to establish some kind of monitoring plan. "Teachers may need to write down the assignment for some kids with ADHD," says Mary Squire, Ph.D., "This may be necessary for even some of the older children."

Says Annie from Sylvania, Ohio, "My son writes his assignments down and has a friend check it for accuracy. The friend then signs the assignment sheet. Chase enjoys collecting coins, so every day that he brings home his assignment sheet signed and with the right textbooks he receives $2.00 to use for coin shopping on Saturdays with his dad. If he misses a day, he loses a coin from his collection because he's in the negative (down $2.00). The next day if he brings the assignment sheet home signed, he's now $2.00 up and he gets the coin back. The following day if he brings home the assignment sheet signed, he gets $2.00." This is a great idea for children who collect something they value because children with ADHD often respond better when they must work to keep something they already have.

Assignment Sheet for Elementary School Children
Encourage your child to use an assignment sheet as soon as he starts receiving homework assignments. If the school does not provide an assignment sheet, design one of your own and make enough copies to last the entire school year. All sheets should be kept in a loose-leaf notebook that your child carries to and from school every day.

Unclear Assignments or No Books
There may still be times when your child is unclear about an assignment. It's helpful if the teacher accepts calls at home, but if this is not possible be sure your child has the phone numbers of a few classmates he can call. If a phone call must be made, your child must be the one to make it no matter his age. You may have to get on the line to help write the assignment down if he's forgotten his spelling book, for example, but the call must be made by your child because homework is his responsibility, not yours.

If your child consistently forgets to bring home his books or brings home the wrong textbooks, you may want to purchase a second set of books that remain in the house. "This also allows for highlighting and writing notes in the margins, which is necessary for many ADHD children," says Mary Squire, Ph.D. This is, of course costly and many teachers discourage it. If you prefer not to buy extra textbooks, you might insist that your child bring home every textbook every night, whether he has homework or not (reward him daily for remembering his books until it is no longer necessary), or make photo-copies of chapters to keep at home.

Your Homework Responsibilities
Homework should be a part of your child's daily schedule and listed on his chart. This means it should be done at the same time each day whenever possible. It is your responsibility to see that your child has a proper area for studying and completing homework, whether that spot is the desk in his bedroom or the dining room or kitchen table. This area should have sufficient lighting and be as free of distractions as possible. (Siblings are distractions so it is your responsibility to keep them out of the study area.) If you find that your child is unable to concentrate in a quiet room, it may be because he needs background sound. The hum of a small fan or a tape playing softly, with the tranquil sound of summer rainfall, may be just what is needed to help him concentrate. And, remember to turn off the television set.

Provide your child with a box of school supplies that are to be used only during homework time. This saves you and your child from the nightly hunt to find those items needed to complete homework. When homework is finished, the box should be put away in the same place.

Encourage your child to do his homework on his own. Encouraging independent work does not mean that you are not available to assist. It means that you are available to help get him started by making sure he understands what the assignment is and assisting him with the first problem. It also means helping your child break larger projects into smaller steps. "Set mini-goals for assignments," advises Dr. Squire. A book report can be overwhelming to some children, but if you break it into smaller parts (title, author, illustrator, the setting, list of characters, main idea in two or three sentences, etc.), the assignment will be much easier to complete. Twenty-five math problems can be broken down into five-problem sections. "Or children can do every other problem," offers Dr. Squire. "But always talk with a teacher about this ahead of time. Reward your child after completing each mini-goal." Rather than having your child study an entire list of twenty spelling words the night before a test, have him learn to spell five words a night for four nights. Many assignments can be broken down into smaller parts or divided over several days so the task becomes manageable. "Children then can see the progress they are making," adds Dr. Squire.

While doing homework, offer your child the opportunity to take short breaks every ten to fifteen minutes. Encourage him to get up and move around, stretch, take a drink of water, or use the bathroom. Use a timer to signal when he must return to his homework. If your child is having difficulty in a certain subject, help him budget his time so he can spend a short period of time reviewing work in that area. "If there is a subject area in which my son is having difficulty, I try to teach him the next lesson just before the teacher presents it in the classroom," says Julie from Newark, Ohio. "Then he will not miss the point of the lesson because of his short attention span and get frustrated. As well, my son is able to answer the in-class questions the teacher asks and this increases my son's self-esteem."

When homework is completed, praise your child for starting his homework on time, sitting quietly and working, writing legibly, and finishing it in an appropriate amount of time. "An after-school dose of medicine may help children who have difficulty working on homework," suggests Dr. Squire. (Be sure to check with your physician before adding another dose of medication on your own.)

Slow Pokes

For children who take forever to do their homework, play Beat the Clock. Together, you and your child determine how much time he will need to complete his homework, including breaktime. Tell your child how much time he has to do his homework, then set the timer. (Note: you will need a second timer for breaktime). Reward your child for completing his homework within the time frame, using the chart system (he gets a sticker or another reward). After three or five days of successfully completing homework, your child earns a special privilege, such as a trip to his favorite restaurant. For older children, you may wish to increase the number of successful days to ten (or whatever you feel is appropriate) before your child earns a privilege. As your child develops the ability to stay on task and completes his homework within the time frame, you can increase the number of successful days it takes to earn a privilege. Always praise your child once homework is completed. Compliment him for staying on task, neatness, controlling frustrations, and finishing the assignment. Ideally, praise for completing the assignment correctly should come from the teacher, but since this does not always happen, parents should praise their child for a job well done.

"If you use Beat the Clock watch your child carefully," suggests Bruce Pasch, M.D. "Some impulsive children will rush through their homework making careless errors. Or, Beat the Clock may encourage impulsivity in slow pokes who are slow because they are checking themselves."

The Rejectors

For children who refuse to do their homework, remove all privileges. This means no television, telephone calls, visiting friends, using the computer, basketball practice, etc., until homework is completed. If he intentionally forgets assignments or his textbooks and is not able to do his homework, he still loses all privileges for the evening. If this continues for a week, take away all privileges on the weekend also. It's important that the child realize he always has a choice. He can do his homework and the privileges are automatically reinstated, or he can refuse to do the work and lose all privileges. This is a frustrating situation, but it's important to control yourself. Don't argue with your child. Don't make idle threats. Don't yell or scream. State the rules in a firm, but positive, voice and be consistent every night. For example: "You may watch televison after your homework is completed," not "You can't watch television because your homework isn't done." When homework is completed, immediately follow through with rewards and remember to praise your child for completing homework during the scheduled time frame.

The Speeders, Forgetters, and Insisters

My nine-year-old used to complete his homework in a matter of minutes. He could do twenty math problems and study twenty spelling words in five minutes. Sounds impressive doesn't it? The problem is that most of the math answers were wrong and he couldn't have passed the spelling test if his life had depended on it. Maybe you have a child who's a "speeder." Speeders often sit down to do their homework without being told (this pleases Mom and Dad greatly and speeders know it), but then always have something more important to do and rush through their assignments. Speeders almost always have to re-do their homework because of wrong answers or sloppiness.

Some children are "forgetters." They often forget their assignments or books and then say they can't do their homework. Speeders and forgetters can be handled the same way. At the usual scheduled homework time, children must still sit down and do schoolwork no matter what. No time-off is given for short assignments, no assignments, or forgotten books. Speeders must work on homework for a predetermined length of time. Forgetters work on math, or language arts, or write a book report assigned by the parents. Parents can base assignments on subjects and skills the child is studying or is expected to study in upcoming months. Assignments should be created in advance and kept on file, so parents always have work prepared—even when schedules are hectic. Parents should always find more to do than the teacher assigns, providing the student the incentive to bring home assignments. Eventually, speeders learn to slow down and do it right the first time, and forgetters remember their assignments and textbooks.

The insisters are the children who maintain they completed their homework at school or that they didn't have any homework. "If you hear this too often," advises Jenny from Seattle, Washington, "then call the teacher and find out for yourself."

Falling Behind on Homework

If your child has trouble with his homework for an extended time period (two weeks), make an appointment with his teacher. Is he having the same problems in school with class assignments? Are other children struggling with homework assignments? Maybe your child has missed some basic points days or weeks earlier that may account for his difficulties. Or, if other children are having trouble with homework, maybe the homework is not grade-appropriate. Just as you want to know what's happening in school, the teacher wants to know what is going on with homework assignments, so keep in touch. School failure may contribute to, or worsen, a student's low self-esteem, depression, or anxiety.

For further tips and hints on motivating children to complete homework, you may want to read the books *Homework Without Tears: A Parent's Guide for Motivating Children to do Homework and Succeed in School* by Lee Canter (HarperPerennial, 1987), and *The Homework Solution: Getting Kids to do Their Homework* by Linda Agler Sonna (Charlotte, VT: Williamson Publishing, 1990). For hints on improving your child's schoolwork, refer to *1,001 Ways to Improve Your Child's Schoolwork: An Easy-to-Use Reference Book of Common School Problems and Practical Solutions* by Lawrence J. Greene (Dell, 1991).

When Homework Isn't Turned In

Discovering that completed homework is not being turned in to the teacher is incredibly frustrating and commonly occurs with children who have ADHD. If this is a problem for your child, schedule a three-way meeting involving you, your child, and his teacher. It's imperative that your child participate in this meeting—his contribution is crucial. Together develop a turn-in-homework plan. Then arrange to meet again in two weeks to see if the system is working.

If problems continue with homework (forgetting books or assignments, not turning in homework) ask the teacher if your child can complete his homework at school sometime during the day.

Hints for Junior High and High School Students

As your child encounters more demanding school days and homework sessions you may want to share these tips with him:

1. **Pay more attention in class by participating during class.** Judy, a former high school teacher and a parent of a child with ADHD, from Toledo, Ohio, says this is best accomplished by:

   - Sitting close to the teacher in lecture-style classes where students not only hear better, but will have fewer distractions
   - Taking notes in classes and using a tape recorder
   - Partaking in class or group sessions (this includes asking questions when the student doesn't understand something and offering answers when they do)
   - Coming to class prepared (homework is done and/or student has studied a lesson the night before it is presented in class)
   - Writing a summary of the lecture after the class. "Always ask a teacher if she has an outline of the lecture," suggests Judy. "If she does, maybe she'll share it."

2. **To organize all class materials using a color-coding system.** (Blue folder for math papers, blue sticker or blue book cover on math book; red folder for history papers, red sticker on history book or red book cover, and so forth). All folders are then kept in one loose-leaf notebook. On the outside of the notebook is a color-coded listing for each subject. Then when he's on the way to history class, for instance, he can stop by his locker, check the front of his notebook and see that he needs all red covered or red stickered books or materials for history class. The notebook also holds other school supplies your child uses frequently. Completed homework is always

placed in the appropriate color-coded folder in the loose-leaf notebook.

For older children changing classes, help them draw a map showing the location of their locker and the route they must take to each class. Color-code each classroom according to the color used on books and file folders.

3. **Use an assignment folder.** This entails creating an assignment sheet to fit the child's schedule, making a copy for each week school is in session, and placing all of the sheets in a folder, which remains in the loose-leaf notebook at all times. The assignment sheet lists the days of the week across the top; the subjects are listed down the left-hand side. A new sheet is started every Monday. Janet Robinson, R.N., Ph.D. suggests that parents use the color-coding system on the assignment sheet also. "My son must enter his assignments next to the proper color. If there is no assignment that particular day, he is to write 'No Assignment' next to that subject. Parents can give points for entries next to each subject."

Older students, with different classes on different days, should buy a daily planning calendar to keep track of classes throughout the school year, noting for example, where and what time they meet, and designated study period times. In this planner they can write down test dates, essay and term paper due dates, and outline plans to study for tests and write papers.

4. **Set a specific time period and place to study and complete homework each day.** Negotiate a plan with your older student and put it in writing. Older students can earn such privileges as use of the car or telephone for staying on task during homework time. Likewise, students can lose telephone time or the use of the car for not staying on task.

5. **Take notes, even when reading chapters for homework assignments.**

An Assignment Notebook that Really Works!

Teachers and educational professionals now place more emphasis on teaching organization and planning skills than ever before. Educators often cover these areas within the broader topic of study skills. Since it is difficult to find well-designed organizers and planners for their students, some educators design their own.

Catherine Pidek, a speech and language therapist in suburban Chicago, is one educator who created her own materials for her students. She is now the president of her own company, called Success by Design, which specializes in designing student planners and making them available to schools across the country. A sample page from one of Success by Design's homework planners is shown here. If you would like a free catalog of their materials, call 1-800-327-0057. Planners are available for students in grades three through twelve.

Study Hints for Students with ADHD

Because students with ADHD have difficulty organizing materials, concentrating for extended periods of time, and selecting important information from written and auditory direction, it's imperative that students tackle assignments with a game plan. In this section, we will cover some of the types of assignments that older students may have difficulty with. If a specific type of assignment is not listed here, parents should be able to alter some of the following tips to meet their child's specific needs.

Reading Chapters in a Textbook

A textbook chapter can appear monumental to a student with ADHD, but when broken down into sections the task becomes less overwhelming and threatening. When studying chapters in a textbook, students should use the popular SQ3R Method:

  S—Scan the chapter
  * Reading the title of the chapter
  * Reading each subtitle
  * Studying any illustrations, graphs, charts, etc.
  * Reading the study guide questions at the end of the chapter
  * Reading the chapter summary

  Q—Make up questions using the subtitles (for example, if the subtitle reads "**Jury**" ask yourself, "What is a jury?" "How many people sit on a jury?" "When is a jury used?")

  R—Read to answer your questions
  R—Write the answers down
  R—Review what you wrote at the end

  Keep all notes to review at a later date, when you will be tested on this material.

Studying for Tests

Before beginning to study for a test, the student must be sure he knows exactly what information he will be tested on. He can clarify this with the instructor or another classmate. Once he has determined exactly what will be covered, he goes through his color-coded folder and pulls notes from classes

_____, _____ _____, 19___
DAY   MONTH   DATE

Subject	Assignments	Date Due	Test Day
Reading			
English/ Language Arts			
Spelling			
Math			
Science			
Social Studies			

Things To Take Home

1._____

2._____

3._____

4._____

5._____

Things To Bring To School

1._____

2._____

Messages

ANS

and homework sessions. If the test covers chapters five and six, and the test will be given in five days, that gives him two days to study each chapter, chapter notes, and old tests and quizzes. The student details this plan in his planner. For example:

Monday, January 18	Study one-half of chapter five. Review notes and summaries.
Tuesday, January 19	Finish studying chapter five. Review notes and summaries.
Wednesday, January 20	Study one-half of chapter six. Review notes and summaries.
Thursday, January 21	Study remainder of chapter six. Review notes and summaries.

Major Assignments

A major assignment, such as a twelve-page report on alcoholism due in six weeks, not only has to be broken down into manageable parts, but must be worked on during an established time each week. The schedule might be like this:

Week One: The student gathers the resource materials he'll need to write the report. Articles are copied; books are purchased or borrowed from the library. If the books have been borrowed, the student reads through them and takes notes (because books usually cannot be loaned for extended periods of time).

Week Two: The student decides which main topics to include in the report and lists them on index cards using numbers.

1. Define alcoholism
2. Who is at risk?
3. How does alcoholism affect the abuser?
4. How does alcoholism affect the family?
5. What can the abuser do to help himself?
6. What can families do to help the abuser?

Week Three: Take notes on each topic, listing them on index cards using the number assigned to each topic. The number should be placed in the top left-hand corner on each index card. All number 1 cards are then paper clipped together, as are number 2 cards, and so forth. Notes should be written in the students *own* words and in complete sentences. This will make the rough draft relatively simple to write.

Week Four: If the instructor requires an outline, this is the next step. With the notes numbered by topics, the student determines the order the facts should be presented in, using a formal or simple outline form.

Week Five: The student begins writing the rough draft. The rough draft does not have to be perfect. If the student is not sure of the spelling of certain words, he should not stop to look them up in the dictionary; he should just circle the word. At this stage, he is only trying to get his thoughts down in paragraph form, beginning with the number 1 cards and so on. He will skip lines so words or sentences can be inserted if needed. After the student completes his rough draft, he sets it aside for one day, then reads it again slowly, one line at a time, making the needed corrections in spelling, punctuation, etc.

Week Six: Before beginning the final draft, the student reviews the points he needs to remember when rewriting. (Did the instructor ask students to write on every line or every other line? What are the margins to be?) After the student completes his final draft, he sets it aside for one day. Then he carefully re-reads it, line by line. Spelling and punctuation should also be checked (check for spelling errors by reading the paper from the bottom up), as well as the overall look of the paper.

Using a computer

Computers are a tremendous help to children with ADHD. The features of a good word-processing program allow students to check for spelling and grammatical errors immediately. Most important, the quality of work is usually much better than if they had written the assignment by hand. Viewing their work on the screen allows them to see what they have actually written rather than what they think they have written. For example, children who have difficulty forming and spacing letters often think they've placed a period at the end of the sentence, but have not actually done so. Their handwriting often makes it difficult to determine where a sentence has ended and where the next sentence begins. Errors can be easily corrected on screen. Computers can be used not only for homework assignments, such as writing sentences with spelling words for the younger student, but also for note-taking and major writing assignments for older students. Some high school and college students with ADHD carry laptop computers to class with them.

Providing an Appropriate Education to Children with Attention Deficit Hyperactivity Disorder

(From the *ERIC Digest*, The Council for Exceptional Children)

Schools must provide appropriate educational services to students who have been identified as having ADHD. In September 1991, the Department of Education issued a policy clarification on the topic of children with attention deficit disorders (Davila, Williams, & MacDonalt, 1991). The memorandum was intended to clarify state and local responsibility under federal law for meeting the needs of children with ADHD in the educational system as a whole. . . . The report recognizes that:

- Regular classroom teachers are important in identifying appropriate educational adaptations and interventions for many children with ADHD.
- State and local districts should take the necessary steps to promote coordination between special education and regular education programs.
- Regular education teachers and other personnel need training to develop a greater awareness of children with ADHD and of adaptations that can be implemented in regular education programs to address the instructional needs of these children.

Federal Laws Affecting Children with ADHD

(From the *ERIC Digest*, The Council for Exceptional Children)

Both the Individuals with Disabilities Education Act (IDEA) and Section 504 of the Rehabilitation Act of 1973 provide coverage for children with ADHD. When the disability adversely affects educational performance, eligibility for special education should be approached through the processes of IDEA. When the disability does not affect educational performance but does substantially limit one or more major life activities, eligibility should be approached through Section 504. The following are highlights of each law as it affects the education of children with ADHD.

1. Individuals with Disabilities Education Act, Part B:

- Requires that state and local districts make a free appropriate public education (FAPE) available to all eligible children with disabilities [if they qualify by discrepancy criteria].
- Requires that the rights and protections of Part B of IDEA are extended to children with ADHD and their parents.
- Requires that an evaluation be done, without undue delay, to determine if the child has one or more of thirteen specified disabling conditions and requires special education and related services.
- Requires that children with ADHD be classified as eligible for services under the "other health impaired" category in instances where ADHD is a chronic or acute health problem that results in limited alertness that adversely affects a child's educational performance. Children with ADHD can also be served under the categories of "learning disabilities"

or "seriously emotionally disturbed," if the evaluation finds these conditions are also present.

- Does not allow local districts to refuse to evaluate the possible need for special education and related services for a child with a prior medical diagnosis of ADHD solely because of that medical diagnosis. On the other hand, a medical diagnosis of ADD does not automatically make a child eligible for services under Part B (IDEA).
- Requires that a full and individual evaluation of the child's educational needs must be conducted in accordance with requirements in Part B (IDEA). These requirements include: a multidisciplinary team must perform the evaluation, and at least one teacher or other specialist with knowledge in the area of ADHD must be on the team.
- Requires that a due process hearing take place, at the request of the parents, if there is a disagreement between the local district and the parent over the request for evaluation, or the determinations for services.

2. Section 504 of the Rehabilitation Act of 1973:

- Prohibits discrimination on the basis of disability by recipients of federal funds (i.e., the public school system).
- Provides appropriate education for children who do not fall within the disability categories specified in Part B (IDEA). Examples of potential conditions not typically covered under Part B (IDEA) are: communicable diseases (HIV, tuberculosis), medical conditions (asthma, allergies, diabetes, heart disease), temporary medical conditions due to illness or accident, and drug/alcohol addiction.
- Requires that a free, appropriate public education be provided for each qualified child who is disabled but does not require special education and related services under Part B (IDEA). A free, appropriate education (FAPE) under Section 504 includes: regular or special education and related aids and services that are designed to meet the individual student's needs and are based on adherence to the regulatory requirements on education setting, evaluation, placement, and procedural safeguards.
- Guarantees parents the right to contest the outcome of an evaluation if a local district determines that a child is not disabled under Section 504.
- Requires the local district to make an individualized determination of the child's educational needs for regular or special

education or related aids and services if the child is found eligible under Section 504.

- Requires the implementation of an individualized education program (IEP). One means of meeting the free, appropriate public education requirements of Section 504 is to follow the IEP guidelines as set forth in the regulations for Part B (IDEA).
- Requires that the child's education must be provided in the regular education classroom unless it is demonstrated that education in the regular environment with the use of supplementary aids and services cannot be achieved satisfactorily.
- Requires that necessary adjustments be made in the regular classroom for children who qualify under Section 504.

Establish the Proper Learning Environment

Parents must become advocates for their children and offer concrete suggestions to teachers that will provide the proper learning environment for children and youth with ADHD. Remember most teachers want to help students with ADHD but many may not fully understand this disorder to be truly effective. To achieve a learning environment appropriate for your child, suggest that teachers:

1. Place students with ADHD near the teacher's desk, in the first row, so the child is within ear, eye, and touch range. With his back to the rest of the class, the student with ADHD can then keep classmates out of view.
2. Surround students with well-behaved role models, preferably students whom they view as meaningful others.
3. Avoid distracting stimuli by seating ADHD students away from air conditioners, high-traffic areas, pencil sharpeners, doors, or windows. (But *not* in a hallway or closet!)
4. Avoid transitions when possible, physical relocation (monitor them closely on field trips), changes in schedule, and disruptions because students with ADHD do not handle change well.
5. Provide a stimuli-reduced area for studying. All students should have the right to use this area, not just the student with ADHD (try not to make the student with ADHD feel different).
6. Use privacy boards to block out distractions or have student use a study carrel when doing work at his seat.
7. Allow students to use headphones or soft-foam earplugs during seatwork.

8. Remind teachers that medication improves, but does not cure, the symptoms of ADHD. The child may still not have skills that equal those of other students and extra assistance may be needed.
9. Tape a checklist for assignments on the student's desk so he can check off assignments as they are completed.
10. Permit students to use learning devices such as a tape recorder, computer, spell-check, calculator, or a word processor.
11. Write a contract with a student outlining what is to be done and what reward will be earned for staying on task.

Parents should review these guidelines carefully and not hesitate to ask teachers to make adjustments for their child. (Note: some suggestions selected from the *ERIC Digest*, published by The Council for Exceptional Children.)

Delivering Instructions to Students with ADHD

When giving instructions, teachers should:

1. Maintain eye contact during verbal instruction. Get the child to repeat instructions.
2. State directions clearly and briefly. Be consistent. Follow with written instructions on the chalkboard in the same place each day.
3. Streamline complex directions. Do not give multiple instructions.
4. Make sure ADHD students comprehend instructions before they begin the task. Break instructions down into steps if necessary, and give next step after completing preceding step.
5. Repeat directions, when necessary, in a favorable manner. Have them repeat certain directions to make sure they understand.
6. Encourage students to seek assistance from peers or from teachers (most children with ADHD will not ask for help) explaining to the child when and how he may ask for help.
7. While students are working independently, circulate and check some of the ADHD child's work. This will increase on-task activity. Provide the student with a prompt if he is off task such as tapping the student's shoulder, or addressing the student.
8. Reduce the amount of the work, not the quality (one hundred math problems can be reduced to fifty, for instance) when necessary.
9. Make sure student's desk is not cluttered with materials not needed for current assignment.
10. If necessary, modify the grade scale.

11. Set quotas of productivity and correctness of work.
12. Offer the student choices. For instance, would he prefer writing the book report or giving it orally.
13. Gradually decrease the amount of support, but keep in mind that students with ADHD may need more help for a longer period of time than the average child.
14. Color code all classroom subjects (science is red, math is blue, language arts is green, etc.). This will help all students, not just those with ADHD.
15. Use colored chalk that corresponds with the subject to write assignments on the board.
16. Assist students with color coding textbooks and folders.
17. Require a daily assignment notebook.
18. Make sure each student writes down all homework assignments correctly each day (use colored stickers in assignment notebook). Homework assignments should be written on the chalkboard and left there until the end of the school day. The teacher should assist a child who is not able to do this on his own, writing it out for them.

   - Teachers should sign the assignment notebook each day to let parents know that homework assignments have been recorded accurately. Parents should sign the notebook before it's returned to school indicating assignments have been completed and were put in backpack.
   - Teachers should use the notebook for daily communication with parents. Parents can also use the notebook to express concerns or ask questions of the teacher.

19. Help student organize his notebook, desk, and locker.

(Note: some suggestions selected from the *ERIC Digest*, published by The Council for Exceptional Children.)

Giving Assignments to ADHD students

When describing assignments, teachers should:

1. Make sure the class is quiet before giving directions or assignments.
2. Be sure they have the attention of the student with ADHD. They may need to touch his shoulder or back.
3. Give only one task at a time.

4. Give students (and parents) a copy of an assignment sheet for predictable homework on a weekly or monthly basis if possible.
5. Do not give homework assignments at the end of the class or the end of the school day when children are tired and ready to move on to other activities.
6. Ask for homework assignments at the beginning of each school day. Many students with ADHD will not remember to turn them in without a verbal reminder.
7. Monitor ADHD students frequently in a supportive fashion.
8. Modify assignments as needed—shorten or allow for less written work if child has motor problems. Confer with special education personnel to identify specific strengths and weaknesses of the child with ADHD. If necessary, develop a customized education program.
9. Test knowledge, not attention span. Decreasing volumes of work expected may actually improve compliance and accuracy.
10. Allow additional time for certain types of tasks. Do not penalize students with ADHD who need extra time. Some take longer to get started, process information, organize materials, and complete assignments. Remember you are testing knowledge, not how quickly he can complete a task.
11. Remember that students with ADHD are easily frustrated. Stress causes children to tire and decreases their self-control, leading to unacceptable behavior. They need a lot of encouragement.

(Note: some suggestions selected from the *ERIC Digest*, published by The Council for Exceptional Children.)

Behavior Modification and Enhancing Self-esteem

When working with students who have ADHD, teachers should:

1. Be proactive. Try to look at activities ahead of time and think of possible problems that mights arise. Problem solve before problems arise.
2. Stay calm, state the infringement, and avoid arguing with the student—discipline with dignity.
3. Set consequences for misconduct (time-out, etc.). Try not to take away recess. Children with ADHD need this time to release energy.
4. Deliver consequences immediately.
5. Post classroom rules and invoke rules consistently. Students with ADHD may need extra reinforcements.

6. Make sure the consequence fits the crime.
7. Avoid ridicule and criticism. Keep in mind that children with ADHD have trouble staying in control.
8. State rules for unstructured times, such as in cafeteria, hallways, library, recess, gym class, camp experiences. Children with hyperactivity and/or impulsivity must be monitored closely as these children are often risk takers. Accidents can and do happen.
9. Reward more than you punish—catch the student being good—to build self-esteem.
10. Immediately praise all positive behavior and performance. Acknowledge improvements, no matter how small.
11. Replace rewards if they are not stimulating enough to change behavior.
12. Look for ways to encourage the student.
13. Teach the child to reward himself or herself through positive self-talk and thinking aloud skills ("You did very well remaining in your seat today. How do you feel about that?" or STAR: Stop, Think, Act, Review).

(Note: some suggestions selected from the *ERIC Digest*, published by The Council for Exceptional Children.)

Other Educational Recommendations

(From *The ERIC Digest*, The Council for Exceptional Children.)

1. [Arrange for] educational, psychological, and/or neurological testing to determine learning style and cognitive ability and to rule out any learning disabilities
2. [Use] a private tutor and/or peer tutoring at school.
3. [Enroll the child in] a class that has a low student-teacher ratio.
4. [Employ] social skills training and organizational skills training.
5. [Administer] training in cognitive restructuring (positive self-talk, such as, "I did that well" or "Whenever, I do that, I always seem to . . .")
6. Use a word processor or computer for schoolwork.
7. Use a tape recorder for lecture notes.
8. [Encourage the child to participate in] individualized activities that are mildly competitive or noncompetitive, such as bowling, walking, swimming, jogging, biking, karate. (Note: Certain children with ADHD with motor skill deficits or social skill deficits may do less well than their peers in team sports).

9. [Encourage the child to become involved] in social activities such as scouting, religious groups, or other youth organizations that help develop social skills and self-esteem.
10. Allow children with ADHD to play with younger children if that is who they fit in with. Many children with ADHD have more in common with younger children than with their same-age peers. They still can develop valuable social skills from interacting with younger children (for example, reading to younger children, learning to play cooperatively, sharing).

(Note: some suggestions selected from the *ERIC Digest*, published by The Council for Exceptional Children.)

Definition of Learning Disabilities

(From a factsheet titled "Learning Disabilities" published by NICHY)

The regulations for Public Law 101-476, the Individuals with Disabilities Education Act (IDEA), which was formerly P.L. 94-142, the Education of the Handicapped Act (EHA), define a learning disability as a "disorder in one or more of the basic psychological processes involved in understanding or in using spoken or written language, which may manifest itself in an imperfect ability to listen, think, speak, read, write, spell or to do mathematical calculations." The federal definition further states that learning disabilities include "such conditions as perceptual handicaps, brain injury, minimal brain dysfunction, dyslexia, and developmental asphasia." . . . Definitions of learning disabilities vary among states. . . .

The label "learning disabilities" is all-embracing; it describes a syndrome, not a specific child with specific problems. The definition assists in classifying children, not teaching them. Parents and teachers need to concentrate on the individual child. They need to observe both how and how well the child performs, to assess strengths and weaknesses and invent ways to help each child learn. It is important to remember that there is a high degree of interrelationship and overlapping among the areas of learning. Therefore, children with learning disabilities may exhibit a combination of characteristics. These problems may mildly, moderately, or severely impair the learning process.

Characteristics

Learning disabilities are characterized by a significant difference in the child's achievement in some areas, when compared with his overall intelligence. Students who have learning disabilities may exhibit a wide range of traits, including problems with reading comprehension, spoken language, writing, or reasoning ability. Hyperactivity, inattention, and perceptual coordination problems may also be associated with learning disabilities. Other traits that may be present include a variety of symptoms, such as uneven and unpredictable test performance, perceptual impairments, motor disorders, and behaviors such as impulsiveness, low tolerance for frustration, and problems in handling day-to-day social interactions and situations.

Learning disabilities may occur in the following academic areas:

1. Spoken language: delays, disorders, or discrepancies in listening and speaking;
2. Written language: difficulties with reading, writing, and spelling;
3. Arithmetic: difficulty in performing arithmetic functions or in comprehending basic concepts;
4. Reasoning: difficulty in organizing and integrating thoughts; and
5. Organization skills: difficulty in organizing all facets of learning.

Educational Implications

Because learning disabilities are manifested in a variety of behavior patterns, the Individual Education Program (IEP) must be designed carefully. A team approach is important for educating the child with a learning disability, beginning with the assessment process and continuing through the development of the IEP. . . .

Some teachers report that the following strategies have been effective with some students who have learning disabilities:

- Capitalize on student's strengths;
- High structure and clear expectations;
- Use short sentences and a simple vocabulary, emphasizing important facts or details so the student understands the importance of the material being presented;
- [Provide] opportunities for success in a supportive atmosphere to help build self-esteem;
- Flexibility in classroom procedure (e.g.: allow use of tape recorders for notetaking and test-taking when students have trouble with written language);
- [Use] self-correcting materials, which provide immediate feedback without embarrassment;
- Use computers for drill and practice and teaching word processing;
- Positive reinforcement of appropriate social skills at school and home; and
- Recognize that students with learning disabilities can greatly benefit from the gift of time to grow and mature.

Parenting Tips for Coping with the Child who Has ADHD and a Learning Disability:

- Accept the fact that aspects of your child's learning disability are medically determined. Remember your child does not have an *inability* to learn—he has a *disability* that makes learning more difficult, but definitely not impossible.
- Read as much as possible about learning disabilities. The knowledge will empower you. Attend conferences. Join a parent support group.
- Become an advocate for your child. Find out what services are available for your child within the school system and your community.
- Provide tutoring for your child if you can afford it. Tutoring usually decreases the amount of stress parents often feel from having to help their child with a great amount of a schoolwork. However, tutoring does no good if you haven't identified the specific problem.
- Try not to become overwhelmed by your child's disability. In two-parent families, parents should take turns helping their child with schoolwork.
- Keep your academic expectations realistic. Don't expect A's and B's in areas where your child is unable to achieve anything but C's. Many learning-disabled children go to college, but some do not.
- Set realistic behavioral expectations. Children respond best to behavior modification techniques, such as tangible rewards.
- Encourage and support your child. Praise what he does well and praise improvements. Do not focus on his failures.
- Be empathetic. Be sure your child understands that you realize how frustrating this is for him.
- Know what your child's true disability is. Make sure you get an understandable explanation and specific suggestions for how you can help your child at home.

For more information on learning disabilities consult the following books: *The Misunderstood Child: A Guide for Parents of Learning Disabled Children*, 2nd ed., by Larry B. Silver, M.D. (Blue Ridge Summit, PA: TAB, 1992); *Help Me to Help My Child: A Sourcebook for Parents of Learning Disabled Children*, by Jill Bloom (Boston: Little, Brown, 1991); *Why Is My Child Having Trouble at School?: A Parent's Guide to Learning Disabilities*, by Barbara Novick and Maureen Arnold (New York: Random, 1991), and *Keeping a Head in School*, by Melvin Levine (Cambridge, MA.: Educators Publishing Service, Inc., 1990).

Commonly Asked Questions about Special Education Services

(From "Questions Often Asked About Special Education Services," published by NICHY)

Where do I begin if I believe my child needs special education services?

Begin by asking questions and developing a better understanding of the Individuals with Disabilities Education Act (IDEA). This law guarantees a free, appropriate public education to children with disabilities. The tips and suggestions on the following pages will help you obtain special education and related services for your child.

You may also want to talk to parents of children who are already receiving special education services. Local parent organizations can assist you. For information about parent groups or statewide disability organizations, contact the National Information Center for Children and Youth with Disabilities (NICHY), P.O. Box 14922, Washington, DC 20013-1492 1-800 695-0285.

What are the purposes of the IDEA?

The major purposes of the IDEA are to: (1) guarantee the availability of special education programs to eligible children and youth with disabilities; (2) assure that decisions made about providing special education to children and youth with disabilities are fair and appropriate; and (3) financially assist the efforts of state and local governments to educate children with special needs through the use of federal funds.

Are services available to very young children?

Services to very young children are also covered under the IDEA. Through Part H, the Program for Infants and Toddlers with Disabilities, states may make early intervention services available to eligible infants and toddlers (birth through two years old). Under the IDEA, states *must* provide special education and related services to eligible preschool children (ages three to five).

Services for these children are provided in different ways than services for school-age children. For more information about early intervention and preschool programs, contact NICHY and request a copy of *Assessing Programs for Infants, Toddlers, and Preschoolers with Disabilities: A Parent's Guide.*

What is the first step toward obtaining special education services?

The first step is to arrange for your child to receive an evaluation. The term "multifactored evaluation" refers to the total process of gathering and using information to determine whether a child has a disability and the nature and extent of the special education and related services that the child needs. The public schools are required to conduct this evaluation of your child at no cost to you.

What is included in an evaluation?

The evaluation process should look at the whole child and include information about your child's total environment. Tests are an important part of an evaluation, but the family's input is also important. Additionally, the evaluation process should include:

- Observation by professionals who have worked with your child;
- Your child's medical history, when it is relevant to his or her performance in school; and
- Information and observations from the family about your child's school experiences, abilities, needs, and behavior outside of school, and his or her feelings about school.

A multidisciplinary team should be involved in performing the evaluation. The team conducting the evaluation may include the following professionals, as appropriate:

- School psychologist;
- Speech and language pathologist;
- Occupational therapist;
- Physical therapist and/or adaptive physical education therapist;
- Medical specialist(s);
- Educational diagnostician(s);
- Classroom teacher(s); and
- Others.

Professionals will observe your child and may administer tests that examine your child's:

- Speech and language functioning;
- Personality and adaptive behavior patterns;
- Academic achievement;
- Potential or aptitude (intelligence);
- Perceptual ability; and
- Vocational interest and aptitude

All tests must be given to your child individually in his or her primary language. The tests must also be given in a way that does not discriminate on the basis of disability or racial/cultural background.

The law states that schools may not place children into special education programs based on the results of only one test. Many tests are needed to measure areas that might be problematic. However, the law does not mention the specific tests to be used. There are many tests that measure the same thing. A specialist may choose to use a certain test as long as the test is considered to be nondiscriminatory and measures what the specialist says it will measure.

How can my child receive an evaluation?

There are at least three ways in which your child may be selected to receive an evaluation:

1. You can request an evaluation. You can call or write the director of special education or the principal of your child's school. If the school refuses to evaluate your child, you must be given a written notice that explains the reasons for refusal. This notice must also give you a full explanation of your rights under the IDEA. It is very important that you keep a copy of this letter, as well as all other correspondence that you have received or sent concerning your child.

2. The school may ask permission to evaluate your child. A school may recommend a child for evaluation based on observations or results from tests given to all children in a grade. If your child is thought to need further testing, the school must tell you. You, as a parent, must give written permission before the school can evaluate your child.

3. A teacher or doctor may suggest that your child be evaluated. Your child's teacher may recommend that your child have an evaluation. Again, you must give permission in writing before the school can conduct the evaluation.

Some schools will be able to conduct a child's entire evaluation within the school. Other schools may not have sufficient personnel to conduct all of the testing needed and will have to contract with outside persons or agencies to conduct some or all of the testing. [The school must also do the testing within a reasonable time frame, usually ninety days, from the time they receive a written request.] If your child is evaluated by a specialist outside of the school, the school must make arrangements and will state in writing exactly what type of testing is to be conducted. All of the evaluation procedures arranged for or conducted by the school system are to be done at no cost to you.

In some cases, once the evaluation has begun, the outside specialist may recommend further testing. Because this additional testing will go beyond what the school originally requested, it is important that the school be contacted to agree to any additional testing and any additional costs that may be incurred.

Here are two more considerations to keep in mind: (1) It is generally a good idea to ask any professional working with or evaluating your child about his or her credentials and prior experience working with children like yours. (2) If, for any reason, you will be having your child retested, be aware that when the same tests are repeated in a short time period, the validity of the results will be seriously weakened. Be sure to talk to all evaluators about any previous testing that has taken place.

What is done with the results of my child's evaluation?

Information gathered from the evaluation procedures will be used to determine whether or not your child is eligible for special education and related services. If your child is found to be eligible, the testing results will form the basis for developing your child's Individualized Education Program (IEP).

What is an Individualized Education Program (IEP)?

An Individualized Education Program (IEP) is a written statement of the educational program designed to meet a child's special needs. Your child's IEP should include statements of your child's strengths and weaknesses and should describe the instructional program developed specifically for your child. The IEP has two purposes: (1) to establish the learning goals for your child, and (2) to state the services that the school district will provide for your child.

The IDEA requires that every child receiving special educational services have an IEP, that parents be included in the development of this IEP, and that the child's parents are entitled to receive their own copy of the IEP (upon request) in order to keep track of progress and to maintain home records.

Who develops my child's IEP?

According to the law, the IEP should be developed at the IEP meeting, by the following participants:

- Your child's teacher(s)—if your child has more than one teacher, your state may specify in its law which teacher(s) should participate;
- A representative of the public agency (school system) other than your child's teacher;
- You, the parents—one or both;
- Your child, when appropriate; and
- Other individuals, at your discretion or at the discretion of your child's school.

What type of information is included in an IEP?

According to the law, an IEP must include the following statements regarding your child:

- His present level of educational performance, which could include information concerning: academic achievement, social adaptation, prevocational and vocational skills, sensory and motor skills, self-help skills, and speech and language skills;

- Specific special education and related services to be provided and who will provide them;
- Dates for when the services will begin and how long they will continue;
- Percentage of the school day in which your child will participate in special education programs;
- Annual goals;
- Short-term instructional objectives (individual steps which make up the goal);
- Transition plan, when applicable; and
- Appropriate objective criteria and evaluation procedures to be used to measure your child's progress toward these goals on at least an annual basis.

Is it the school's responsibility to ensure that my child reaches all of the goals in his IEP?

No. The IEP is a guideline for individualized instruction, not a contract. The school is responsible for providing the instructional services listed in an IEP.

When is the IEP meeting held and may I attend?

The law is very clear that parents have the right to participate in the meeting where their child's IEP is developed. The school staff will try to schedule the IEP meeting at a time that is convenient for parents (and other team members) to attend. If the school suggests a time that makes it impossible for you to attend, explain your schedule and needs to the person who is making the arrangements. Often, an alternative time or date can be arranged. However, if no mutually agreeable time can be set, the school may hold the IEP meeting without you. In this event, the school must keep you informed by telephone or mail.

The law makes provisions for the changing needs and growth of children. At least once a year, whether you request it or not, a meeting must be scheduled with you to review your child's progress and to develop your child's next IEP. A full reevaluation must be conducted every three years. A reevaluation may occur more frequently if you or your child's teacher(s) request it.

What should I do before an IEP meeting?

The IEP meeting is scheduled for the purpose of developing your child's Individualized Education Program. You can prepare for this meeting by looking realistically at your child's strengths and weaknesses, talking to teachers and/or therapists, visiting your child's class or other classes which may be appropriate for him or her, and talking to your child about his or her feelings about school. It is a good idea to write down what you feel your child will be able to accomplish during the school year. It also helps to make notes about what you would like to say during the meeting.

What occurs during an IEP meeting?

The IEP meeting will take place after the specialists have tested your child and recorded the test results. In most cases, the school will have held a meeting to look at your child's test results and determine whether he or she is eligible for services. You may or may not have been invited to attend the eligibility meeting. If you were not at the eligibility meeting, then the results of the tests will usually be discussed with you at the IEP meeting. The specialists who evaluated your child will explain what they did, why they used the tests they administered, the results of your child's tests, and what your child's scores mean.

As you listen to the results of the tests (either eligibility tests or measures of progress), make sure that you understand what the tests are meant to measure and how the performance of your child compares with other children who are the same age. Take notes on what you hear, and ask questions if you do not understand.

During the IEP meeting, you will be asked to share the special things you know about your child, including how your child behaves and gets along with others outside of school. You will also be asked about your child's school experiences and personal life. After this discussion, everyone involved will have a better idea of your child's needs. This will allow the team to discuss and determine:

- What educational goals and objectives are appropriate for your child;
- What type of special education your child needs;
- Which related services are necessary to ensure your child benefits from his or her special education;
- What assistive technology devices or services your child needs to benefit from special education; and
- What placement alternatives exist, and which is most appropriate for your child.

As a parent, you should understand why the school proposes certain special education services and/or related services (such as therapy) for your child, and you should be comfortable with these ideas before listing them in the IEP. If you hear something about your child that is surprising to you, or different from the way you perceive your child, you will want to bring this to the attention of the other members of the team. To design the most appropriate program for your child, it is important to work closely with the other team members and share your feelings about your child's educational needs.

Before you sign the IEP, ask any questions you have, so you are sure you understand what is being said. Signing the IEP means that you agree to the services, goals, and other matters listed in the IEP. [If you are unsure of any part of the IEP, have it examined by an outside source such as an educator, tutor, psychologist, etc., before you sign it!]

It is helpful to remember that the IEP can be changed. If you are unsure about some of the ideas being presented, set a date for evaluating progress and a time to get together again to discuss the results of the evaluation. You may request a review or revision of the IEP at any time.

What if I disagree with the school about what is appropriate for my child?

It is important to know that before the school system can place your child in a special education program for the first time, you, as parents, must give your written consent. School districts can only override your lack of consent through the use of certain procedures specified in federal and/or state law.

Even if your child has been receiving special educational services for some time, you have the right to disagree with the school's decisions concerning new IEPs or educational placements for your child. If you do not agree with what has been proposed in your child's IEP, then you should not sign the IEP. . . .

How can I get services for my child increased?

Suppose that your child gets speech therapy two times a week, and you think this needs to be increased to three times a week. What do you do?

First, talk with your child's speech pathologist and request an IEP review meeting with the purpose of increasing speech therapy. Discuss your child's needs and ask to see the evaluation of his or her progress. If your child is not making progress with the current schedule, talk to the IEP team about the need for making changes in the IEP. The school personnel will either agree with you and change the IEP, or they will disagree with you.

With any disagreement, you can appeal the decision of the IEP team. . . . Appealing a decision can mean bringing in a third party to mediate your concerns, or it may mean requesting a due-process hearing. Your local department of special education can provide you with your state's guidelines for providing services in your state and for appealing decisions.

Rights and Responsibilities of Parents of Children with Disabilities

(From "Rights and Responsibilities of Parents of Children with Disabilities," the *ERIC Digest,* The Council for Exceptional Children.)

What are your rights, as a parent, in the special education process?

The Individuals with Disabilities Education Act (IDEA) clearly defined the rights of children with disabilities and their parents. A fundamental provision of the law is the right of parents to participate in the educational decision-making process. This includes the right to:

- A free, appropriate public education for your child. "Free" means at no cost to you as parents. "Appropriate" means meeting the unique educational needs of your child.
- Be notified whenever the school wishes to evaluate your child, wants to change your child's educational placement, or refuses your request for an evaluation or a change in placement.
- Initiate an evaluation if you think your child is in need of special education or related services.
- Informed consent. "Informed consent" means you understand and agree in writing to the evaluation and educational program decisions for your child. Your consent is voluntary and may be withdrawn at any time.
- Obtain an independent evaluation if you disagree with the outcome of the school's evaluation.
- Request a reevaluation if you suspect your child's present educational placement is no longer appropriate. The school must reevaluate your child at least every three years, but your child's educational program must be reviewed at least once during each calendar year.
- Have your child tested in the language he or she knows best. For example, if your child's primary language is Spanish, this is the language in which he or she must be tested. Also, students who are deaf have the right to an interpreter during the testing.
- Review all of your child's records. You may obtain copies of these records, but the school may charge you a reasonable fee for making copies. Only you, as parents, and those persons directly involved in the education of your child are allowed access to personal records. If you feel that any of the information contained in your child's records is inaccurate or misleading or violates the privacy or other rights of your child, you may request that the information be changed. If the school refuses your request, you then have the right to request a hearing in order to challenge the questionable information in your child's records.
- Be fully informed by the school of all rights that are provided to you under the law.
- Participate in the development of your child's individualized education program (IEP). The school must make every possible effort to notify you of the IEP meeting and then arrange it at a time and place that is convenient for you. Remember your child's IEP cannot be implemented without your written consent.
- Have your child educated in the least restrictive school setting possible. Every effort should be made to develop an educational

program that will provide the greatest amount of contact with nondisabled children.

- Request a due-process hearing to resolve differences with the school that could not be resolved informally.

What are your responsibilities, as a parent, in the special education process?

Parental responsibilities to ensure that a child's rights are being protected are less clearly defined than are parental rights. These rights vary considerably depending on the nature of the child's disabling condition and other factors. In accepting these responsibilities, some of the following suggestions may be helpful:

- Develop a partnership with the school or agency. You are now an important member of the team. Share relevant information about your child's education and development. Your observations and suggestions can be a valuable resource to aid your child's progress.
- Ask for clarification of any aspect of the program that is unclear to you. Educational and medical terms can be confusing, so do not hesitate to ask.
- Make sure you understand the program specified on the IEP before agreeing to it or signing it. Ask yourself whether or not what is planned corresponds with your knowledge of your child's needs.
- Make sure your child is included in the regular school activities program. Do not forget nonacademic areas such as lunch and recess and other subjects such as art, music, and physical education.
- Learn as much as you can about your rights and the rights of your child. Ask the school to explain these rights as well as the policies and regulations in effect in your district and state before you agree to a special education program for your child.
- Monitor your child's progress. If your child is not progressing, discuss it with the teacher and determine whether or not the program should be modified. As a parent, you can initiate changes in your child's educational program.
- Discuss with the school or agency any problems that may occur with your child's assessment, placement or educational program. It is best to try to resolve these problems directly with the agency, school, or district. In some situations, you may be uncertain as to which direction you should take to resolve a problem. Most states have protection and advocacy agencies

that can provide you with the guidance you need to pursue your case.

- Keep records. There may be many questions and comments about your child that you will want to discuss, as well as meetings and phone conversations you will want to remember. It is easy to forget information useful to your child's development and education that is not written down.

- Join a parent organization. In addition to offering the opportunity to share knowledge, experiences, and support, a parent group can be an effective force on behalf of your child. Many times parents find that as a group they have the power to bring about needed changes to strengthen and broaden special services.

As the parent of a child with a disability, what can you offer the IEP process?

In the final analysis, parents of children with a disability should be involved in the process as much as they want to be and can be. Varying degrees of involvement are possible. The following are suggestions for ways in which parents can become involved:

- Before attending an IEP meeting, make a list of things you want your child to learn. Discuss any differences between your list and the school's or agency's list. Take notes about aspects of your child's behavior that could interfere with the learning process. Describe the methods you have found to be successful in dealing with these behaviors.

- Bring any information the school or agency may not already have to the IEP meeting. Examples include copies of medical records, past school records, or test or evaluation results. Remember, reports do not say all there is to say about a child. You can add real-life examples to demonstrate your child's ability in certain areas.

- Find out what related services are being provided. Besides your child's teacher, many other specialists and professionals may have contact with your child through provision of related services. Ask each professional to describe the kind of service he or she will be providing and what growth you might expect to see as a result of these services.

- Ask what you can do at home to support the program. Many skills the child learns at school can also be used at home. Ask to meet with the teacher when your child is learning new skills that could be practiced at home.

- Make sure the goals and objectives on the IEP are specific. This will ensure that everyone teaching your child is working toward the same goals. Ask questions to make sure that you understand and agree with each of the goals and objectives before signing the IEP.
- Periodically, ask for a report on your child's progress. After the meeting is over, your job as parent is not finished. You should follow your child's progress throughout the year.
- Regard your child's education as a cooperative effort. If at any point you and the school cannot reach an agreement over your child's educational and developmental needs, ask to have another meeting. This would allow time for you and the school or agency to gather more information and data. If after a second meeting there is still a conflict over your child's program, you should ask for a state mediator or a due-process hearing.

What resources are available to help you?

Local and state education agencies have information to help guide you through the special education process. Since there is great variation in the specific criteria and procedures employed by school districts, it is important that you familiarize yourself with the information they provide. You will find your local director of special education and his or her staff helpful in accessing such information and guiding you through the process.

Additional resources are available from national organizations. Some of them will also be able to direct you to local and state chapters that can provide more locally based support. Almost all of the states now have federally supported parent information and training centers. Any of the contacts cited here may be able to help you locate such a center in your state:

Children with Attention Deficit Disorders (CHADD)
499 N.W. 70th Ave., Ste. 308
Plantation, FL 33317

The Council for Exceptional Children
1920 Association Dr.
Reston, VA 22091

Learning Disability Association of America
4156 Library Rd.
Pittsburgh, PA 15234-1349

National Information Center for Children
and Youth with Disabilities (NICHY)
P.O. Box 1492
Washington, DC 20013-1492

Change Begins with Parents and Teachers

Parents *must* find the time to learn as much as possible about ADHD and then share this knowledge with educators, beginning with their child's teacher. Statistics show that for every classroom of children in the United States, one or two children will have ADHD. If every parent of a child with ADHD took the time to educate one teacher each year by providing him or her with information on teaching children with ADHD, inviting him or her to attend a conference or workshop (or parent support group meetings), and donating a book on ADHD to the school library, it would make an enormous difference, not just for our children but for future generations of children with ADHD. Don't just talk about the changes that need to be made; reach out and educate.

CHAPTER EIGHT

The Adolescent with ADHD

Adolescence is defined as "the period of physical and psychological development between childhood and adulthood." For parents with teenagers, this is the time to let go—often a difficult concept for parents but particularly so for those with an adolescent who has ADHD.

"How can I possibly let go?" asks one mom from Oklahoma. "I worry about my son from the time he wakes up until he goes to bed. He's still so unorganized. I have to remind him of everything from taking his clothes to the cleaners to putting gas in the car to completing his homework. He can't even remember to take gym clothes to school. I worry about his driving, going out with the guys, having dates, etc."

"My daughter is always screaming at me, 'Get out of my face. Leave me alone,' says Kathy from Salem, Oregon. "I know I need to give her some room, but who's going to help her if I'm not around. She wants to date, but she's so immature compared to other girls her age. I'm afraid some guy is going to come along and sweet talk her into having sex. What if she gets pregnant?"

"My son keeps saying he can't wait until he's twenty-one so he can drink," admits another mom from Arkansas. "I've read that children with ADHD, especially those who are hyperactive and impulsive, are at risk for abusing drugs and alcohol, so, of course, I'm worried."

"When my daughter drives without medication, she never sees a stop sign. With medication, she's a pretty decent driver," explains one mom. "The rule in our house is that if she wants to drive she has to take Ritalin one-half hour before she leaves the house and she must be back within three hours. We had to limit her time because she rarely remembers to take her medication when she's out."

Yet, like all parents, parents of teenagers with ADHD know that their children are beginning to move on, and they, too, must begin the process of letting go. So how do committed parents let go?

Janet Robinson, R.N., Ph.D., of Sylvania, Ohio, is a mother of an eighteen-year-old son with ADHD who says, "At some point, we have to let them assume total responsibility and the best way to do that is step by step, giving them as much as they can handle where it's appropriate. We don't own and we can't control the consequences of our kids' ADHD. It's painful, but don't be afraid of your child's pain. Although we can walk through it with them, we can't take it away from them. Going through the pain does build character. The kids learn the lessons they need to learn."

Letting Go Step by Step

How do you let go step by step? You begin by examining your child's history. Does he telephone you when he arrives at a friend's house as you have requested? Does he follow the house rule that says he must come right home from school? If you check on him, will you find him where he says he'll be? If yes, then he is ready for more responsibility; if no, then he must be taught to follow the rules before he can be granted more freedom.

Once a child is ready for more freedom, you begin letting go by negotiating the limits. If he wants to make a stop at a friend's house after school for a few hours twice a week and you are uncomfortable with two or three hours, reach a compromise. ("If you can show me that you will come home after spending one hour at your friend's house, then I will increase that time to two hours next month.") If your child wants to use the car on Saturday until midnight but you are uneasy about letting him stay out that late, give him permission to use the car but only until 10:00. Once he has proved that he is responsible and can get home by 10:00, then you can increase the time to 11:00 or later.

Once your child solicits more latitude, make sure the freedom you offer comes with clear-cut limits. For example: "Yes, you may use the car until 10:00, but you must tell me where you are going and call me when you arrive." Not only will you know where your child is, but you will find out if your child is responsible enough to follow the rules. When your child follows the rules, use praise to acknowledge his compliance. ("Thank you for calling me when you got to the mall. It shows me how responsible you are.") Remember to always praise the behavior you want to continue.

What do you do if your child abuses a new privilege? Don't overreact. Screaming or threatening will cause more harm than good. Stay calm, but take the privilege away from him. You might tell him, "I'm sorry you didn't call me when you got to the mall. Because you didn't call you may not use the car for one week. However, next week I will give you another opportunity to prove that you can follow the rules."

Monitor your child carefully and give one new freedom at a time. Don't tell your child he can use the car Saturday night to drive fifty miles to the school his friend attends and then spend the night.

ADHD Symptoms in Teens

Despite past predictions that children with ADHD would outgrow this disorder when they reached adolescence, we now know that this is not always the case. Many children with ADHD (approximately 50 to 60 percent) will have symptoms that will persist into adulthood. These people will display and have to cope with many of the same symptoms that plagued them as children.

Some of the symptoms an adolescent will have to cope with, as well as their families and teachers, are: a short attention span, low frustration tolerance, impulsivity, a need for immediate gratification, distractibility, low self-esteem, and poor peer relationships. The symptoms of hyperactivity usually decrease as the child matures, but signs may still be evident and are often perceived as restlessness, such as tapping fingers, feet, or a pencil, and wiggling legs. On the other hand, some teenagers may be underactive (sometimes referred to as "hypoactive"), often appearing lethargic or spacey.

Short Attention Span

A short attention span creates problems for the teenager, especially in the school environment where students are expected to hear and remember instructions and complete more elaborate classroom and homework assignments. Often, teens with ADHD do not remember or record assignments accurately and, consequently, the work is not completed. Other problems include being unable to distinguish between important details and not-so-relevant materials. Teachers generally describe these students as lazy, forgetful, or disorganized. This deficit may only affect specific subjects—the student may do well in other classes—which is confusing to those closest to the student, like parents and teachers.

Says Stephanie, the mother of a sixteen-year-old from Lincoln, Nebraska: "My son never had any real difficulties in school until he reached ninth grade, then suddenly he was having all sorts of problems. He became so frustrated, despite the fact that he was trying. Eventually he fell behind in his schoolwork and his self-esteem was very low. One day I had a call from the school. They wanted to know why he wasn't in school. As it turned out he had skipped several days of school. When we confronted him, he said there was no point in going to school. He couldn't do the work even when he really tried. We found a tutor for him and that has made a difference. This year his more difficult classes are now in the morning and that seems to have made a difference also. His concentration has always been better earlier in the day because he takes medication in the morning, but often forgets to take it after lunch."

Poor grades can result in depression or in unacceptable behaviors, such as truancy. A tutor may be the answer in many cases, or the child may need to be placed in special education classes. Summer school is an option for other students. This allows the student to concentrate his efforts on one subject for a shorter period of time.

Low Frustration Tolerance

Students with ADHD may become especially frustrated when attempting to complete a major assignment, especially one they find boring and/or complicated, because they are so impatient and their frustration threshold is low. They also may have difficulty waiting in traffic, obeying stop signs, and adhering to speed limits because they are in hurry to get where they are going. A high percentage of adolescents with ADHD have an accident in their first year of driving. In fact, many teens with ADHD are involved in car accidents each year—a result of their short attention span, their impulsiveness, and their low frustration tolerance.

Impulsivity

Teens may have little self-control, often act without thinking first. Poor impulse control may make it extremely difficult for a teenager to say no to peers who encourage him to try drugs or have a beer or two before driving to a party. "I've taught my daughter to stop and think before deciding to do something," explains Leah from Eau Claire, Wisconsin. "If she makes the wrong decision I help her examine the consequences. I encourage her to look at the behavior and think of other ways, other options, she might have chosen instead. You can't just tell your child once to stop and think, you must do it repeatedly so it becomes second nature. The earlier you begin working with your child on poor impulse control, the easier it will be for her during adolescence."

Immediate Gratification (Insatiability)

Like the younger child with ADHD, a teenager may also beg and plead for something he wants now. "I spent an entire day with my daughter looking for the perfect dress, but once we got home she decided the outfit wasn't really quite right for the dance she was attending and begged me to take her shopping again to find something else," explains Barbara, the mother of the seventeen-year-old. "This is really typical for my daughter. Once she gets what she *must* have, she often is not satisfied."

Sometimes, in teens with ADHD, need for immediate gratification leads to far more serious behavior. One ADHD adult I know was extremely handsome as a teenager, had a sense of humor, and was considered quite a catch years ago. He admits that when he wanted to sleep with a girl he usually got his way. How? He begged and pleaded and wouldn't give up until the girl consented. However, once he had sex with her he was no longer interested because there were many other girls who were just as appealing. Consequently, at ages fifteen and seventeen, he fathered babies (which were placed for adoption at birth).

Distractability

Children with ADHD are easily distracted. In class, their attention may be diverted from the teacher by noises in the hall or by another student in the room. One teenager, Tracy, said that she would enter math class and tell herself over and over to pay attention. "The next thing I knew the class was over and I hadn't heard a word the teacher said. Yet I did hear the two girls behind me whispering and I heard the pencil drop in the back of the room and I remember seeing the janitor walk past the door," she says. One mother of a sixteen-year-old said it was not uncommon to send her daughter to the grocery store to pick up three items and have her return with only two, which often were not the items she had specified. "Unless I write the items down, she can't remember them," the mother says. "Once I sent her to the grocery store and she went to the post office instead." To avoid this, make directions clear, simple and brief. Have your adolescent repeat the directions back to you or, better yet, write them down.

Poor Peer Relationships

Like children with ADHD, some teenagers with the disorder are immature for their age, often displaying inappropriate age behavior, and have younger friends. If these same teenagers are also demanding and bossy, it is easy to understand how they can alienate their peers. Adolescents who are not liked by their peers appear to be at risk for engaging in antisocial behaviors that result from poor self-esteem. Some may also be at risk for developing psychological problems. Studies have shown that young children with poor social skills usually have poor social skills as teenagers and adults.

Children who were extremely aggressive with peers as youngsters often do not outgrow their antisocial tendencies. They are often at increased risk for substance abuse and criminal behaviors as teenagers. (The use of medication in the treatment of ADHD does not lead to substance abuse. On the contrary, failing to medically treat ADHD may lead to substance abuse and/or criminal behaviors in some individuals.)

"Parents should model appropriate social skills and make their child's friends feel welcome in their home," suggests Sally, the mother of a sixteen-year-old daughter. "Demonstrating appropriate social skills to their friends will help your child learn how to be nice to his friends and teach him how to welcome friends into his home. Obviously we can't make a child become a friend to our daughter, but we can help set the stage for a comfortable and pleasant interaction. As parents, we can also teach our children how to start a conversation and, especially, how to end one. My daughter, who easily gets distracted, would just walk away in the middle of a conversation or, if on the phone, would abruptly say 'good-bye' and hang up. It's not easy to teach these skills, particularly if one spouse has ADHD and has difficulty with social skills. My husband, who has ADHD, often gets up in the middle of a conversation with my daughter or me, and makes a phone call. My daughter has witnessed this repeatedly. Teaching her the proper way to talk with people was not easy because of the way her father handles situations. But with work, patience, and time, I did get through to her."

Low Self-Esteem

Frustrations that arise from troubles with schoolwork, underachievement, the inability to make or keep friends, continuous negative feedback, and the realization that they are different than others, will adversely affect the adolescent's self-esteem. Over the years, it becomes easy for him to see himself as a failure, even in areas where he may excel. It's imperative that parents focus on their child's strengths and abilities and encourage him to develop them more fully. Express pride in their accomplishments and note areas of improvement.

"When my daughter expresses frustrations about not being like the other girls, I run through my mental list," offers Sandy from Spokane, Washington. "For instance, if she tells me how well her friend does in math, I remind her how well she does in drama. Parents can always find something about their child that is particularly positive to compliment."

Parents of teenagers with ADHD should be aware that poor self-esteem and feelings of failure, anger, and isolation can result in depression. Depressed teenagers may turn to drugs or alcohol, exhibit out-of-control behavior, or even harbor thoughts of suicide. Parents who are troubled by their teen's behavior should not hesitate to seek professional intervention. Parents who are having considerable difficulty reaching their teenager, are losing self-control when faced with noncompliant behavior, or are retreating to inappropriate techniques that perpetuate unacceptable behavior, should also seek professional help. Through therapy, parents can improve their self-control, for instance, and learn how to teach their teenager self-restraint. Through therapy a teenager's self-esteem can be bolstered. The adolescent can also learn strategies for dealing with the stress that results from heightened demands.

Some Suggestions for Parent/Teacher Activities

(From NICHY's "Transition Summary," no. 7, Sept. 1991.)

To feel good about what one has to offer as an individual, one has to feel good about oneself. Therefore, parents and teachers can start teaching self-determination by focusing on the individual's disability. Parents and teachers should keep in mind the following when helping children and youth feel good about being a person with a disability:

- **Be open about the disability.** Your view of the disability will be reflected in your child's body image and self-concept. If you cannot accept the disability or overreact to it, your child will react the same way.
- **Avoid demeaning and negative terms like "hardship" and "burden."** If you perceive the disability as something negative, so will your adolescent.

- **Don't hide the disability.** Both of you know the disability is there. You are the best source of accurate information regarding his disability and can help him understand it. If the teenager cannot get the information from you, he will try to figure it out alone or ask others who may give erroneous answers.
- **Avoid comparisons with others.** Phrases such as "Why can't you be like . . ." and "If John can do it, why can't you?" not only focus on an ability the child does not have but implies that this ability is something that the parents value and see missing in their teenager.
- **Stress positive, coping strategies.** Get to know good role models. Your teenager can learn many positive things from adults with disabilities who live and work in your community.

The second step is for parents to provide their teenagers with opportunities for structured choice. [For example, you might tell your teen:]"You get to plan dinner for Tuesday. This is the menu for the rest of the week, and this is our budget for food." (This reflects a higher level of decision making, because the teenager needs to know something about nutrition and the price of the food. This task also reflects the importance of the teenager's input for the good of the family unit.)

Parents can assist in planning activities that the teenager can perform independently by (1) providing a checklist of the steps the child needs to follow or (2) using an approach where a parent, mutual friend, or more responsible peer "shadows" the teen as he proceeds through the activity. The "shadow" intervenes only if necessary. Both of these procedures should provide the teen with enough flexibility to begin taking some independent action, but there should be sufficient structure, if necessary, to guide the teenager.

As early as possible, parents should involve the child in meetings and conferences that are directly related to the child's well-being (IEP, [parent-teacher conferences,] etc.). Parents may need to help professionals relate to their child by requesting that they phrase their comments so that he can understand what is being said and its implications. The child may not want to or know how to contribute meaningful information during the meeting, but by observing the interactions of others, there is an opportunity to learn by example. Parents who communicate effectively can also pattern assertive behavior without being overly aggressive.

Skills necessary for self-determination *must* be taught to all children and youth; it is especially important for children and youth with disabilities. Expecting youth who have been overprotected and restricted in terms of self-determination to be functioning, independent adults is akin to expecting a nation that has lived under an oppressive, totalitarian system for centuries to govern by democratic principles immediately after a revolution. Self-determination just doesn't happen; it requires a great deal of preparation and practice.

Discipline Strategies That Work with Teenagers Who Have ADHD

You don't have to be a genius to understand that many of the discipline techniques (token and chart systems, for example) you use with the younger child who has ADHD lose effectiveness as the child matures. Other strategies that you may have been using may continue to be effective into the teenage years (see chapter seven for techniques that work with younger children). The following list includes some of those strategies, but also others that are appropriate for use with teenagers:

1. **Time-out**
   While it's true that time-out is most appropriate for younger children (ages two through ten years), you may find it works with your teenager (especially if you have used it consistently for years). If your older child still complies when sent to time-out then by all means use it. "My daughter is seventeen, almost eighteen, and we still use time-out," comments Barbara from Omaha, Nebraska. "We send her to her room when she needs to calm down, to collect herself. And she goes without an argument. We don't use the term 'time-out' anymore. At this age, we just tell her to go to her room."

2. **Grounding**
   Grounding is a popular punishment for all teenagers and it does work with adolescents who have ADHD, when it is used properly. The problem with grounding is that many parents do not use it appropriately probably because they don't understand how it is meant to be used. A parent who grounds his or her teenager for coming home ten minutes late on Saturday night for one month, has misused the grounding technique. Not only must the teenager stay home for four weeks, but he also misses contact with friends for one month. So what, you say? Consider the facts.

   Withdrawing your adolescent from friends and activities for long periods of time can seriously impair his social network. Remember, teens with ADHD sometimes have difficulty with social skills. If he has one or two close friends, he's probably worked hard to make and keep those relationships. Cutting him off from his friends for weeks may cause his social network to collapse. He may also rebel or fall into a state of depression. (Besides, grounding your teenager for extended periods is hard work for parents to enforce.)

   So how should grounding be used? Grounding works best when the rules have been established first and the teenager is forewarned that if he is late he will then be grounded next

Friday and Saturday night, or he'll be grounded for the rest of the week. Grounding is most effective when used for short periods of time only.

3. **Withdrawing the use of the car**

   Driving is a privilege. Driving and using the family car is an even bigger privilege. When a teenager abuses that privilege, then it may become necessary to withdraw it entirely. If your teenager gets a ticket for speeding, has been drinking and driving, is responsible for causing an accident, or uses the car to go someplace other than where he said he was going, it is appropriate to suspend the use of the car. Be sure your child knows the rules regarding the use of the car and the consequences of abusing those rules.

4. **Ban the use of the telephone**

   Suspending the use of the telephone is another common discipline technique. A teenager who abuses the privilege of using the family telephone after being warned not to tie it up for more than the allotted time, or fails to do homework because he is on the phone all evening, should lose the use of the telephone for a few days. This is a logical and fair removal of a privilege. Losing the use of the car for one month would not be a reasonable or just price to pay for violating phone privileges. Losing the telephone for a month also would not be fair. Always be sure the crime fits the penalty.

5. **Write a contract**

   Contracts can be made with teenagers. A negotiated agreement is made between the parent and the middle or high school student and can work for such things as violating curfews, skipping school, and other similar major infractions. Let's say your daughter has been bugging you to let her get her hair colored and so far you've resisted because she's been skipping classes. The contract might read:

   I, Heather, agree to go to my classes every day.
   When I go to all my classes for one month,
   I can go to the beauty salon and have my hair highlighted.

   Signed:

   Heather

6. **Negotiate**

   You can negotiate with your teenager as long as both parties are willing to work to find a solution to the problem. Both parties must be willing to compromise. To negotiate, you first must define the problem. Then in a respectful manner, together, you find some solutions to the problem and discuss the pros and cons of each until you reach an acceptable conclusion you both can live with. Once you've reached an agreement, set a defined time for a trial period, then renegotiate the terms if necessary.

7. Use "I" statements

Remember, "I" statements focus on you not on your teenager. "When you miss your curfew and don't call to tell me where you are, I feel frightened because I'm afraid you've had an accident." (See chapter six for more information on "I" statements.)

8. Cost-response

Cost-response appears to work well with teens who have ADHD. Instead of earning rewards, rewards are given first and the child must work to keep them.

You can give teens a number of hours per week that they can use the telephone or car. The teenager then works to keep those hours, but is penalized for inappropriate behaviors (not doing chores, abusing privileges, etc.) by losing precious time from this weekly allotment. (A weekly allowance can also be handled the same way.)

9. Family meetings

Plan a meeting once a week for all family members. A secretary should be chosen at each meeting to note the minutes, so that there is always a record of important decisions and rules. Use the meeting to go over the family rules, and solicit your teenager's input. Show respect for his opinion. If a rule needs to be changed, make the necessary changes. If you don't feel comfortable with a change at this point, explain why, but write down and consider all ideas. This will tell your teenager that his opinion is valuable.

Meetings also can be used to allow all members of the family to discuss whatever is on their minds (routines that need to be readjusted, mom needs more help with housekeeping chores, where to go on vacation, who will help a sibling with a scouting project, etc.). The family meeting focuses on all family members, not just the child with ADHD. Set rules for meetings, such as no prolonged arguments will be permitted, and respect must be shown for others' opinions. Remember though, a family cannot be a true democracy; parents must keep some executive veto power. If you find you must veto, make sure you explain your reasons for refusing to consent. For detailed information on the family meeting, refer to *The Parent's Handbook* by Don Dinkmeyer and Gary D. McKay (Circle Pines, Minnesota: American Guidance Service, 1989).

10. **Offer a choice**

    This is a great technique for oppositional teenagers. Offer a choice of activities. ("Would you like to prepare lunch or dinner today?" "Would you like to run the vacuum or fold the laundry?" "Would you like to plant the flowers or trim the bushes?") Although your teen has a choice, be sure he realizes that if he doesn't choose one of the tasks, you will assign one. As mentioned in chapter six, offering mini choices also directs debate away from important non-negotiable rules.

What Not to Do

If your child has a special talent or interest, such as playing the piano, **do not take this away from him or her.** This one precious gift is just too relevant and necessary for your child's self-esteem to be used as a punishment for undesirable behavior. (Too often parents react hastily and take away the first thing that comes to their mind—usually, whatever is most important to the child. Often the undesired behavior can be changed with the loss of another privilege.) Restricting or pulling your teenager out of something so important to him will only yield negative results. When your teenager has something in his life that he feels good about, he is more apt to have positive feelings about himself, his schoolwork, and his family. If you take away that one activity, your child may have nothing worthwhile left.

If your teen has a part-time job he particularly enjoys, do not force him to quit. You may ask him to reduce his hours if he's working too late, or is falling behind in his homework. Parents should consider the job's role in fostering their teen's sense of independence. A job not only teaches responsibility, it enables a teen to acquire valuable skills and knowledge and earn and manage money.

Do not preach, nag, lecture, or argue because your adolescent will only tune you out. (Remember the many times you didn't listen to your parents? And when you did listen, you probably disagreed, verbally or mentally, with everything they said to you.) Arguing with your teenager is a no-win situation.

If you have the urge to argue, nag, lecture or preach, leave the room immediately! If the problem is something that must be addressed, do it later. When everyone has settled down, arrange a meeting with your teenager. A restaurant is an excellent spot for this type of conversation because participants are more apt to keep themselves under control in a public place. Or, write your teen a note explaining your feelings and arrange to talk (possibly before bed or after dinner).

If you find yourself arguing, nagging, preaching, or lecturing more often than not, you *must* attempt to alter your behavior. These tactics only perpetuate the unacceptable behavior you are trying to modify. Concentrate on changing your normal response patterns. I know how difficult it is to change your behavior when you have a child who is difficult and strong-willed. But, I'm also familiar with the guilt one feels after such episodes. It takes time, effort, desire, and awareness to change negative responses into positive ones, but it can be done.

Living with the Teen Who Has ADHD

Several parents have offered excellent suggestions and advice for living with teens who have ADHD. Here are some of the most helpful:

- "Don't threaten your son or daughter unless you plan to enforce the threat," suggests Bill from Knoxville, Tennessee. "Threats that are made [often in anger] but never implemented teach your child that you do not mean what you say. If the infraction is serious, tell your teenager that you need to think about the situation and discuss it with the other parent before delivering the consequence." It is imperative that parents follow through because teens with ADHD need the stability of knowing what to expect.
- Set realistic expectations. Think ADHD and you are less apt to expect perfection. Always focus on your child's assets and abilities, rather than on his shortcomings. Believe in your child, even when he doesn't believe in himself.
- "Remember there is more than one way to do something," cautions Faith from Marietta, Georgia. "Our way is not always the best, even though we'd like to believe it is." Parents of children with ADHD become accustomed to telling their children how to do things. As children mature, we must accept the fact that they may have found their own way of handling life's challenges.
- Listen to your child. Children who talk but are not heard by their parents often drift away from their families over the years. Be open to what he has to say. Don't be judgmental. Teens with ADHD need to be *heard*—possibly even more than other teens—because *they* are always listening to others' instructions.
- Look ahead. "When your teenager enters high school, look ahead with him at career choices, colleges, junior colleges, or no college," suggests Helena from Hartford, Connecticut. "Too many parents leave this job to school guidance counselors.

Nobody knows your teenager better than you. Many ADHD symptoms are qualities that are greatly admired in adults and there are occupations that people with ADHD experience relatively few problems with." There are ADHD adults who head corporations, are police officers, attorneys, and great salespeople. Some are computer programmers, hairstylists, entertainers, construction workers, truck drivers, psychologists, and teachers. Some of these people have ADHD and are also learning disabled. So, don't lose hope.

- Talk with your younger teen about potential problems they may encounter. Children learn about drugs and alcohol, drinking and driving, AIDS, and teenage pregnancy in school, but parents need to reinforce these issues. Let them know about the temptations they will face when they begin dating, how their impulsiveness may come into play, and the choices they'll have to make. Give them time to consider these choices before they're confronted with them. They're more apt to listen to you before a problem develops, rather than after.

- "Set ground rules for dating," advises Allison from Council Bluffs, Iowa. "Ask your teenager to tell you about the person he or she wants to date. Tell your daughter that you want to meet the fellow she's planning to go out with (he's to come up to the door when he picks her up, for instance). Likewise, tell your son you want to meet the girl he's dating. Make sure you know the date's name and where he or she lives. [Try to meet the other parents also.] After the date, encourage your teenager to tell you how the date went. Know where your teenager is going (be sure he knows what types of places are off limits) and what time he plans to be home, or give him a time to be home. [Make sure he has at least one quarter in his pocket to call home if needed.] Decide how often he or she can date (once a week, for instance, during the school year, and twice a week during summer vacation). If you haven't done so already, talk with your son or daughter about sex." Although establishing and periodically reiterating rules usually works with most teens, those with ADHD need to hear rules much more frequently (possibly before every date). Because teens with ADHD may have poor self-control, be impulsive and insatiable, and have difficulty delaying gratification, repeating rules and expectations will help them avoid situations that may lead to an unwanted pregnancy, drug abuse, or other problems that can result from socializing and peer pressure.

- "Remember your teen needs structure and that he has trouble with organization," continues Helena. "Establish rules, give clear, simple directions for tasks, and teach him ways to organize himself [he can't do this on his own] and manage his environment. Encourage him to make use of bulletin boards, calendars, and daily planners and to make notes for daily tasks, activities, and schoolwork. He may need to use lists [of things to do] and daily planners for his entire lifetime." If you are having problems teaching your child to organize himself, look for classes in the community that teach organization skills. Memory skill classes are also available.

- "For years, when our children are younger, we are their advocates," says Judy, a former high school teacher in Toledo, Ohio, and parent of a child with ADHD. "It's imperative that parents teach their teenagers to advocate for themselves in school [and later, on the job or in a marriage]. When an older student comes to a teacher and says, 'I have attention deficit problems and I can't organize my schoolwork very well,' or 'I have problems with spelling and writing. I try my hardest, but I may need more time than the average to complete essay questions,' or whatever the problem is, teachers are very impressed and are willing to help in anyway they can. Somehow it's different when the student makes the appeal in high school than when the parent does. Maybe it shouldn't be, but that's the way it is for a lot of teachers."

- "Look at your fears," advises Jolene from Madison, Wisconsin, "and analyze how realistic they are. Ask yourself, 'What is the very worst that can happen and how likely is it that it will happen?' Talk about your fears with others in a parent support group or with a therapist. It will help you deal with your fears and to take control of your feelings."

- "Always be available for your teenager to help keep him on task with homework, chores, daily tasks, etc.," says Leslie from Huntington, West Virginia. "Set aside fifteen minutes a day and give your teenager your undivided attention. Like youngsters, older children appreciate special time with mom or dad."

- Elicit their compliance on the basis that everyone is responsible for the family's success. For example: "If you limit your time on the telephone, I'll have enough time to make arrangements to have your friends over this weekend and for your sister's birthday party."

The Adopted Teenager with ADHD

Teenagers who were adopted will be dealing with a number of issues during adolescence that parents should be aware of. (Of course, younger children may also wrestle with adoption-related issues, which will likely differ.) These include, but are not limited to:

- A struggle to develop a sense of identity because they have been separated from their biological families ("Who do I look like, what do my birth parents look like, and how alike or different am I from my adoptive parents?").
- The realization that things may have been different had they stayed with their birth families, especially if they are the only person in the adoptive family who has ADHD and/or learning disabilities. For example, would their biological parents be more like them? Would they have been better equipped to understand their ADHD symptoms (and problems) than their adoptive parents? Some teenagers may be angry at their birth parents for the role they may have played in passing along their impulsivity to them. Be sure you let them know that no one is to blame for the ADHD.
- The teen feels different than other teenagers and does not fully understand the effects a learning disability or ADHD may have on him, often labels himself as stupid or dumb, which he may then view as the reason he was placed for adoption in the first place. Not only will he feel different because of the ADHD and/or learning disability, but he will also feel different because he was adopted. His self-esteem is then hit doubly hard.
- Teenagers may wonder if they really fit in with their families, especially if they exhibit major differences in their abilities, interests, and personalities than their adoptive families. The child with ADHD who has an average IQ, for instance, may wonder if his adoptive parents are disappointed in him, especially if they are professional people with advanced degrees. The day will come when the adoptive child will realize that his parents could have adopted a different child—one with a higher IQ or one that did not have ADHD. The child may ask himself: "Would they have been happier with another child? Am I good enough for them?" Adoptive parents must let their teen know that they love and accept him for the very special person he is.

Whether your child was born to you or adopted, you must remember that he did not choose to have ADHD. But with the proper intervention and lots of love, patience, and understanding from the people who love him the most, your child has a good chance at having a great life.

What's Next?

(From NICHY's "Transition Summary," no. 7, Sept. 1991)

This section presents suggestions for how students with disabilities can work with their families and school professionals to put together an action plan for transition after high school. The key words here are *plan* and *action*. There's a saying that goes "Plan your work, and then work your plan." Planning requires action—information gathering, self-assessment, weighing of alternatives, decision making. "Working the plan" also requires action—following through on decisions that have been made, evaluating progress, gathering more information and making new decisions, as necessary.

Leaving secondary school is an eventuality that all students must face. Under IDEA, preparing for this transition has become more than a personal choice. Each student's IEP must now include a statement of the transition services needed by the student, beginning no later than age sixteen. The transition plan must also include, where appropriate, a statement of interagency responsibilities or linkages (or both) before the student leaves the school setting. [Much of the following is excellent advice for all students, not just those with IEPs.]

In Junior High School: Start Transition Planning

- Become involved in career exploration.
- Visit with a school counselor to talk about interests and capabilities.
- Participate in vocational assessment activities.
- Use information about interests and capabilities to make preliminary decisions about possible careers: academic versus vocational, or a combination.
- Make use of books, career fairs, and people in the community to find out more about careers of interest.

In High School: Define Career/Vocational Goals

- Work with school staff, family, and people and agencies in the community to define and refine your transition plan. Make sure that the IEP includes transition plans.

- Identify and take high school courses that are required for entry into college, trade schools, or careers of interest.
- Identify and take vocational programs offered in high school, if a vocational career is of interest.
- Become involved in early work experiences, such as job tryouts or internships, summer jobs, volunteering, or part-time work.
- Re-assess interests and capabilities, based on real world or school experience. Is the career field still of interest? If not, redefine goals.
- Participate in on-going vocational assessment and identify gaps of knowledge or skills that need to be addressed. Address these gaps. If you have decided to pursue postsecondary education and training prior to employment, consider these suggestions:
  - Identify postsecondary institutions (colleges, vocational programs in the community, trade schools, etc.) that offer training in any career of interest. Write or call for catalogues, financial aid information, and applications. Visit the institution.
  - Identify what accommodations would be helpful to address your special needs. Find out if the educational institution makes, or can make, these accommodations. Many colleges maintain advisors and tutors for individuals with learning disabilities.
  - Identify and take any special tests (e.g., PSAT, SAT, NMSQT) necessary for entry into postsecondary institutions of interest. SATs can now be taken untimed by youth with ADHD. For information on taking untimed SATs, contact the College Educational Testing Service, 1441 Lower Ferry Rd., Trenton, New Jersey 08618, (609) 771-7137.

CHAPTER NINE

The Impact Children with ADHD Have on Their Families

Managing Life

The family raising a child with ADHD encounters an immense task—keeping the family unit as normal as possible with a child who does not conform or meet expectations (yours and society's). Families need balance to progress, yet children with ADHD manage to keep families unbalanced in varying degrees. These degrees change, often daily, and confusion develops. One thing is always certain and that is "nothing is ever certain." We often can't predict how our child will act from one situation to the next, or one day to the next, which leaves parents feeling like they are on an emotional roller coaster. Visiting friends, going to the grocery store, your place of worship, or out for dinner, is not a matter of just picking up and going. This is a privilege that belongs to other families. Instead, decisions to leave the house with the child who has ADHD are usually made, and well thought out, in advance. To not think ahead may result in a disastrous experience for all.

Because of the uncertainty and confusion, not to mention the ramifications of inappropriate behavior and a parent's reaction to the stress, numerous problems often confront the family. Some families are drawn and stretched in every direction. The child usually becomes the center of the attention, with other family members (usually mom) trying to pull it all together and maintain a sense of balance.

Balancing a family in which one or more members have ADHD is like trying to put together a solid green puzzle made up of fifteen hundred pieces. The difference, of course, is that you can dump the puzzle back into the box and forget about it. When it's your family, you have to keep working at it day after day. Every member of the family is affected. The mother's role usually needs to be redefined (with other family members taking on some of the responsibilities of caring for the child) or the child with ADHD becomes her all-consuming focus. Role overload is the result, a situation that can become highly problematic for some mothers and even result in depression or drug abuse. Mothers of children with ADHD are often critical of their parenting skills and are apt to blame themselves for the difficulties their children experience.

Unless you or your spouse grew up with a family member who had a disability, you are not equipped for parenting a child with special needs. You are not prepared to lose your parental autonomy to well-meaning professionals, and feelings of resentment and loss of self-esteem often develop. Your child with ADHD may require special education classes, which means you will be more involved in his education than most other parents and this adds additional stress. You may recognize the need to reach out to other families with children who have ADHD for support, yet hesitate because you are uncomfortable sharing family matters with others. Marriages often are at risk because of the constant turmoil, stress, and the unpredictability of daily living. As noted in other chapters, siblings of children with ADHD suffer also.

The intent of this chapter is not to paint a bleak picture for families struggling to raise their children, but to provide insight into the various feelings experienced by family members and the types of situations that can develop within the family. You may want to look at this chapter as preventive medicine.

Privacy between Spouses

With the addition of children to the family, husbands and wives find that their sexual intimacy is affected. Spontaneity is abandoned. Workload also becomes a consideration, as mother becomes, in many cases, the primary caretaker. If mother has a full-time job outside of the home, plus the responsibility for the majority of housework and meeting the needs of all her children, she then has two jobs and is often too exhausted to engage in sexual intimacy with her spouse. Now add the addition of a child with ADHD, plus the focused time that must be spent with the child, financial concerns, and job-related pressures, and you have a horrendous strain on the marital relationship.

In the 1990s, almost all couples have less time to spend together, due to job and childcare demands. However, parents of children with ADHD need to examine issues that may be less obvious to them such as anger, frustration, and disappointment—intense feelings that may involuntarily affect your marital relationship. Resentment or frustration can build if one spouse feels the other is not a contributing partner in managing household chores, shopping, homework, and caring for the overall needs of the children. When negative feelings become overwhelming and a spouse finds fault with the other, avoidance may be the outcome! (See the introduction by Mary D. Squire, Ph.D., for additional information on the strain on marital relationships and the family.)

"Our sexual relationship was greatly affected by the birth of our son," says a woman from Kansas. "We expected some changes initially, but felt that once our baby began to sleep through the night, we would have more time for each other. He was almost thirty-six months old before he began sleeping through the night. During those months we were both totally exhausted from a lack of adequate sleep. Sex was the last thing on our minds. Unfortunately, our sexual life never returned to where it once was. Now, at age five, our son who is very impulsive and hyperactive, leaves me exhausted by the end of the day. I usually go to bed early, an hour or so after he falls asleep, because I am so tired and he awakes so early each morning. One of us has to get up with him, and since my husband won't, he's my responsibility. For all practical purposes our sex life is over."

In retrospect, this mother advises that parents make an extra effort to keep their sex life alive. "Take advantage of grandparents who offer to baby-sit your child," she adds. Ask if your child can spend one night every other weekend. Drop them off a few hours before their bedtime and pick them up first thing Saturday morning, for instance. In reality they are only watching your child a total of a few hours, but you have all night with your spouse. Or find a baby-sitter that will spend the night while you check into a nearby motel."

One very frustrated parent told a good friend of their similar dilemma. One day when the friend was watching the nine-year-old, she asked the child what she did when she awoke during the night. The child replied that she always went to her parents' room. When the friend asked "Why?" the child shook her head and said, "I don't know. I just always do." The friend suggested that the next time she awoke that she just use the bathroom and go back to bed. She explained that unless it was an emergency she shouldn't go into her parents' bedroom because they needed their sleep to care for her the next day. The child said, "Okay." From that day on the child no longer wandered into her parents' bedroom during the night. Sometimes it takes a supportive and caring friend, a therapist, or the child's doctor to reach your child. Please don't be afraid to reach out to others that are in a position to help.

Uncooperative Grandparents

"I've given up on my mother and father," says another mother. "They don't believe that my daughter has a medical problem and see my husband and me as the reason she acts the way she does. Consequently, we don't do much with them because every time we are all together the strain is unbearable. They become upset with my daughter and raise their voices. She cries and it hurts to see her get so upset. We visit them but only for a short period of time—a half hour here and there. Hopefully, as she matures, we'll be able to spend more time with my family. I really could use the emotional support that my parents could offer us if things were different."

Some parents were raised during the time when children were to be seen, but not heard. If this is true in your case, you have probably received more than your share of questions and suggestions about your child-rearing practices. ("Why can't you control that child? What that child needs is a good spanking. Then he'll learn who's the boss in your house. When you were younger, we never let you . . .") If this has gone on for some time, you may already resent your parents' interference in your family's life.

As discussed earlier, grandparents need to know the truth so they can understand that not all children can be parented the same. You and your spouse are probably the only people who are going to teach your parents about ADHD. Provide them with reading material or videos on ADHD, invite them to attend a support group meeting with you or ask them to attend an ADHD conference, or introduce them to other parents with ADHD children. It may take a long time before you reach them, but once you get through life will be much better.

I knew I had finally reached my father when one day my son came flying through their house and a relative raised her voice to him. My dad responded, "Raising your voice won't help because his medication wore off twenty-five minutes ago. He can't help it. He's not running to make you angry." It took me seven years—and my patience was tried many times during those years—but I was eventually heard. Persistence can and does pay off.

"My mother-in-law is a former teacher. I expected her to understand ADHD, but she didn't," says one father. "Everytime she started questioning why we did this or that, or offering suggestions, I calmly explained why it wouldn't work with our daughter. I finally got through to her, and as it has turned out she's an excellent grandmother to our daughter. She's very patient and will explain or repeat directions calmly. Even the temper tantrums don't get to her. She remains calm and can settle our daughter down quickly when necessary. Parents need to realize that instead of getting upset with grandparents' reactions to their child, they must patiently teach their parents about ADHD, even if it takes years. Children need grandparents in their lives."

"We have had critical grandparents to deal with," says Julie from Newark, Ohio. "I inundated my mother-in-law, who lives far away, with literature about ADHD. After she read it all (and hopefully understood ADHD more), she rarely criticized our parenting methods or our choice to use medication for our son.

But what about grandparents who literally believe you are abusing your child by medicating him? Like Julie, from Newark, Ohio, you can flood them with information and hope they'll take the time to read it. Or you can take the tough-guy approach and tell grandparents in no uncertain terms that your child is your responsibility and that you will no longer listen to their criticisms or accusations. You might phrase it like this: "Mom and Dad, you know nothing about attention deficit hyperactivity disorder. John and I have conferred with Jessica's pediatrician, a child psychologist, and a pediatric neurologist and they have recommended that Jessica take Ritalin so she can succeed in school. Despite what you may think, we did not make this decision haphazardly. We can no longer tolerate your interference in this matter. John and I will send you information on ADHD. We hope you will take the time to become informed. Until that time, we do not want to discuss this with you nor do we intend to listen to your criticisms. I'm sorry it had to come this, but we find your remarks very upsetting. We need your love and support, not your accusations." Sometimes it becomes necessary for parents to cut ties with family for an indefinite period of time to maintain their own sanity and concentrate their energies on their child and their family unit.

Unique Demands from Non-ADHD Siblings

When a child becomes the focus of mom's and dad's attention, stress-related problems will develop with other siblings. Factors that will influence the amount of stress a sibling feels depend on many variables, including:

1. The severity of the ADHD (mild, moderate, severe) and how it affects the life-style of the family. Is the family often governed by the behavior of the child with ADHD? Is the family limited by the number of things they can do together as a unit because of the child?
2. The age of the child with ADHD. (Is the child the oldest or the youngest, for instance?)
3. How the parents react to the child with ADHD. Are parents patient and understanding? Or do they frequently display anger and frustration with the child?
4. The temperament and personality of the child with ADHD. Is he demanding and nasty? Does he constantly pick on or grab at the sibling, disregard rules of privacy, etc.? Or is he basically a pleasant child?

Siblings should be encouraged to express their feelings about their brother or sister with ADHD, even if those feelings are negative. Parents should listen carefully and express empathy. You might say it this way: "I know it's difficult to see and hear your brother running around the house causing trouble and upsetting everyone. We all need to be patient until he learns that those behaviors are not appropriate. Thank you for sharing your feelings with me." Encourage your child to treat his sibling with kindness and compassion—the same way he would treat a friend who had a medical problem.

In general, most older non-ADHD children will feel empathy for their sibling with ADHD, especially when parents have made a point of explaining the disorder to them. Yet, depending on how parents manage homelife, some siblings may feel unimportant, ignored, and even angry at times because of the amount of focused time that is bestowed on the child with ADHD.

Parents must make an effort to spend quality time alone with each of their children, not just with the child who has ADHD.

Many parents say that the biggest problems they experience with their non-ADHD children is related to behavior. Not surprisingly, when the non-ADHD sibling was younger, parents report that the sibling copied or mimicked the behavior of the child with ADHD in what they felt was an attempt to get the same attention, even if the attention resulted in punishment. Remember, charts work just as well with children who do not have attention deficits or hyperactivity as they do for the child with ADHD. Other parents expressed concern about the younger sibling. Was the younger sibling really mimicking the inappropriate behavior or actually displaying their own symptoms of ADHD?

One mother reported her daughter suddenly couldn't do her homework once she realized that her older brother had a tutor. "She wanted a tutor also, so for a time I acted as her tutor while continuing to emphasize the good work she did on her own. Eventually, she reached the point where she insisted that she could do her work without my help."

Another parent wrote that her son required extended care beyond what was normal for his chronological age because of fine motor difficulties. "By the time my daughter was four she was dressing and bathing on her own," says the parent. "When she realized her older brother couldn't dress himself without help or take a bath without assistance, she told me she couldn't do these things for herself anymore. I tried to explain to her why her brother couldn't do these things for himself yet, but she was too young to really understand. To encourage her to once again dress and bathe herself, I started using a chart. Everytime she got dressed or bathed on her own, I gave her a sticker. For every three stickers, I gave her an inexpensive trinket. Before I knew it, things had returned to normal and we were able to stop using the chart system."

For children with fine motor disabilities, talk with your pediatrician about occupational therapy in which children can learn to button clothes, tie shoes, zip clothing, and improve writing skills. For children who have difficulty bathing because they can't hold a bar soap and use a wash cloth, buy liquid soap with a pump and a sponge with a wooden or plastic handle. Transfer shampoo and conditioners to pump bottles that prevent children from spilling or pouring too much on their hair. An occupational therapist can provide helpful hints for all types of fine motor difficulties your child may experience.

Parental Isolation and Curtailed Social Activities

Some parents feel a degree of confinement in terms of interests and activities they enjoy. They may not be able to attend as many social functions or participate in activities outside of the home like they used to.

Parental isolation may occur when it consistently becomes difficult to find a reliable baby-sitter to care adequately for your child (all of your friends go out together on a weekly or semiweekly basis, but you are not able to go). Feelings of isolation also may develop when you are unable to attend certain functions due to your child's behavior—you begin to feel alienated from other parents. This may be especially true when your child's relationships with peers suffer. Parents often become friends with the parents of their children's classmates. These friendships are often formed through scouting, team sports, and school functions. If your child experiences difficulties getting along with classmates or teammates, other parents may unconsciously or consciously alienate you from their group. If your child has difficulties with team sports and is unable to participate due to poor coordination skills or attention problems, you lose the opportunity to form friendships with other families who attend school games and practices.

But, you don't have to settle for parental isolation according to one mom, who says, "I wanted my son to be involved in Boy Scouts, yet I didn't feel comfortable sending him off to meetings alone as I was never sure what his behavior would be like. So I made the decision to be the den leader. That way my son could participate and I could keep an eye on him. As a result, I've worked closely with other parents and have made some new friends. Bobby is not able to play the team sports he would like to participate in, but I do take him to the school games when he wants to go. Many of the Boy Scouts play sports, so I see some of the families at the games and I sit with them. I also do other volunteer work around the school."

Isolation may also occur when friends invite you and your spouse to their home for dinner and you don't return the invitation because you are so uncomfortable with your child's behavior. Eventually the invitations stop. "This has happened to us many times over the last ten years," says one mom. "Taking people out to dinner instead isn't quite the same in many peoples' minds. I think they are offended, but trying to have a dinner party with our two children in the house won't work even with a baby-sitter. When our children finally reach that magical age, I'm going to invite every one I know over to my house for a sit-down dinner." Invitations don't have to be for a sit-down dinner. Try outdoor entertaining during the warmer months. Invite your friends over for a barbecue, pool party, or another informal get-together. Encourage guests to bring their children along and make it a family gathering.

Parental Stress and Related Health Problems

Stress can also threaten the body's welfare. As parents we face stressful, and sometimes overwhelming situations, almost daily with our child who has ADHD. Writes one mother from Aurora, Illinois: "I can't help but feel I should be reading your book instead of contributing to it. There are so many times my frustration with the noise, confusion, and destruction involved with ADHD have me so overwhelmed. I often have to remove myself from some situations by time and space, try to relax (deep breathing in my own time-out) and then consider my next move. My natural reaction would be rashness, anger, and loss of control. On my worst days, my son is spinning while my daughter hangs on my legs crying. I have Irritable Bowel Syndrome and have lost substantial weight attempting to deal with the stress levels present in my home and my life."

Not surprisingly, many parents who submitted tips for this book also enclosed letters. A few courageous parents were willing to share more than a handful of parenting tips. One of them permitted us to excerpt her letter with the hope that it will help others avoid what she has faced. As you read the following, keep in mind that although no definitive statistics are available at this time, the substance abuse, depression, and other problems she describes are alarmingly common.

> *I grew up in an affluent setting, was well educated, got married, and was finally enjoying my teaching career. I was a good teacher in difficult circumstances. I had good rapport with students and parents, was well respected, and I had good control in my classroom. I felt as if I could handle anything. I was confident and successful.*
>
> *When I became pregnant, I was excited, but scared. It was a difficult pregnancy and I almost lost my baby. The thirty-six hours of excruciating labor further added to my doubts. My beautiful son, Anthony, was finally in my arms and I was filled with wonder, anticipation, and fear.*
>
> *In the past, I thought nothing of relaxing with a glass of wine or two. It calmed me down, and I enjoyed how it made me feel. After nine months of abstaining from alcohol, I couldn't wait to receive the celebratory wine that accompanied the first hospital dinner.*
>
> *As soon as I was home, alone with my son, I discovered an extremely irritable, colicky baby who wouldn't stop crying. The sadness of being at home alone while my friends were teaching, made it worse. Our pediatrician recommended drinking a beer to help my breast milk and to calm my nerves. This sounded like a great idea and I wholeheartedly participated.*
>
> *Anthony was either very happy or very miserable and that affected all of those around him, especially me. It was difficult to go out and I often felt that he would never stop crying. I asked myself, "Is this what motherhood is all about?" I couldn't understand how I could handle thirty-six sixth graders, but one baby, my precious son, could cause me to feel such powerlessness, frustration, and disappointment in both him and me.*
>
> *So I began to self-prescribe the medicine, alcohol, which could temporarily dull the pain, emptiness, and mask the feelings of inadequacy.*

While munching on a sandwich at lunch, a beer (or two) would be a regular accompaniment. After Anthony would go down for a nap, I would reward myself for such hard work and treat myself to a glass of wine.

As Anthony grew we were thrilled with his development, but his temperament was even more extreme. The hopes of him "growing out of it" diminished, but we had no clue that this behavior was related to ADHD. I thought his problems were attributed to "bad" mothering and this was my punishment.

I desperately needed a break, so I began a part-time job, when Anthony started preschool. This was a great time for me, and I was allowed to gather back some of my own value and worth. I easily gave birth to a beautiful daughter. When Anthony turned three, we moved to another city, and I settled into the role of wife and mother of two. I began to see such a difference in my two children. Sara was a delightful, happy baby who was easy to please. However, Anthony didn't like her at all, and an intense sibling rivalry developed from the start. I was beginning to feel those unacceptable feelings mothers aren't supposed to feel: anger, resentment, and loss of a "normal" child.

As my depression increased and my self-esteem and confidence decreased, my dependence on alcohol grew. I would drink over any stress. Although I rarely got drunk or lost control, I still craved the relief that the alcohol would provide. To those around me I was doing well, but inside I was crumbling.

Now I don't want the reader to believe that I am blaming or excusing my behavior. No one made me drink that glass of wine. People encounter far greater stress and cope in healthier ways than I did. I understand that alcohol dependency is influenced by many factors. Those include a strong hereditary component and a history of abuse, both of which pertain to me. I also read an article describing the relationship between drug and alcohol abuse and living with a difficult or disabled child. The findings did cite a strong correlation. Although it's not an excuse to drink, it shows that I was not alone in how I coped with my stress and anxiety.

When Anthony turned three several things had gone from bad to worse. His behavior was more overt; his anger was immense, self-esteem low, [and] he was having trouble at school, and with his peers. I drank even more heavily, as our home became a battleground. I started to suspect ADHD, but at this point the negative consequences of my depression and drinking were beginning to show, so my input at school and with my husband was disregarded. I was the "identified patient" and although my problems at home did contribute to Anthony's symptoms, it was frustrating that no one looked past this. This delayed Anthony's diagnosis and the treatment he so desperately needed . . .

In the summer of 1992, with the help of family, and a caring ther-apist, I entered a treatment facility for alcoholism. I had reached my bottom, and it was finally time to surrender. My family needed a whole healthy mother and wife and I began to learn the tools to be effective in this role. I have had to deal with my past pain, and the role I allowed my son's ADHD to play in my mental health. I now cope with the strength of a twelve-step group, therapy, a women's support group, and CHADD. I haven't felt the need to take another drink since I entered treatment. Anthony's ADHD is still very difficult to handle at times, but I understand his pain and see his courage.

He was finally properly diagnosed last year, began medication and counseling and we experienced a dramatic improvement. He is a suc-cessful, hardworking third-grader, who still struggles with the symptoms of ADHD, but he is on his way. Finally knowing what we are dealing with, it makes things much easier . . .

Being in recovery, and providing the advocacy, support, and strength my son needs, has been a difficult balance to achieve and one I struggle with daily. I know for me to be the best for my family, I need to first take care of myself. I realize it's easy to become enmeshed in our ADHD children and although these children need and require additional support, they especially need our help so they can someday be able to meet their own needs. I believe by modeling to my family when things get really tough that I seek help and support, then Anthony will hopeful-ly feel comfortable doing the same.

Therefore, I urge all parents who are struggling to successfully raise an ADHD child to be aware of the stress involved and to find healthy outlets to reduce the stress. Also, if you recognize yourself in my story . . . I hope and pray you can borrow a piece of courage and ask for help.

Marital Stress

"A strain on a marriage? I've thought that there would never be a time that we wouldn't be discussing our son's problems and how to manage it and him," says Mary from Troy, New York. Is this the right school? Is this the best response to his behavior? It went on and on. Guilty feelings on some days when you didn't even seem to like your child. I'm surprised we're still mar-ried and I am still sane."

Mary says three things helped her cope:

1. "Talking with a neighbor whose older child was being evaluat-ed for ADHD. Just sharing feelings helped tremendously."
2. "Working with a wonderful child psychologist to help us with our son's behavior. She not only helped with him but with me.

When I'd walk into her office and flop in the chair, she would say, 'He's been driving you up a wall, right?' Just her simple statement made me feel that she really understood how I was feeling."

3. "All day, five-day-a-week school. Initially, we started out with one-half-day kindergarten because I really felt that was what is best for kids. But in my son's case, structure was more important. I was told that these children do best with a lot of structure. So at the school's suggestion we went to full day. He's doing better in school and after school also."

"My advice is to communicate with your spouse," says Debra from Crownpoint, Indiana. "Pull together on what actions to take and carry through on those actions consistently. Meet with teachers, doctors, and other professionals together, whenever possible. Find a support group for children with ADHD."

"My husband has ADD and both of our children have ADHD," explains Gail, who is from Montana. We didn't know my husband had attention deficits until a few years ago. Now, I understand why he's always acted the way he does (doesn't finish projects he's started, is always doing three different things at the same time, never seems to be paying attention when people try to talk with him, unorganized—I could go on and on), but it's difficult parenting two children with ADHD when your spouse can't follow through on things that you agree on. He has little patience for the children. The very things he hates in them are the same symptoms he displays. I feel like I am in a no-win situation. My husband doesn't realize what effect his ADD has on our family and on me, and he's not willing to try medication or therapy. We've tried marriage counseling, but half the time he forgets about the sessions or shows up a half-hour late. He has a winning personality and is a good talker. Usually by the time we leave a session, he's the 'good' guy and I'm the person who causes all the problems in our home. The stress and anxiety between us and with the children is very obvious. In the meantime, I try to keep a positive attitude by remembering that my husband and children are not intentionally trying to make me miserable. I found that if I mentally dwell on the characteristics I don't like, I tend to get angrier and angrier. One's thoughts can sneak up and create havoc, so I no longer permit myself to dwell on the negative. If my husband starts a project and doesn't finish it, for instance, I either finish it myself or hire someone else to do it."

"I work full time. It's distressing to get a call at two in the afternoon from your child's teacher telling you how out of control your child was that day," says a Diane, the mom of an only child. "While you are talking to the teacher, a problem arises at work, and then your husband calls to tell you he has to work late. When you get home, your child is still wound up and he demands dinner right away.

I have not been on a vacation in six years! My husband works a lot of long hours at night. I have a spa membership I have only used a few times in the last few years. I have a stationary bike that's in my dining room that I rarely get a chance to use.

How are we supposed to cope? The only time I can find peace in my home is in the morning. A cup of coffee on the porch swing at 6 A.M. is the closest thing to heaven I can find on earth. If I don't get my 6 A.M. break, the day is off to a bad start. I collect my thoughts at this time."

Julie, from Newark, Ohio, has a son with ADHD and says, "My husband and I have had many stress-filled talks about 'what to do with him.' Whenever our son is having particularly difficult problems at school, I become so frustrated that I make myself ill. My blood pressure would be much lower if I did not have a child with ADHD. I can directly trace my gastrointestinal problems to incidents involving my son.

"My husband and I make a concerted effort to seek out calm and peace. We live out in the country where it is peaceful. We vacation where it is quiet and calm. Other people may think we are boring because of this, but they do not realize that it is necessary for our mental health—we have all the excitement we can handle just with our son."

Taking Care of Mom and Dad

It's easy to understand how parents can become stressed out or burned out. Couples often feel isolated, not just mom. They find they have little time to go out and have fun with friends, and even less time for each other. Mothers fight stress and depression from juggling everything, and dads find extra work to do at the office. Friends and relatives often blame the parents for the problems in the home. Marriages are pushed to the limits, causing a breakdown in communication, and sometimes collapsing under the strain. One parent wrote about her marriage of twenty years, which was ending in divorce. "My husband says he's had it. He wants a divorce so he can have a chance at some happiness and peace before he's too old. He's forty-five and our son with ADHD is fourteen. Well I've had it too, but moms aren't suppose to walk out. It's not motherly."

So what can parents do to preserve their sanity, keep their marriages intact, and not buckle under the pressure? Here are some suggestions:

- Keep the lines of communication open with your spouse.
  Neither of you is to blame for your child's disability, so support each other. Make a date with your spouse every week or every other week and go out and enjoy yourself. Do not talk about your child on your night out. This time is reserved for you and

your relationship. Remember that relationship (in many cases) was there before your child.

- Compliment yourself out loud daily, either in private or in front of your child.
- Remind yourself daily that your child did not choose to have ADHD, nor does he do things intentionally to make your life miserable. (I have a note posted on my bathroom mirror that I read the first thing every morning. It says, "Please remember, this was NOT my choice Mom.")
- Never look at yourself as a bad parent. (In fact, you are probably a much better parent than most, although you may not feel like it at times.) Instead, look at yourself as a good parent of a child who has a disability. Remind yourself that your family is not like most families and, considering the challenges you face, you're doing remarkably well.
- Hang a copy of the serenity prayer somewhere where you can see it and read it every day. (Mine is in my kitchen next to the sink.) When you read it, carefully think about what it says ("God grant me the serenity to accept the things I cannot change, Courage to change the things I can, and the Wisdom to know the difference"). You cannot change the fact that your child has ADHD but some of his actions you can help change slowly. Recognize and accept what you can and cannot change in him.
- Do something nice for yourself every day because you deserve a break (take thirty minutes to read a book, soak in the tub, watch television, pursue a hobby, work a crossword puzzle, write a letter, or polish your nails), even if it means getting up earlier or postponing your bedtime.
- Don't take everything seriously. Look at the long-range implications of a given act. If there are none, then ask yourself, "What am I upset about?"
- Look for funny or humorous things that your child does and then laugh out loud with him. I remember one morning when my oldest son, then four, was throwing a major temper tantrum in my bathroom. He kept throwing himself up against the bathroom vanity. I turned away in an attempt to ignore him, when suddenly the screaming and yelling stopped. When I looked over at him, I burst out in uncontrollable laughter. He had caught his bib overalls on the knob on the drawer and was literally hanging by his shoulder strap, feet off the ground. For a brief second, I felt his embarrassment and shock, but then he, too, burst out laughing. We laughed for weeks over that incident. Look for funny and amusing situations in your life.

- When the day is over, evaluate it. Take delight in those things you did right. If you handled a situation poorly, decide how you'll handle it the next time but don't dwell on mistakes.
- Don't try to be a perfect parent. Perfect parents don't exist. Even if other families look picture-perfect to you, remember those familles have their own challenges to face.
- Find a caring, nonjudgmental friend, or a therapist, you can talk with. You need someone to talk with when you truly believe you can't handle life with your child any longer.
- Locate an ADHD support group for parents in your area and attend the meetings. This is an excellent place to vent frustrations and meet others parenting children with ADHD.
- Find an energetic teenager (preferably one between sixteen and nineteen years old) who enjoys children. This teenager can help lighten your load a few evenings a week until your child's bedtime. The sitter can entertain your child while you clean house, prepare dinner, run errands, spend some time alone with your spouse, or just relax. Many children with ADHD cannot be left unattended.
- Exercise at least three times a week. This can be an opportunity to spend time with your spouse as well. Exercise has been shown to reduce stress. A daily walk of a mile or two in your neighborhood can make you feel so much more fit and relaxed.
- Ask for help and delegate tasks to other members of the family. Parents must share responsibilities equally.
- If you find you are fighting depression, drinking, or using drugs to cope and get through the day, talk with your spouse and seek professional help immediately. Don't wait until the situation gets further out of control.
- Use behavior management techniques every moment of the child's day.
- Take a vacation from your child as often as possible. If you can't get away for a week then get away on a weekend. And don't feel guilty about being away from your child. You'll come back with renewed strength, a better outlook on life, and more patience.
- Set realistic expectations for your family life. Letting go of the dream you once had is the first step toward acceptance—things will never be perfect, so don't expect perfection from yourself or your child.
- As a family, focus on the positive qualities your child possesses, rather than the negative. Make a list of your child's strengths and review the list when you become discouraged. Also, work

on positive language. For example, substitute "energetic" for "hyperactive," "assertive" for "demanding," "decisive" for "impulsive," etc.

- Lower your expectations. It's okay not to have a perfectly clean house every day.
- Remember always that there are families who are struggling in far worse ways than you may be able to imagine. Your child is a challenge, but could you imagine life without him? Of course not!

Afterword

We are all fortunate to be parenting a child with ADHD in the 1990s. Never before have parents had the resources that they have now. There are many excellent books we can turn to for information, parent support groups that offer intellectual and emotional support, and national organizations that provide educational information to parents and teachers. There are also magazines and newsletters, and national conferences and local workshops for parents and educators. Plus, a growing number of professionals now specialize in ADHD. If you haven't read the foreword and introduction to this book be sure to do so. Both Drs. Pasch and Squire work with children who have ADHD, and are parents of children with this disorder. (Please check the bibliography and the appendix for a listing of some of the resources available to you.)

However, we are only fortunate if we take advantage of all the resources available to us, including support from other parents. Unfortunately, some parents of children with ADHD would rather conceal. As one parent remarked, "ADHD is where adoption was thirty years ago—in the closet. I am amazed at the number of parents I know whose children have been diagnosed with ADHD, yet they don't want to talk about it." When parents are engrossed in their own feelings about having a child with extra challenges, they cannot effectively contend with the needs of their children. Until parents can openly admit that their child has a disability and work through their own feelings, they cannot adequately provide the support their child so desperately needs.

Many of today's health and parent organizations (both local and national would never have been formed if it hadn't been for courageous adults with disabilities or their families. How is it that one family accepts their child's disability so fully that they want to organize and reach out to other parents facing the same challenges, while another family struggles in silence? It is because of their acceptance and attitude! One family meets the challenges head-on because, despite the disability, they see their child as a remarkable human being of immeasurable value. They find hope in learning about the disability and giving support to other parents attempting to cope with the same disability. They do not sit and wonder who's to blame. Rather, they live life fully realizing that what happened yesterday cannot be changed. Your attitude can make this job of parent either rewarding or rewardless. The choice is yours.

As parents we must make commitments to our children because they desperately need all of our love, patience, understanding, and strength if they are to become healthy, functional adults. Our role as parents will not always be easy. We may face many challenges as our children grow and mature. But remember, ADHD is an obstacle placed in our path. The size of that obstacle is determined by the beholder. If we see it as overwhelming, it will be just that. If we can look at it as only a detour, we can find ways to adapt and adjust. Our purpose as parents is to provide our children with the opportunities to be the best they can, to raise healthy children in mind and spirit, and then send them on their way with our blessings. As parents of children with ADHD, our parenting road is just bumpier than most but that road is not necessarily impossible to travel. Take it one day at a time. When you wake up in the morning do so with renewed spirit. Ask for strength to make it through the day with love and patience, and forget about yesterday. The recovering alcoholic takes it one day at a time. We would be wise to do the same.

I encourage all parents to take a good look at their child. If your child has an interest in a special area, do what you can to enhance and support that interest. That one gift, talent, special interest, or hobby can be the bright light in the life of a child who faces daily frustrations. Hobbies and special talents are areas where children with ADHD can excel, gain competence, and build self-esteem. Believe me, as a parent your heart will soar with joy when you witness your child succeeding and excelling in an area special to him or her. Often those memories are enough to get you through that next demanding day with a smile on your face and love in your heart.

I hope that you can release any negative thoughts, discover your child's qualities, and share him with the world by standing behind him, not in front of him. Reach out to others who are raising a child with ADHD. Let them find a comforting friend in you. Become an advocate in the schools and community. Please join me. Together we can make a difference!

I would enjoy hearing from you. If you have a computer, you can reach me on CompuServe's ADD Forum where I am a daily visitor. The ADD Forum is an online support community for parents, adults with ADD, and professionals. My number is 74347, 3231. If you do not have a computer, you may write me at:

Colleen Alexander-Roberts
Taylor Publishing Company
1550 West Mockingbird Lane
Dallas, Texas 75235

Appendix

Parent Support Groups

Attention-Deficit Disorder Association (ADDA)
P.O. Box 972
Mentor, OH 44061
1-800-487-2282

Attention Deficit Information Network, Inc.
475 Hillside Ave.
Needham, MA 02194
(617) 455-9895

Children and Adults with Attention Deficit Disorders (CHADD)
499 NW 70th Ave., #308
Plantation, FL 33317
(305) 587-3700

Information on ADHD and Learning Disabilities

American Speech-Language-Hearing Association (ASHS)
10801 Rockville Pike
Rockville, MD 20849-1725
(301) 897-5700

Closer Look
Parent's Campaign for Handicapped Children and Youth
P.O. Box 1492
Washington, DC 20013

ERIC Clearinghouse on Handicapped and Gifted Children
Council for Exceptional Children (CEC)
1920 Association Dr.
Reston, VA 22091-1589
1-800-438-8841

Information Center for Handicapped Children
605 G St., NW, 2nd Fl.
Washington, DC 20001

The Learning Disabilities Network
72 Sharp St., Site A-2
Hingham, MA 02043
(617) 340-5605

Learning Disability Association of America (formerly ACLD)
National Headquarters
4156 Library Rd.
Pittsburgh, PA 15234
(412) 341-1515

National Center for Learning Disabilities (NCLD)
99 Park Ave.
New York, NY 10016
(212) 687-7211

National Clearinghouse for Professionals in Special Education
1800 Diagonal Rd., Ste. 320
Alexandria, VA 22314

National Information Center for Children and Youth with Disabilities (NICHY)
Box 1492
Washington, DC 20013
(703) 893-6061(Local)
1-800-695-0285

National Institute for Learning
Disabilities
107 Seekel St.
Norfolk, VA 23505
(804) 423-8648
 National Parent Network on Disabilities
1600 Prince St., Rm. 115
Alexandria, VA 22314
(703) 684-6763

Orton Dyslexia Society
8600 LaSalle Rd., Chester Bldg., Ste. 382
Baltimore, MD 21204
(410) 296-0232

Parent Advocacy Coalition for
Educational Rights (PACER)
4826 Chicago Ave., South
Minneapolis, MN 55417
(612) 827-2966

The Parent Educational Advocacy
Training Center
228 South Pitt St., Ste. 300
Alexandria, VA 22314
(703) 836-2953

Tourette's Syndrome Association
National Headquarters
42-40 Bell Blvd.
Bayside, NY 11361
(718) 224-2999

Gifted Children
National Association for Gifted Children
1155 15th St. NW, Ste. 1002
Washington, DC 20005
(202) 785-4286

Resources for Adoptive Families
Adoptive Families of America
333 Highway 100 North
Minneapolis, MN 55422
(612) 535-4829

National Adoption Information
Clearinghouse
Cygnus Corporation
11426 Rockville Pike, Ste. 410
Rockville, MD 20852
(301) 231-6512

**Transition and Vocational
Education Information**
National Clearinghouse on
Postsecondary
Education for Individuals with
Disabilities
The HEATH Resource Center
One Dupont Circle, Ste. 800
Washington, DC 20036-1193
(202) 939-9320 (in DC only)
1-800-544-3284

National Center for Youth with
Disabilities (NYCD)
University of Minnesota
Box 721
420 Delaware St. SE
Minneapolis, MN 55455
(612) 626-2825
1-800-333-6293

Job Accommodations Network (JAN)
1-800-526-7234

**ADHD Resources, Books, Tapes,
and Videos**
(request a free catalog)
A.D.D. WareHouse
300 Northwest 70th Ave., Ste. 102
Plantation, FL 33317
(305) 792-8944

The ADD Resource Center
1344 Johnson Ferry Rd., Ste. 14
Marietta, GA 30068

**Resources for Learning and
Teaching (book publishers)**
Write and request a book catalog from:
American Guidance Services (AGS)
4201 Woodland Rd.
P.O. Box 90
Circle Pines, MN 55014-1796

Developmental Learning Materials
(DLM)
One DLM Pk.
Allen, TX 75002-1302

Free Spirit Publishing, Inc.
400 First Ave., North, Ste. 616
Minneapolis, MN 55401-1724

For Help with Teenagers
ALCOHOL AND DRUGS
Alcoholics Anonymous (AA)
307 7th Ave., Rm. 201
New York, NY 10001
(212) 647-1680

Al Anon and Alateen
Box 862
Midtown Station
New York, NY 10018-0862
(212) 302-7240

National Clearinghouse for Alcohol and
Drug Information (NICADI)
P.O. Box 2345
Rockville, MD 20847-2345
1-800-729-6686

Cocaine (and crack)
1-800-COCAINE

Alcohol and Drug Helpline
1-800-252-6465

DRINKING AND DRIVING
Students Against Driving Drunk
P.O. Box 800
Marlboro, MA 01752
508-481-3568

OUT-OF-CONTROL TEENAGERS
Tough Love
Community Service Foundation
Box 70
Sellersville, PA 18960
(215) 766-8022

RUNAWAYS
National Runaway Hotline
1-800-448-4663

Runaway Hotline
1-800-231-6946
1-800-392-3352 (in Texas)

DEPRESSION
D/ART Public Inquiries
5600 Fishers Ln., Room 15C-05
National Institute of Mental Health
Rockville, MD 20857

SUICIDE PREVENTION
Crisis Intervention and Suicide
Prevention Program
4200 N. Oak Park Ave.
Chicago, IL 60634

American Association of Suicidology
2459 South Ash
Denver, CO 80222

The Samaritans
Suicide Services
500 Commonwealth Ave.
Boston, MA 02215
(617) 247-0020

SEXUAL HEALTH
Planned Parenthood hotline
1-800-829-PPFA

Schools
National Association of Independent
Schools
4 Liberty Square
Boston, MA 02109

Parents' Legal Rights
National Committee for Citizens in
Education (NCCE)
410 Wilde Lake Village Green
Columbia, MD 21044
1-800-NETWORK

Bibliography

Attention Deficit Hyperactivity and Learning Disabilities

Adelman, Howard S. and Linda Taylor. *An Introduction to Learning Disabilities.* Glenview, IL: Scott, Foresman and Co., 1986.

Armstrong, Thomas. "Driven to Distraction." *Parenting*, October, 1990, 32, 34, 38.

_____. *In Their Own Way: Discovering and Encouraging Your Child's Personal Learning Style.* Los Angeles: Jeremy P. Tarcher, Inc., 1987.

Attention Deficit Disorder (ADD). Reston, VA: The Council for Exceptional Children.

Bain, Lisa A. *A Parent's Guide to Attention Deficit Disorders.* New York: Dell, 1991.

Cummings, Rhoda W. and Cleborne D. Maddux. *Parenting the Learning Disabled: A Realistic Approach.* New York: Bantam, 1985.

Fowler, Mary Cahill. *Maybe You Know My Kid: A Parent's Guide to Identifying, Understanding and Helping Your Child with Attention-Deficit Hyperactivity Disorder.* New York: Birch Lane, 1993.

Friedman, Ronald and Guy T. Doyal. *Attention Deficit Disorder and Hyperactivity.* 2nd ed. Danville, IL: Interstate Printers and Publishers, Inc., 1987.

Garber, Stephen W., Marianne Daniels Garber, and Robyn Freedman Spizman. *If Your Child is Hyperactive, Impulsive, Distractible . . . Helping the ADD (Attention Deficit Disorder)/Hyperactive Child.* New York: Villard, 1990.

Hallowell, Edward M., M.D. and John J. Ratey, M.D. *Driven to Distraction: Attention Deficit Disorder in Children and Adults.* New York: Pantheon, 1994.

Hartman, Thom. *Attention Deficit Disorder: A Different Perception.* Grass Valley, CA: Underwood Books, 1993.

_____. *Focus Your Energy: Hunting for Success in Business with Attention Deficit Disorder.* New York: Pocket Books, 1994.

Ingersoll, Barbara D. and Sam Goldstein. *Attention Deficit and Learning Disabilities: Realities, Myths and Controversial Treatments.* New York: Doubleday, 1993.

Learning Disabilities. Washington, DC: National Information Center for Children and Youth with Disabilities.

Lippert, Joan. "Help for Your Hyperactive Child," *Healthy Kids 4–10 Years*, Winter 1990, 40–44.

McCarney, Stephen B. and Angela Marie Bauer. *The Parent's Guide to Attention Deficit Disorders.* Columbia, MO: Hawthorne Educational Services, 1990.

McNamara, Barry E. and Francine J. McNamara. *Keys to Parenting a Child with Attention Deficit Disorder.* Hauuppauge, NY: Barron's Educational Series, Inc., 1993.

Moss, Robert A. *Why Johnny Can't Concentrate: Coping with Attention Deficit Disorder.* New York: Bantam, 1990.

Parker, Harvey C. *The ADD/Hyperactivity Workbook for Parents, Teachers and Kids.* Plantation, FL: Impact Publications, Inc., 1988.

Phelen, Thomas W. *All About Attention Deficit Disorders: A Comprehensive Guide.* Glen Ellyn, IL: Child Management, Inc., 1992.

Silver, Larry B. *The Misunderstood Child: A Guide for Parents of Children with Learning Disabilities.* rev. ed. Blue Ridge Summit, PA: TAB, 1992.

Taylor, John F. *Helping Your Hyperactive Child.* Rocklin, CA: Prima Publishing and Communications, 1990.

Weiss, Lynn. *Attention Deficit Disorder in Adults.* Dallas, TX: Taylor Publishing Co., 1992.

_____. *The Attention Deficit Disorder in Adults Workbook.* Dallas, TX: Taylor Publishing Co., 1994.

Books for Children and Adolescents

Cummings, Rhoda and Gary Fisher. *The School Survival Guide for Kids with LD (Learning Differences).* Minneapolis: Free Spirit Publishing, 1991.

Galvin, Matthew. *Otto Learns About His Medicine.* New York: Magination Press, 1988.

Gordon, M. *Jumpin' Johnny. Get Back to Work: A Child's Guide to ADHD/Hyperactivity.* DeWitt, NY: GSI Publications, 1992.

Hartman, Thom. *You Are Not Defective: A New Look at Attention Deficit Disorder Written Specifically for Adolescents.* Atlanta, GA: Mythical Intelligence, 1993.

Krementz, Jill. *How It Feels to Be Adopted.* New York: Knopf, 1988.

Moss, Deborah. *Shelly the Hyperactive Turtle.* Kensington, MD: Woodbine House, 1989.

Munsch, Robert. *Love You Forever.* Canada: Firefly, 1986.

Parker, Roberta N. *Making the Grade: An Adolescent's Struggle With ADD.* Plantation, FL: Impact Publications, Inc., 1992.

Quinn, Patricia A. and Judith M. Stern. *Putting on the Brakes: Young People's Guide to Understanding Attention Deficit Hyperactivity Disorder (ADHD).* New York: Magination Press, 1991.

Children's Activities

Hickman, Danelle and Valerie Teurlay. *101 Great Ways to Keep Your Child Entertained While You Get Something Else Done: Creative and Stimulating Activities for Your Toddler or Preschooler.* New York: St. Martin's, 1992.

Bergstrom, Joan M. *School's Out: Now What? Creative Choices for Your Child.* Berkeley, CA: Ten Speed, 1984.

Choosing a Doctor

Ripley, Suzanne. *A Parent's Guide: Doctors, Disabilities, and the Family*, Volume 1, Number 2, May, 1990, Washington, DC: The National Information Center for Children and Youth with Disabilities.

Ward, Michael J., Ph.D. *Self-Determination Revisited: Going Beyond Expectations*. NICHY Transition Summary, Number 7, September, 1991, Washington, DC: The National Information Center for Children and Youth with Disabilities.

Chores

McCollough, Bonnie Runyan and Susan Walker Monson. *401 Ways to Get Your Kids to Work at Home*. New York: St. Martin's, 1981.

Communicating with Children

Faber, Adele and Elaine Mazlish. *How to Talk So Kids Will Listen and Listen So Kids Will Talk*. New York: Rawson, Wade Publishers, Inc., 1980.

_____. *How to Be the Parent You Always Wanted to Be*. New York: Hyperion, 1992.

Developing Social Skills

Duke, Marshall and Stephen Nowicki. *Helping the Child Who Doesn't Fit In*. Atlanta: Peachtree, 1993.

Greene, Melissa Fay. "The Left-out Child," *Family Life*, September/October 1990, 104–108.

Gifted Children

Dunn, Rita, Kenneth Dunn, and Donald Treffinger, *The Giftedness in Your Child: Unlocking Every Child's Unique Talents, Strengths, and Potential*. New York: John Wiley and Sons, Inc., 1992.

Walker, Sally Yahnke. *The Survival Guide for Parents of Gifted Children: How to Understand, Live With, and Stick Up for Your Gifted Child*. Minneapolis: Free Spirit, 1991.

Organizational Skills

Crary, Elizabeth. *Pick Up Your Socks and Other Skills Growing Children Need*. Philadelphia: Childswork Childsplay, 1990.

Parenting Adopted Children

Bothen, Linda. *When Friends Ask about Adoption: Question and Answer Guide for Non-Adopted Parents and Other Caring Adults*. Chevy Chase, MD: Swan Publications, 1987.

Melina, Lois R. *Raising Adopted Children: A Manual for Adoptive Parents*. New York: Harper and Row, 1986.

_____. *Making Sense of Adoption: A Parent's Guide*. New York: Harper and Row, 1989.

Schaffer, Judith and Christina Lindstrom. *How to Raise an Adopted Child*. New York: Crown, 1989.

Parenting Adopted Children with ADHD or Learning Disabilities

Alexander-Roberts, Colleen. "Gifted Kids with Attention Deficit Hyperactivity Disorder: What You Should Know and How You Can Help," *OURS*, September/October, 1992, 16–19.

Severson, Randolph W. *Can't You Sit Still? Adoption and Attention Deficit Hyperactivity Disorder*. Dallas: House of Tomorrow Productions, 1992.

Positive Discipline

Dinkmeyer, Don and Gary D. McKay. *The Parent's Handbook*. Circle Pines, MN: American Guidance Service, 1989.

Kersey, Catherine C. *Don't Take It Out on Your Kids: A Parent's and Teacher's Guide to Positive Discipline*. Washington, DC: Acropolis, 1990.

Phelan, Thomas. *1–2–3– Magic: Training Your Preschoolers and Preteens to Do What You Want*. Glen Ellyn, IL: Child Management Press, 1985.

Robin, Arthur and Sharon Foster. *Negotiating Parent-Adolescent Conflict*. New York: Guilford Press, 1989

Varni, James W. and Donna G. Corwin. *Growing Up Great: Practical Steps for Parenting Your 6 to 10 Year Old*. New York: Berkley, 1993.

Windell, James. *Discipline: A Sourcebook of 50 Failsafe Techniques for Parents*. New York: Collier, 1991.

Wyckof, Jerry and Barbara C. Unell. *Discipline Without Shouting or Spanking: Practical Solutions to the Most Common Preschool Behavior Problems*. New York: Meadowbrook Books, 1984.

School Related

Bean, Reynold. *How to Help Your Children Succeed in School*. Los Angeles: Price Stern Sloan, Inc., 1991.

Bloom, Jill. *Help Me to Help My Child: A Sourcebook for Parents of Learning Disabled Children*. Boston: Little, Brown and Co., 1991.

Canter, Lee. *Homework Without Tears: A Parent's Guide for Motivating Children to Do Homework and Succeed in School*. New York: HarperPerennial, 1988.

Fiske, Edward B. *Smart Schools, Smart Kids: Why Do Some Schools Work?* New York: Simon and Schuster, 1991.

Gearheart, Bill R. *Learning Disabilities: Educational Strategies*. 5th ed., Columbus, OH: Merrill Publishing, 1988.

Higbee, Kenneth L. *Your Memory: How It Works and How to Improve It*. Englewood Cliffs, NJ: Prentice-Hall, Inc., 1977.

Jones, Claudia. *Parents Are Teachers, Too: Enriching Your Child's First Six Years*. Charlotte, VT: Williamson Publishing, 1988.

_____. *More Parents Are Teachers, Too: Encouraging Your 6- to 12-Year Old*. Charlotte, VT: Williamson Publishing, 1991.

_____. *Parent's Are Teachers, Too: Enriching Your Child's First Six Years*. Charlotte, VT: Williamson Publishing, 1991.

Kelley, Mary L. *School-Home Notes: Promoting Children's Classroom Success*. New York: The Guilford Press, 1990.

Levine, Melvin D. *Keeping a Head in School: Students Book About Learning Abilities and Learning Disorders*. Cambridge, Massachusetts: Educators Publishing Service, Inc., 1990.

Mercer, Cecil D. and Ann R. Mercer. *Teaching Students with Learning Problems*. Columbus, OH: Merrill Publishing, 1989.

Novick, Barbara and Maureen Arnold. *Why Is My Child Having Trouble at School?: A Parent's Guide to Learning Disabilities*. New York: Random House, 1991.

Porter Sargent Staff. *Handbook of Private Schools*. 71st ed. Boston: Porter Sargent, 1990.

Rief, Sandra F. *How to Reach and Teach ADD/ADHD Children*. West Nyack, NY: The Center for Applied Research in Education, 1993.

Scheiber, Barbara and Jeanne Talpers. *Unlocking Potential: College and Other Choices for Learning Disabled People*. Bethesda, MD: Adler and Adler, 1987.

Sonna, Linda Agler. The Homework Solution: *Getting Kids to Do Their Homework*. Charlotte, VT: Williamson Publishing, 1990.

Teaching Children with Attention Deficit Disorder. Reston, VA: The Council for Exceptional Children.

Thiel, Ann, Richard Thiel, and Penelope B. Grenoble. *When Your Child Isn't Doing Well in School*. Chicago-New York: Contemporary, 1988.

Townsend-Butterworth, Diana. *Your Child's First School: A Handbook for Parents*. New York: Walker, 1992.

Wade, Theodore E. *The 5th Edition Home School Manual: For Parents Who Teach Their Own Children*. Auburn, CA: Gazelle Publications, 1991.

Self-Esteem

Youngs, Bettie B. *How to Develop Self-Esteem in Your Child: 6 Vital Ingredients*. New York: Fawcett Columbine, 1991.

Sibling Rivalry

Faber, Adele and Elaine Mazlish. *Siblings Without Rivalry: How to Help Your Children Live Together So You Can Live Too*. New York: Avon, 1987.

Special Education

Rights and Responsibilities of Parents of Children with Handicaps. Reston, VA: The Council for Exceptional Children.

Providing an Appropriate Education to Children with Attention Deficit Disorder. Reston, VA: The Council for Exceptional Children.

Questions Often Asked About Special Education Services. Washington, DC: National Information Center for Children and Youth with Disabilities.

Social Skills

Drew, Naomi, ed. *Learning the Skills of Peacemaking*. Minneapolis: Free Spirit Press, 1987.

Temper Tantrums

Hall, Nancy. "Taming Temper Tantrums," *Working Mother*, July 1993, 42–43, 46.

Welch, Martha G. *Holding Time*. New York: Fireside, 1989.

Index